THEATER OF THE DEAD

THEATER
OF THE
DEAD

A SOCIAL TURN IN CHINESE
FUNERARY ART, 1000–1400

JEEHEE HONG

UNIVERSITY OF HAWAI'I PRESS
HONOLULU

21 20 19 18 17 16   6 5 4 3 2 1

Library of Congress Cataloging-in-Publication Data
Hong, Jeehee, author.
Theater of the dead : a social turn in Chinese funerary art, 1000–1400 / Jeehee Hong.
pages cm
Includes bibliographical references and index.
ISBN 978-0-8248-5537-6 (cloth : alk. paper)
1. Sarcophagi, Chinese—Themes, motives. 2. Sarcophagi—Decoration—China. 3. Tombs—Decoration—China. 4. Funeral rites and ceremonies, Ancient—China. 5. Theater in art. I. Title.
NB1810.H66 2016
726'.8095—dc23
2015034531

Illustrations in this book were funded in part or in whole by a grant from the Meiss/Mellon Author's Book Award of the College Art Association.

Publication of this book has been assisted by grants from the following organizations:

ASSOCIATION FOR ASIAN STUDIES

FURTHERMORE:
A PROGRAM OF THE J. M. KAPLAN FUND

MILLARD MEISS PUBLICATION FUND
OF THE COLLEGE ART ASSOCIATION

Designed by Julie Matsuo-Chun

CONTENTS

ACKNOWLEDGMENTS

It took many turns and years for this book to materialize. I am deeply grateful for numerous teachers, friends, and colleagues who guided me through at various phases. At the inception of this project at the University of Chicago, Wu Hung believed in the potential from the beginning, and mentored me in shaping many unsorted intellectual interests into a tangible work that became the foundation of this book. Judith Zeitlin introduced me to an exciting new field of study—Chinese drama—and made it possible for me to work with a corpus of literature with which I had never been familiar. Ping Foong provided many invaluable suggestions, leading to common interests that promise to bring productive intellectual exchanges in the future. Rebecca Zorach's unbounded interest in visual issues outside of her areas of research—which are already immense—were great resources at the outset of this project.

During several research trips in China, roughly from 2005 to 2014, I received indispensable help from local scholars. Zhang Qingjie in Shanxi Provincial Institute of Archaeology, Tian Jianwen in the Museum of Jin-dynasty Tombs in Jishan, Wang

Jinxian in Changzhi Municipal Museum, and Yang Linzhong at Provincial Archaeological Institute for Southeast Shanxi generously assisted me with accessing tombs and temples, and shared their first-hand knowledge of the sites and materials, without which my research and writing of this book would have been simply impossible. Yan Baoquan and Wang Fucai of the Department of Chinese Literature in Shanxi Normal University in Linfen kindly shared their thoughts and information about materials exhibited in the Museum of Chinese Theater located at the university. A group of graduate students at the Department of Archaeology in Zhengzhou University helped me facilitate my regional trips; I thank them for their warm hospitality and discussions over nice local beers. Dong Rui of the Department of Art in Henan University assisted me with acquiring photographs of several objects at the Henan Provincial Museum. In Beijing, Wang Guixiang of the Department of Architecture in Tsinghua University helped me to clarify certain issues that went beyond my immediate areas of research.

Two years in the Department of Art History at Dartmouth College as an Andrew W. Mellon Postdoctoral Fellow provided me with essential time and support for reshaping and polishing the project. I want to express my appreciation to Allen Hockley and Adrian Randolph for their enduring support during the process.

Over the years, I have been extremely fortunate to have excellent friends eager to discuss issues and questions raised in the book manuscript with both sincere critiques and reassurances—often along with gastronomic comfort. I thank Bonnie Cheng, Wen-shing Chou, Karl Debreczeny, Kristina Dy-Lyacco, Rivi Handler-Spitz, Christina Normore, Iiyama Tomoyasu, Li Qingquan, Julia Orell, Peggy Wang, Wasana Wongsurawat, Yudong Wang, and Zheng Yan for their generosity of spirit and brilliant insights. Special thanks to Jeffrey Moser, Julia Orell, Peggy Wang, and Yudong Wang for meticulously reading parts of the manuscript and offering feedback. At the early stages of writing, Stephen Frankel's editorial assistance was indispensable.

At the final stage of the preparation for the image preproduction, helping hands from many different parts of America and China were vital. Michael Hatch, Stephanie Su, Jin Xu, and Zhiyan Yang provided image reproductions on short notice. Liu Jie and Sun Bo helped to track down image sources in China.

I feel very lucky to have been surrounded by a caring community at Syracuse University who made the last stages of writing more enjoyable. Norman Kutcher, Romita Ray, and all of my colleagues at the Department of Art and Music Histories deserve special credit for fostering such a steady and productive intellectual environment.

The final revisions of this book were supported by an American Research in the Humanities in China Fellowship from the American Council of Learned Society. Subvention grants from various sources made it possible for me to reproduce images in this book: the office of the Dean of Humanities at Syracuse University, the Association for Asian Studies First Book Subvention, Furthermore: A Program of the J. M. Kaplan Fund, and the College Art Association's Millard Meiss Publication Fund and Meiss/Mellon Author's Book Award.

I am immensely grateful to those who literally made it possible for this book to exist. I appreciate Patricia Crosby at the University of Hawai'i Press for her early interest and my editors Stephanie Chun and Brian Ostrander for their patience and hard work at various stages of the publication. Meticulous copyedits by Brian Bendlin shaped the book into its present form.

Finally, my deepest thanks go to every member of my family near and far who have always wholeheartedly encouraged me and expressed happiness for what I do. I dedicate this book to them.

PRELUDE

THEATER IN TWO WORLDS

A modest single brick decorated with bas-relief, stored in the National Museum of China in Beijing, carries unusual historical weight (fig. Pr.1). Reportedly found in an eleventh-century tomb in Yanshi County, Henan Province, it had been in the hands of a private collector until its historical value was confirmed by scholars and acquired by the museum. Delicately carved on the surface is an image of a woman wearing a long tunic and pants—a fashionable outfit among urban women in the late eleventh century—and a hooded garment embellished on top with a large bouquet of flowers. Clues that the woman was no ordinary figure, aside from her appearance and manner of dress, include three characters carved at the upper-right-hand corner of the relief. Her name was Ding Dusai, one of the most popular actresses performing in Bianjing, the capital city of the Northern Song dynasty (960–1127). As a member of an independent troupe, the so-called Actresses of the Outdoor Stage (Lutai dizi), Ding performed a series of skits with her fellow actresses as part of the entertainment program at the Pavilion of the Treasured Ford (Baojin lou) during the Qingming spring festival.[1] As twelfth-century author and former

FIGURE PR.1. Actress Ding Dusai.
Brick relief. Northern Song,
11th–12th centuries. 28.4 × 9.3 cm.
National Museum of China.

Bianjing resident Meng Yuanlao implies in his colorful memoir of life in the capital during that time, Ding was apparently well known and the subject of much conversation for those interested in theatrical performance; she was one of only a very few performers among the many of her day whose names were mentioned in Meng's account. This relief, as modern scholar of Chinese drama Liu Nianzi has pointed out, turns out to be the earliest representation of an actor in Chinese history.[2]

Indeed, the middle period in China—from the Song dynasty through the Yuan dynasty (1206–1368)—was the era of theater. Facilitated by rapid urbanization, streets in major urban areas in the Central Plain, and particularly in Henan and Shanxi provinces, were by the eleventh century becoming hubs for all kinds of performance.[3] People of every status had access to different sorts of performances, old and new, ranging from traditional acrobatics to increasingly popular theatrical performances (i.e., variety plays, or *zaju*), for which Ding was renowned. While emperors and high-ranking officials enjoyed a variety of shows performed at court by imperial troupes, commoners had access to performances on improvised stages on the streets, in commercial theaters, or on temple stages, where they would drop by to have a peek at a skit or two. There people of every walk of life would meet: ordinary folk could walk into a theater and sit next to a literatus, who might find himself in the company of Daoist or Buddhist monks.[4]

Without a doubt, the bas-relief depicting Ding is evidence of this burgeoning enthusiasm for theatrical culture. One cannot help but wonder, however, why an image of the actress was placed in the tomb space where it was found. It seems that the significance of this image connected with the theater was not limited to the visual mimicry of everyday life intended for theater enthusiasts. Although prototypical scenes of theatrical performance seen by contemporary spectators belonged to the realm of the living and were associated with merriment and amusement, some of these representations were chosen to occupy spaces designed for the dead—where, it was presumed, they would remain permanently. In this way, through various images of actors and model theaters, the earthly passion for theatrical entertainment was transferred to the underground abode for the dead.

THEATER AND TOMB: TRANSPOSITION OF SPECTACLES

This book examines carefully selected examples of theater-themed images that engage two very different types of performance site: theater and tomb. The subtext connecting all of these examples is that a distinctive mode of visual theatricality mediated the disparate realms of the living and the dead—a concept that is articulated throughout the book.

Reflecting the long period of development of theatrical performances in China and their representations in tombs, the temporal scope of the present volume spans from the eleventh through the late thirteenth centuries, comprising parts of the Song, Liao (907–1125), Jin (1115–1234), and Yuan dynasties. This period, often characterized as a time of political turmoil and cultural ruptures due to ethnic migrations in each dynasty, can be freshly viewed through the continuity manifested in the development of theatrical performances, their representations, and their roles in funerary contexts. After the development of *zaju* in the Song dynasty, later forms of theatrical performance such as scripts from actors' guilds (*yuanben*), which flourished in the Jin during the thirteenth century, and the Yuan *zaju,* emerged; both featured some of the basic characters of the Song *zaju* but also had more sophisticated role types as well as elaborate narrative structures. The geographic scope of this book is concentrated in northern China, where theatrical performances initially developed and matured. Most representations of theatrical performance were found in tombs in the northern and central regions, which featured the most vibrant performance culture of the time, and especially in the northern Henan and southern Shanxi provinces.[5]

The Ding relief is only one of numerous images of actors and model theaters that have been excavated since the mid-1950s in tombs dating from the eleventh through the thirteenth century (see the appendix). As the pioneering research of Liao Ben as well as subsequent studies and collections of these theatrical images colorfully illustrate, they were made in such diverse mediums as brick reliefs, clay figurines, murals, and stone carvings.[6] Some examples show individual actors in frozen theatrical gestures, each molded and carved on a clay brick, as if conceived as collectibles of popular theater idols; some reflect a composite tableau-like composition in which four or five actors engage with one another; still others represent more ambiguous scenes. Some appear in elaborate stage settings, while others are set against empty backgrounds. Some are located opposite representations of the tomb occupants, others are on the same side, and still others are not accompanied by any image of the dead.

It is surprising that these varying details in thematic, compositional, and spatial settings have not drawn much scholarly attention.[7] The main reason seems to be the predominant concentration—on the part of scholars of Chinese drama and theater—on the documentary value of the materials. Indeed, the archaeological discoveries that I examine in this volume have helped to remap the early history of theatrical performance in China, pushing the first appearance of formal theatrical performance from the Jin dynasty back to the Northern Song.[8] Welcoming the archaeological finds as visual evidence, scholars of Chinese drama and theater have sedulously examined the excavated images in order to fill in the blanks in our knowledge about early forms of drama and theater that were only haphazardly recorded in texts from those periods. Yet this overwhelming interest in the documentary value of the excavated material has overshadowed a crucial context that shaped their complex meanings: the transfer of the images from the realm of the living to that of the dead.

There were two types of transposition. The images created as portable objects (in the cases of brick reliefs, figurines, and carvings on sarcophagi) were physically moved from workshops to the underground tomb space.[9] In addition, and at a more fundamental level, prototypical imagery of theatrical performance on which the representations would have been based were transferred into the place of the dead in the form of representations. The seemingly trivial visual details briefly listed above are thus invaluable sources for conceptualizing the processes by which the representations were conceived, designed, produced and, finally, placed in tomb spaces.

Understanding those dimensions helps to imagine how the images that dazzled the living were appropriated and represented in their final destination, their tombs. Where in the society of the living were the prototypes of the images—or, more precisely, theatrical spectacles—located? What sorts of visual sources were available for these representations? Basically, two loci of actual performances, one of which was itself funerary in nature, would have provided the source of the representations. The first is the site of funeral processions or rituals. Apparently, despite persistent government prohibitions against any sort of entertainment during funerary rituals in the middle period, such performances were popularly conducted before and during the rituals.[10] The second type of source for theatrical representations came from a broader range of events that enriched the everyday lives of urban dwellers outside the funerary context. By the late eleventh century, there were at least four nonfunerary locations in urban areas where theatrical performances took place: street corners, commercial theaters, temple stages, and private households.[11] Theatrical performances on the streets were the most casual of these four locations; three or four actors would gather, mark the boundaries of their impromptu stage by simply drawing lines on the ground, and perform.[12] A common occasion for putting on these performances was the seasonal festival, during which people of all social statuses, along with the emperor, could watch *zaju* performances by famous actors and actresses such as Ding. No commercial theater building used for this early phase of drama has survived. But extrapolating from a couple of rare descriptions of such theaters written during this time period, such as Du Renjie's (ca. 1197–1270) "Country Bumpkin Knows Nothing of Theater" (Zhuangjia bushi goulan), we can roughly reconstruct the typical interior of a commercial theater, and we have some idea of the kinds of programs played therein and how the audiences watched the shows.[13] Fortunately, a few thirteenth-century examples of the third popular venue for theatrical performance, temple stages, have survived, which helps us visualize another basic setting for the shows.[14] Although few accounts of the kinds of performances played on these temple stages have been handed down, both excavated and transmitted texts suggest that the plays performed in temples were largely about earthly matters.[15] The last of the four venues, private households, is the only one for which several historical accounts exist. Most of the episodic records describe theatrical shows that were held at the homes of literati.[16] Although the performances in these cases were usually considered to be part of the background setting for a major event, and therefore details of the performances are absent from the record, these texts confirm that actors did perform in private households, just as entertainers of more traditional genres had done in earlier times.

The attempt to identify a specific source for any of these tomb images, despite insufficient data, is a common yet misleading practice in studies of theatrical images and often results in reducing a complex and nuanced picture of the various representations and discourses into an iconographic caricature. The fact is, one person—whether an artisan or the sponsor of a tomb construction—could have seen theatrical performances in virtually all of these venues, which makes it impossible to narrow down the source. From the start, I have deliberately avoided identifying a single site as a visual source of the representations placed in tomb spaces. This approach also helps to avoid the common mistake of artificially contextualizing the contents of performances that occurred in supposedly "mundane" or "sacred" sites—that is, it is only an assumption that performances on the streets or commercial theaters were devoted to earthly matters whereas those on temple stages were about sacred concerns. As mentioned above, even in the case of temple performances, the spectators as well as the content of performances were deeply immersed in the mundane concerns of the everyday world.

Rather than attempting to identify possible prototypes of theatrical images by singling out particular sites through the limited data that is available, I instead examine what linked the visual experiences of theatrical performances to the image making: the power of the spectacle. All of the performance venues mentioned above, regardless of specific location, offered spectacles that were the potential source for their representations in one way or another. The definitions of spectacle range broadly from an ephemeral event to a corporeal object—that is, from the most widely used and still-current definition of it as "a specially prepared or arranged display" (i.e., a public show or display, especially on a large scale, such as a parade) to an obsolete definition of it as "a means of seeing" (such as a window or mirror).[17] What ties the spectrum of all the meanings together is the spectacle's role as medium between the eye and the performance as a "window" onto another "reality."

It is this characteristic that constitutes one of the most notable social functions of the spectacle. The spectacle as a form of mediation tends to alter the order of the everyday world during the duration of a performance and/or thereafter, and to shape the viewers' environment in ways that contest the "normal" order of everyday life.[18] Firmly anchored in the daily world of the living, spectacles experienced in this context offer audiences an opportunity to reflect on their own lives and perhaps provide them with fresh, unforeseen ways to reimagine, challenge, and re-create their lives. By attending to this generative role of the spectacle, this book revolves around the relationships between the contexts of prototypical images of performance and representations of them without being limited by the lack of sources for exactly what audiences would have seen in specific sites.

What, then, happened when the experience of spectacle, serving to invert the normal order of the everyday world of the living, migrated to the space designed for the dead? I contend that the fundamental mechanism of the spectacle as a contester of the existing order, represented and transferred into the tomb space, would manifest particular ways in which contemporaries configured the relationship between the worlds of the living and the dead. In other words, by entering the tomb space, the spectacles formulated in the domain of the living redefined the order of the deceased's realm. The single most important role in this transition, by default, was played by the *representations* of such theatrical experiences.

THE SOCIAL LOCATION OF THEATRICALITY

Someone familiar with the long tradition of Chinese tomb furnishing who views such images of actors and recognizes the cultural traditions of theatrical performance, image making, and funerary practice in China might immediately recall the

FIGURE PR.2. Dancers and musicians. Painted pottery figurines from a tomb in Shaogou, Henan Province. Han. H14–26 cm. Henan Provincial Museum.

variety of small and large figurines made of wood or clay that were buried with the dead since the Warring States period (475–221 BCE). Generally called spirit articles (*mingqi*), these figurines included representations of musicians and dancers (fig. Pr. 2), acrobats, and storytellers as well as male and female attendants.[19] The concept and practice of making *mingqi* have changed over time, but their core function can essentially be defined as accompanying the soul of the deceased to the afterworld. Seen in this perspective, representations of actors such as that of the Ding relief may simply have derived from this figurine-making tradition in funerary contexts, designed to serve the tomb occupant as a performer of the trendiest forms of entertainment at the time.

Yet actor images such as this, made during the middle period, are distinguished from traditional *mingqi* in terms of their nature as representations. Behind the act of representing an existing contemporary entertainer and placing it in a tomb was the enthusiastic endorsement of the lively theatrical scene as a kind of cultural and social statement. The image of Ding, bearing her name and placed within a tomb, conveys a particular value promoted by the maker and the sponsoring family of the deceased. Given the fact that public figures represented in earlier tombs were only individuals of extraordinary stature—deities, exemplars of filial piety, or legendary figures such as the Seven Worthies of the Bamboo Grove (*Zhulin qixian*; see fig. Pr.3)—the inclusion of a named contemporary actress's "portrait" must have been an equally meaningful action, and perhaps more so. This unprecedented appreciation of an existing performer in the context of tomb furnishings thus points to a new use of grave imagery, and may even indicate a changing perception of the tomb space itself at the time. Unlike the predominantly functional value ascribed to the

classical *mingqi,* the bas-relief of the actress Ding proves to be visual testimony to a distinctive cultural taste.

Whose cultural taste was this, and what roles did this practice play in the funerary context? Unfortunately, the original location and nature of the tomb in which the Ding relief was found is unknown.[20] But judging from the data available from excavated tombs with similar theatrical images (see the appendix), we know that only a certain stratum of society placed such images in its tombs. I identify this group as a subset of the "local elite" who could afford rather lavish burials.

Although there is a visible connection between the size and sophistication of the tombs and the occupants' wealth, the generic nature of tomb inscriptions in these burial places, when there are any at all, makes it difficult to define this social group with a single historical term. Most of the inscriptions do not include a funerary epitaph (*muzhi, mubiao,* or *muzhiming*) that would indicate the deceased's basic biography, social standing, or values pursued during his or her life.[21] When there are tomb contracts (*maidi quan*) buried in these graves, they usually follow the formulaic format of traditional tomb contracts, providing little information about the deceased.[22]

Because the local elite I refer to is a distinct social stratum that has never been a main subject of Chinese cultural history, and because defining this group is closely linked to the much-discussed characteristics of the literati, some explanations are in order. The large category of the local elite is borrowed from Dieter Kuhn's characterization of the occupants of relatively elaborate chamber tombs, such as the literati, merchants, and landowners of a local area, who had "wealth, power, and prestige" within that area.[23] But I am referring specifically to those people within the local elites who were not under any pressure to follow the orthodox Confucian funerary decorum encouraged by the government and leading literati, and who were invested in displaying certain cultural assets in their funerary monuments. As the case studies in this volume will show, these two interrelated characteristics are important markers that define this otherwise rarely recognized people as a social group. One clue to identifying this group is the fact that lavish tomb making during the middle imperial period was usually discouraged by the imperial government and orthodox Confucian scholars, at least officially.[24] Among numerous examples, prominent Song dynasty scholar-official Fan Zuyu's statement sums up this view, which defines the humble burial as the teaching of the ancient sages, and the extravagant burial as a wrong custom.[25] For ideological or practical reasons, humble burials (*bozang*) or frugal burials (*jianzang*) had been practiced for more than a millennium before the Song dynasty, but before that period relatively few scholars and high-ranking officials had chosen them over lavish burials (*houzang*). While regulations against luxurious burials had always existed, it was only after the

OPPOSITE PAGE

FIGURE PR.3. Ji Kang, one of the Seven Worthies of the Bamboo Grove. Ink rubbing from modeled brick reliefs found in a tomb in Xishanqiao, Nanjing Province. Eastern Jin. H 88 cm. Nanjing Museum.

tenth century that more scholar-officials adopted visibly plain burials.[26] According to the prominent scholar-official Sima Guang (1019–1086), the most authentic and ideal burial for literati was a simple vertical shaft tomb in which only a coffin would be laid and nothing else.[27] Tellingly, most excavated tombs of scholar-officials, identified by the content of their epitaphs, are plain and largely undecorated.[28]

Corresponding to this phenomenon, none of the tombs in which representations of actors, musicians, furniture, or architectural elements were found include an epitaph that identifies the occupant as a scholar or scholar-official.[29] In fact, the very absence of such information helps determine the particular social group under discussion. It was unreasonable for anyone who had served at the imperial court or who had been renowned as an orthodox scholar to sacrifice his fame by defying the injunction against lavish tomb making, which would have overtly contradicted and damaged his (and his family's) reputation. When the literati did desire a luxurious tomb, they seem to have devised a different way to realize it. A recent discovery of the tomb of the Song scholar-official Han Qi (1008–1075) in Anyang, Henan Province is a case in point. The basic structure and mode of adorning the tomb interior hark back to a classical manner of decorating tombs during the Tang dynasty that was popular among aristocrats and members of the imperial family, with a few murals occupying the walls in the corridor and tomb chamber.[30] This is in sharp contrast to the tombs constructed in the new manner of so-called wood imitation (*fangmu*) brick architecture, which was shunned by literati but was becoming popular among members of the nonliterati local elite in the mid-eleventh century.[31] Although this recent archaeological discovery suggests that some literati of the time were still following the manner of tomb making commonly practiced by the social elite of previous centuries, what stands out in this tomb as conveying an unusual sense of magnificence is a gigantic epitaph placed in the burial chamber rather than any images.[32] With each side measuring five feet, and bearing more than six thousand characters carved on its stone surface, this over-the-top scale of the epitaph would have been one way for Han Qi to make his tomb lavish.[33]

Those who were free from the demands of strict Confucian ideology adorned the entire space of their tombs with elaborate representations without any qualms, however—people such as merchants, landowners, affluent farmers, religious clergy, or some local literati who were only loosely engaged in mainstream Confucian teachings. Among numerous examples, the tomb of a local farmer named Dong Hai in Houma, Shanxi Province (ca. 1196), who owned approximately sixty thousand square meters of land, displays one of the most exquisite sets of reliefs simulating louvered doors and other architectural elements among the middle period tombs (fig. Pr.4).[34] Many of the occupants of these tombs were merchants, which, despite the overall lack of records identifying them as such, is suggested by particular pictorial motifs featured in several tombs made in wood imitation architectural style that indicate their cash-handling occupations (fig. Pr. 5).[35] Although the production cost (e.g., material and labor) for constructing those decorated tombs is itself the best indicator of their wealth, the prominent rendering of such pictorial motifs in tombs and their unusual specificity imply that managing a large amount of cash would have been a part of the occupants' everyday lives and that the accumulation of wealth was highly valued during this era of great prosperity. The occupants of the tombs adorned with conspicuous representations of theatrical performances that are the focus of this book would have been such members of the local elite.[36]

Equally significant is locating the makers of such tombs in middle period society. It is challenging to reconstruct a seamless historical narrative explaining who built and adorned them, a common issue encountered in any studies dealing with the cultural legacy of members of a social group who did not represent themselves with their own writing. From the outset, however, it is vital to recognize the social space shared by the makers and sponsors of the tomb images that fundamentally linked their visual and cultural experiences, which is distinct from the situation in pre-Song times. The makers (i.e., artisans) of most excavated tombs embellished or

FIGURE PR.4. Painted brick reliefs from the north wall, rear chamber, of the tomb of Dong Hai and his wife, Houma. Shanxi Province, Jin, ca. 1196. App. 240×247 cm.

furnished with various representations from the Han to the Tang periods were
barely literate and far from affluent,[37] whereas their patrons had high intellectual
and cultural backgrounds (i.e., they were aristocrats, literati, or officials) and therefore lived starkly different lives from the makers.[38] By contrast, the makers of the
middle period tombs with elaborate images largely belonged to a middle stratum in
the social scale, not clearly distinguished from their sponsors. Artisans during the
middle period officially shared the same social status as that of merchants (*shang*),
one of the major components of the nonliterati elite who sponsored the sophisticated tombs under discussion here.[39] Furthermore, in reality, some artisans also had

FIGURE PR.5. Woman carrying a basket of coins. Mural in a tomb discovered in Qingyundian,
Beijing. Liao.

dual occupations as artisans-cum-farmers. Many civil artisans (*minjiang*)—that is, artisans who worked for private households rather than for the government (i.e., *guanjiang*)—worked primarily as farmers, and their activities as artisans were often secondary, a means of earning additional income.[40] Like successful merchants or landowners, some artisans were quite affluent, so much so that they would some-times get away with paying the tax known as corvée (in the form of compulsory unpaid labor) by bribing local officials.[41]

While recognizing the complex social position of artisans during the middle pe-riod, it is reasonable to think that the artisans and the sponsors of these tombs—such as merchants, well-off farmers, and other members of the local elite who could afford them—would have followed similar basic patterns of living, and it is therefore likely that the sponsors' involvement in developing the ideas for the tomb's images was not completely separate from that of the artisans who actually produced them. In this sense, while the tombs of the local elite during the middle period remained to some extent a locus of social relationships that were still in flux, just as in earlier periods,[42] the social distance between the sponsors and makers had narrowed by then and would have partially overlapped, much more than in the case of those who made and decorated the tombs of early China.

What is not known is the level of visual knowledge that surrounded the making of images of actors and theaters in burial spaces for this "middle" class, and how these images were perceived; I must, however, emphasize the fact that the origi-nal images for such representations were derived from theatrical spaces to which nearly everyone in society had access. The theater was one of the very few venues in middle period China that provided a shared space in which people from all so-cial strata could mingle and have cultural experiences together. The extraordi-nary openness of the theater may be taken for granted and could easily escape our attention, but when one thinks of the social restrictions attached to other cultural spaces of the time (for example, literati communities for poetry or paint-ing), it is clear that the theater was distinguished by a cultural literacy shared by a wide variety of social groups, including the nonliterati elite.[43] Given the theater's unique position in the cultural field of middle period society, my discussion of the images and tomb spaces in the chapters that follow actively engages with ideas about contemporaneous theatrical performances and how they were perceived, whenever relevant, as well as representations of them by different types of cul-tural elites.

The present volume takes into serious consideration the open nature of the source images that intersected many social spheres. Rather than limiting the poten-tial of the theatrical images to the source for their patronage or social history, I consider them as a material agency that harbored multifaceted cultural ideas and practices.[44] Recognizing such representations that were generated within that open realm as providing the most tangible link between the theatrical and ritual envi-ronments and the people who inhabited them, this book specifically delves into "vi-sualities" of the theatrical images by addressing such questions as how people saw performances in various circumstances, to what kinds of images they were exposed, what inspired them to represent theatrical images in specific ways, and what kinds of visual or ritual experiences (specifically, funerary ritual experiences) shaped the meanings of those theatrical images.[45]

THEATRICALITY IN TWO MODES

Although representations of dancers, musicians, or acrobats already appeared in Chinese tombs as early as the Warring States period, it was the images of actors that demonstrated a full-fledged capacity to reveal the power of spectacle as the shifter of a given order of reality. The basic distinction between images of actors and those of other entertainers was made through the visual articulation of the defining characteristics of acting and staging. As I will show throughout this study, a series of dual sensibilities involved in dramatic performance were deeply embedded in the theatrical image, such as self and persona in impersonation, or world and theater in the idea of *theatrum mundi*. The full recognition and utilization of these basic dualisms in the representation of theatrical performances amounted to a particular kind of theatricality. The result was an appropriation of the space for the dead: the theatrical images formulated a new spatial order in the tomb space on both the physical and conceptual levels, distinct from yet intricately interwoven with the everyday world of the living.

This construction of multilayered space in the realm of the dead is the overarching role that the theatrical images in the selected case studies share. Among the many archaeological discoveries of theatrical images listed in the appendix, I have chosen examples that show visual and conceptual novelty in engendering and engaging various dimensions of space in specifically theatrical terms. They were created in brick bas-reliefs (such as the one portraying Ding), clay figurines, carvings on sarcophagi, and paintings—none of which, by the eleventh century, was an entirely new medium in the long tradition of representing performances in funerary contexts. What makes them noteworthy, however, are the ways in which their materiality and modes of representation interacted with their surroundings, which, by restructuring the tomb space, manifest specific ideas about the world of the dead. Thus, what distinguishes the selected examples from traditional representations of entertainment is their complex mode of representation rather than the motifs themselves.

Two distinctive modes of representation coexisted. The first mode, borrowing its visual and conceptual sources from classical depictions of performances, is characterized by a narrativity that integrates ritualized performances into a larger funerary process. In chapter 1, I discuss a rare depiction of a *zaju* performance in this mode. The chapter defines the ritual location of theatrical performance in a funeral, and lays out an important set of issues for understanding a second mode of theatrical images that is explored in the subsequent chapters. This second mode emerged as a different, more complex visual phenomenon by the eleventh century, revealing distinctive connections between the society of the living and the imagined afterworld by embodying the theatricality of contemporary dramatic performances in its fullest form. Apart from the depiction of individual traits through dramatic gestures, facial expressions, and props, which intrinsically characterized these performances as theatrical, this new mode turned the entire space in which performance images were present into a virtual theater that signified something larger than that to which their individual signs referred. Often creating another layer of "theater" in the single tomb space, the images self-reflexively doubled the idea of what they were and what they did—that is, representing actors, theaters, and performances. Constituting the core of the second mode, this concept of theatricality thus refers to the doubling of theatrical modality as opposed to theatrical content.[46] The examples examined in chapters 2–5 variously show how such theatricality was visually and spatially manifested and how it redefined the tomb space.

Although the first new narrative mode—which in part derived from the traditional way of representing entertainment—may have appeared earlier than the second, the two modes do not need to be sequenced in evolutionary terms; both coexisted during the period of the social and cultural phenomena explored in this book. By the same token, the largely chronological arrangement of the selected examples should not be understood as an assertion of clear evolutionary development. We simply do not have sufficient extant examples to describe their development in such terms, nor indeed is it the goal of the present study to reconstruct a history of theatrical images. In what follows, readers will instead find a complex network of visual, ritual, and cultural contexts revolving around the original representations of theatrical performance created for the burial space. Through the spectacles that dazzled the eyes of those whose identities are otherwise lost to history, the reader can ascertain their cultural taste and vision of death so tangibly expressed in material form at the beginning of the second millennium in China.

1

THEATER
AND
FUNERAL

Traditionally, imperial governments and scholars shared negative views on the practice of entertainments during the funerary ritual, which has been traced back as far as the third century. One of the earliest known criticisms was by Qiao Zhou of the Shu Han (fl. third century), who strongly condemned musical performances at a funeral.[1] The critical attitude continued into the middle period on both the legal and moral levels. In Northern Song law, the act of sponsoring performances for parents' funerals was described as unfilial, which was one of the ten major crimes (shi'e).[2] Since children of deceased parents were most often those who conducted funerary rituals, this rule must have been officially applied to the majority of people who prepared funerals. Prominent Confucian scholars of the time were particularly vocal about the inappropriateness of such practices; Sima Guang harshly criticized the common entertainments offered during mourning rituals as a violation of ritual codes and laws,[3] and another revered scholar, Lu You (1125–1210), urged his children and future descendants not to have actors perform at a funeral so as not to distract the mourners.[4] Such criticism prevails in most surviving texts on this matter.

While the increasing weight of the criticism is itself a telling barometer of such performances' popularity, the content of the entertainment on funerary occasions is missing in those accounts; only a handful of rare records let us have a glimpse of how they would have been staged and how the mourners responded to them. A lively performance scene during the funerary process is captured in an eyewitness account by Feng Yan (fl. 756), which gives us some idea of actual practices conducted at the vernacular level in the late Tang period and provides a counterbalance to the disproportional number of records consisting only of prescriptive rules for funeral rites: "Again they stopped the funeral carriage, and set up wooden figures of Xiang Yu and Liu Bang participating in the banquet at Goose Gate. The show lasted quite some time. In the meantime, all the mourners came through the funerary curtain, stopped wailing, and watched the performance."[5] This performance was part of a funeral procession during the Dali reign (766–779) as the coffin of the deceased was being carried on the streets to his tomb site. The main funerary ritual had taken place at the house of the deceased, and now the mourners were walking in the funeral procession, along with a troupe of performers. The latter performance of this celebrated episode of the feast at the Goose Gate (Hongmen) from the Three Kingdoms saga was preceded by the enactment of a combat scene between two celebrated soldiers in history that was performed alongside the procession.[6] These few descriptive passages thus focus on conveying the fascination of the onlookers and provide the details of the theatrical performances as a part of the larger funerary program. Clearly the power of spectacles impelled the mourners to temporarily forget about their ritual duties and instead indulge in watching what was unfolding fantastically before their eyes.

Why were such controversial entertainments regularly performed at funerary occasions? Were there ritual meanings in such performances in the larger context of the mourning process? The classical term that generally refers to any kinds of entertaining performance in funerary occasions, *yuesang*—that is, music (or, by extension, other kinds of entertainment) accompanying a mourning ritual—is not very helpful for defining the function of such performances in the ritual context or their reception during the middle period.[7] The term *sang* can designate any phase in the entire funerary ritual, from the initial ritual of soul calling (*zhao hun*) to the final worship ceremony (*yuji*).[8] All subrituals taking place within a single funeral could occur in various settings, both private and entirely public, involving different audiences (from immediate family to townspeople).[9] The deceased was not simply regarded as a physical body; his or her status would also change according to the particular phase of the death ritual being performed.[10] The ritual meaning of the performance in a funeral was thus inevitably contingent upon the phase of the entire funeral program in which entertainment occurred. Existing textual sources that deal with this issue are terse and heavily prescriptive; with the exception of Feng's account, there is almost no historical record from the early middle period of how spectators-cum-mourners responded to such shows.

ZAJU DURING FUNERALS

While almost all the textual sources are silent about theatrical performances during funerary rituals, some visual representations of contemporary funerary scenes open up an unexpectedly rich context in which the vernacular practice of entertainment for a funeral can be reconstructed and its ritual meaning can be deduced. Among the few representations of theatrical performance found in tombs of the eleventh century, one stands out as a rare depiction of a pictorially coherent narrative of a funerary ritual. A sarcophagus found in a brick chamber tomb in Xingyang, Henan Province (fig. 1.1), bears incised line drawings of a series of events, including a tableau-like scene of an acting troupe (fig. 1.2). This stone coffin belonged to a certain Zhu Sanweng, "the third man of a Zhu family,"[11] identified as such by the inscription carved on the coffin lid. Zhu's coffin—and most likely the entire tomb—was commissioned by his son Zhu Yunjian, and was buried on the eighth day of November (in the lunar calendar) in 1096.[12] Unfortunately, the tomb had been robbed before it was excavated, and this sarcophagus was the only remaining object. Judging from the brief inscription, which does not indicate any official title for Zhu, he must have been an ordinary local man whose family had the means to build a brick chamber tomb and to commission a sarcophagus. Despite the unassuming technique and seemingly insignificant details of the pictorial carvings on the coffin's surface, they provide rich information about the context in which some of the crucial ritual moments of Zhu's funeral occurred.

FIGURE 1.1. Zhu Sanweng's limestone sarcophagus, Xingyang. Henan Province, ca. 1096. H 93 (front)×W 193×D 102 cm. Henan Provincial Museum.

Zhu's coffin follows a standard form of Chinese sarcophagi, composed of four slabs, a lid, and a base; each of the two long side panels is shaped like an elongated trapezoid that is higher at the coffin's head than at its foot (which correspond to the location of the body's head and feet). Each panel presents a pictorially self-contained narrative, but the images on the side panels are also linked thematically, forming a larger narrative. Some elements in the composition and the structure of this pictorial narrative were derived from classical representations of various motifs in tomb murals, as well as other images in different mediums destined for a tomb space. While demonstrating strong ties to earlier pictorial conventions that can be traced back as far as the Han period (221–206 BCE), several details that revolve around the scene of theatrical performance show the pictorial and ritual appropriations of the classical motifs in the contemporary setting of the eleventh century.

The slab on the right side (when standing at the foot of the coffin) can be pictorially divided into three parts (fig. 1.2, left). Beginning with the images at the right of the panel (the narrower end), there are three men preparing food in a kitchen. Two of them seem to be following the orders given by a standing figure, perhaps a chef: one man is adding fuel to a fire in a stove, and another man is making what appear to be dumplings of some sort; images found in other contemporaneous burial sites indicate that dumplings would have been quite a common menu item in middle period funerals as well as in daily life.[13] To the left of the kitchen, in the second part of the panel, a groom stands with his horse, turning his head to the left; this alludes to an upcoming journey, a conventional sign indicating the departure of the deceased for the afterworld in funerary art since the Han period.[14] Following the groom's gaze, the viewer finds two servants carrying a dish and a wine vessel. It soon becomes clear where the food and drink are being delivered and who the groom is waiting for. In front of the food carrier, in the third part of the panel (at the higher end), are four entertainers in dramatically frozen poses, obviously performing for two spectators seated at a table laden with several plates of food and utensils and attended by a servant and a small cat. The inclusion of domesticated animals in a pictorial image was a common practice during the middle period in both funerary and non-funerary art, and here it adds a note of authenticity—a familiar sight in the contemporary domestic space.[15]

Each scene—the preparation of food, the groom with a horse, and the entertainment—is unfailingly reminiscent of classical representations that adorn many tomb walls or coffin surfaces created since the Han period. Often deployed in separate pictorial planes, these motifs are generally understood by students of Chinese funerary art as a banquet for the deceased,[16] but here I will recontextualize them within a funerary context. Whether the two seated spectators depicted actually resemble Zhu and his wife is impossible to determine, but it is clear that they represent the deceased couple because of the motif's strong connection to traditional representations of performances prepared for tomb occupants.

Yet details of each segment are minutely updated with contemporary visual and material culture. It takes just a couple of comparative examples from the Han and Eastern Han periods to show how this scene from a Song period sarcophagus

FIGURE 1.2. Line drawing of carved images on side panels, Zhu Sanweng's sarcophagus.

was "modernized." The traditional food prepared—in earlier examples, the butchering of animals—is here replaced by the steaming of dumplings (fig. 1.3), while a floor mat for the deceased couple is replaced by a table and chairs (fig. 1.4).[17] Most notable of all the changes is that traditional entertainers such as acrobats, dancers, or musicians are replaced by a troupe of four actors with distinctive costumes, makeup, and props; thanks to these particular details, they are instantly recognized as *zaju* actors. The *zaju* (literally, a variety play or show) began to flourish during the Song period and is generally understood by modern scholars as a series of comic skits performed by four or five people in the roles of announcer, leading actors, and supporting clowns.[18] There is no single contemporary text to explain the form of *zaju* systematically, but scholars of Chinese drama have ascertained a basic structure of *zaju* by stitching together fragmented sources written since the thirteenth century and retrospectively tracing back the origins of a more developed form of theatrical performance that succeeded it in the Jin dynasty (i.e., *yuanben*).[19] The identifications of the roles of the actors suggested here are based on these literary reconstructions as well as on other representations of actors found in slightly later tombs.

This late eleventh-century sarcophagus is one of the invaluable archaeological finds that have advanced the study of early Chinese drama since the 1950s.[20] Certain visual theatrics of the four actors depicted on Zhu's coffin are clearly recognizable despite the rather casual carving style (fig. 1.5). The costume and prop of the actor standing at the far left help narrow down his possible role to that which became standardized in the thirteenth century as the second male lead (*fumo*), whose purpose was to make jokes and provoke the other players.[21] His cylindrical hat—nicknamed by contemporaries Su Shi's hat (*Dongpo mao*) or Su Shi style (*Zizhan yang*), after Su Shi (1037–1101), one of the most celebrated literati of the time—as well as his thin bamboo stick (*zhugan zi*) are the visual hallmarks of this role type.[22] The two actors standing in the center of the group represent comic roles, which became the second clown (*fujing*) in the Jin and Yuan theaters.[23] The prominent headgear they are wearing (the hood with a projected knot on top and the triangular hat) are both frequently spotted in later depictions of this comedic duo (see figs. 2.6

and 3.4). Here the actor wearing the knot-topped hood is holding a *paiban,* a wooden clapper frequently used in theatrical and musical performances, and the amusing makeup on the eyelids of the actor wearing the triangular hat confirms his comic role. The fourth actor of this little troupe, standing to the right of the other three and facing the viewer, is the most ambiguous. Given the identifications of the role types of his fellow actors, this figure may represent a male lead (*moni*) or the one who introduces the play (*yinxi*), two other possible role types that became consolidated later in the Jin theater.[24] This figure's gesture remains indecipherable, making it difficult to know if there might be any link to the extremely terse descriptions of these role types in twelfth- to fourteenth-century textual sources.[25] And yet, the distinctly theatrical posture that confronts the viewer's gaze, as well as the proximity to the actor group, suggests that the figure is most likely a member of the troupe.

Are these actors staging a specific play? The answer is no, not only because of the lack of evidence that could remotely identify the performance but, more important, because of the role that the *zaju* scene plays in a larger pictorial narrative. Lü Pin, based on his observation of some stitched lines on the costume of the clown with the pointed hat (fig. 1.5), has suggested that this figure represents a popular actor in the Song period, Li Yishan, who is recorded in a couple of contemporary essays as wearing "torn" and "humble" clothes on stage.[26] Although the peculiar clothing certainly deserves attention, this single visual characteristic cannot be sufficient evidence for identifying the specific actor and play; there may well have been several plays that utilized such clothing to represent the poor or beggars.

Redirecting our focus from the vaguely relevant anecdotal link to the more firmly codified clothing for funerary events of the time, we discover an intriguing visual overlap between the theatrical costume and mourning garb. The small patch of fabric sewn onto the shoulder of the actor's gown, prominently shown to the viewer, strikingly resembles a rectangular piece of fabric stitched onto a type of sackcloth called *zhancui,* the most important of the five garments (*wu fu*) to be worn by the chief mourner for the deceased—ideally for three years. According to the interpretation of Jia Gongyan (fl. 7th century), the term *zhan* is used to express the meaning of deep pain.[27] In principle, the *zhancui* was to be worn by a son mourning his father, a feudal lord mourning the Son of Heaven, a minister mourning the emperor, or a father mourning his oldest son. Since the chief mourner for Zhu Sanweng was identified as his son Zhu Yunjian, it is clear that the wearer of *zhancui* here was supposed to be Zhu Yunjian. According to Zheng Xuan's (127–200) commentary on *Yili* (Ceremonies and rites), a patch of cloth referred to as *cui* (in *zhancui*) was to be sewn onto the chest part, and another piece of cloth, called *fuban*, was to be stitched onto the back.[28] It was implied that the resulting appearance of the raggedness, highlighted by the purposefully unhemmed garment, resonated with the symbolic meaning given to the cloth patches as carrying and bearing the grief on the mourner's body.[29] While the eleventh-century illustration printed in the *Sanli tu* (Newly edited pictures for the three compendia for ritual) of Nie Chongyi (fl. tenth century) presents *zhancui* in a rather simple manner (fig. 1.6, top), the same clothing code is concretely pictorialized in the early fourteenth-century edition of the *Shilin guangji* (Comprehensive record of the forest of matters) by Chen Yuanjing (fl. thirteenth century), showing both *cui* and *fuban*, as well as the unhemmed sleeves.[30] In fact, the costume of the actor standing on the right of this figure, whose role type has been discussed above as most difficult to determine (either *moni* or *yinxi*), also echoes the quintessential form of the mourning skirt—the *zhancui chang* (fig. 1.6, middle).[31] The illustrations in both *Sanli tu* and *Shilin guangji* show distinctive pleats, identical to the one worn by this actor.[32]

These two actors' costumes thus conspicuously evoke an imagery of mourners at a funeral. What was the appeal of inserting the mourners into the scene of the theatrical performance? Why did the coffin designer and/or the sponsor not just have the mourners (e.g., Zhu's son and daughter-in-law) depicted as who they were rather than representing actors in the guise of the mourners, with their theatrical makeup and gesticulations still discernible? The curious merge between the acting and mourning subtly implies the grander scheme of the narrative that goes beyond this theatrical space. The presence of the figures in the mourning robes amid what might otherwise seem a generic entertainment event serves to fix this performance scene to a particular temporality: it alludes to the moment of mourning for the deceased rather than documenting a past event in his life or anticipating the future prosperity of the afterlife.

The ritual element incipient in this *zaju* scene is fully unfolded in the extended funerary discourse depicted throughout the sarcophagus surfaces. This mode of representation, which contrasts sharply with some later examples of theatrical images, heightens the sense of narrativity by emphasizing the conscious flow of time within the single pictorial space.

OPPOSITE PAGE

FIGURE 1.3. Above, Cooking in a kitchen. Detail. Rubbing of a stone carving from a tomb discovered in Yinan, Shandong Province. Eastern Han. **FIGURE 1.4.** Below, The deceased (top left) watching entertainment. Brick relief from Yangzishan, Sichuan Province. Eastern Han. 39.5×48 cm.

FIGURE 1.5. Four actors in *zaju* performance. Detail. Ink rubbing from Zhu Sanweng's sarcophagus.

ACTORS, MONKS, AND THE FUNERARY PROCESSION

Looking at this series of scenes on one side of the coffin (food being prepared and delivered, *zaju* being performed, and the deceased couple watching the performance while enjoying the food), one wonders why these particular events were chosen to be depicted on the limited surface of the sarcophagus. Clearly it is a plausible pictorial narrative, but why were these seemingly trivial subjects selected to adorn the coffin that contained the deceased, the focal point of the entire tomb space? Because a narrative is always potentially part of another narrative, which often alters the meaning of the local narrative, this "banquet" scene should be considered as possibly belonging within a larger narrative.[33] Moving our gaze to the other side of the sarcophagus, we discover an extended arena of the pictorial world where the ritual meaning of the *zaju* performance becomes clear.

Like many sarcophagi with carved designs made prior to the eleventh century, Zhu's coffin utilizes a pictorial scheme that continues from one side panel to the other (fig. 1.2, right). Again, the beginning of the narrative on the panel is located at the narrower end (which, on this side, is the left end of the panel), indicated at first glance by the linear movement of all the figures from left to right. At the far left is an architectural scene featuring a compound consisting of three structures with elaborate roofs, arranged around a central courtyard that—though rather crudely depicted—seems to represent an affluent household. The structure at the left of the

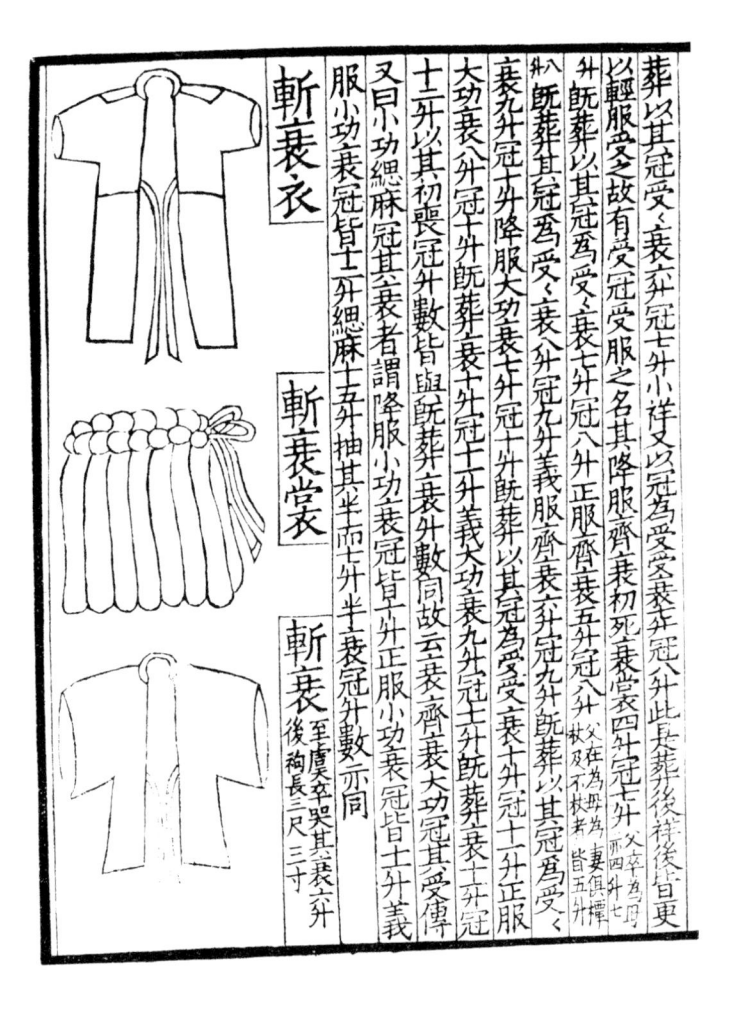

FIGURE 1.6. Mourning jacket (top) and skirt (middle). Woodcut print, 1175. From Nie Chongyi, *Xin ding San li tu.*

courtyard is recognizable as the main gate, with its stone stairs; it is wide open, suggesting that there is an ongoing event that would have moved from inside to outside. Just beyond the other side of the compound, through the smaller gate, a groom stands with his horse, most likely the same one represented on the first panel. The repetition of a figure twice or more in a pictorial space was already commonplace in narrative images by the middle period, which is perhaps most clearly illustrated in the tenth-century scroll painting *The Night Entertainments of Han Xizai (Han Xizai yeyan tu)*: while Han Xizai's presence in every scene of this continuous scroll indicates that it represents a series of distinct spatiotemporal episodes, with each episode separated by partitions or screens, they can be viewed as a continuous series of events.[34] On the sarcophagus, the pictorial convention of repeating the image of the groom and his horse in two successive scenes serves to connect the new pictorial space to the previous one—that is, the reappearance of this figure in a new context signals the continuity of the narrative as well as a shift in time and space.

This continuity is reaffirmed as the viewer sees two familiar figures among the group of people depicted in the next scene (in the middle of the panel): an elderly man and woman who, with clothes, hairstyles, and their central positioning all similar to those of the couple at the table on the first panel, are immediately identifiable as the deceased couple. They are walking forward, led by four Buddhist monks and followed by two attendants. The monks are holding *naobo* cymbals and striking them together; these cymbals were commonly used in a procession by the lead performer, whether Buddhist or non-Buddhist. A few similar representations excavated in tombs from the twelfth and thirteenth centuries suggest that the practice was popular not only in the Central Plain but also in the northwest and south (fig. 1.7).[35] Finally, at the extreme right of the coffin panel, there is a group of three women wearing highly elaborate clothes and headdresses; one is holding an incense burner from which a plume of smoke is rising, and the other two are carrying banners, most likely *mingjing,* the funerary banners that bore the names and titles of the deceased.[36]

The presence of the Buddhist monks and the particularity of these props and clothing suggest that the entire scene represents a kind of funerary procession com-

FIGURE 1.7. Monks performing *zi mingfu* ceremony for the deceased couple. Mural in a tomb excavated in Huaixi Village, Xingyang, Henan Province. Song. H 86 cm.

mon to the experience of the local elite (such as Zhu's family) rather than the kind that conformed to canonical ritual practice. The use of *naobo* cymbals, for example, was condemned by Cheng Yi (1033–1107) and other leading Confucian scholars of the Song period for their Indian origin and inappropriateness for expressing grief.[37] But again, it is in such harshly critical statements by scholar-officials and the imperial court that we are given an unusual glimpse of vernacular funerary practice. An early thirteenth-century author, Wang Yong (fl. 1227), wrote:

> Families in mourning have Buddhist or Daoist priests chant sutras, arrange vegetarian feasts, and conduct wine offerings and Buddhist rites, and call these "investing in the deceased's welfare in the afterworld [*zi mingfu*]." When taking the coffin to the tomb site, they have the priests lead [the processions]; how could this be righteous? As to the *naobo* cymbals, it's just foreign [Indian] music; in the foreign custom, their vulgar music is made by banging *naobo*. But how could they do this to the deceased in a funeral casket [*sangjiu*]? The ordinary folks' ignorance has reached the point where they even play music using drums and flutes. How could this, too, be endured![38]

This passage confirms the ubiquitous sight of monks busily striking cymbals together while leading a funerary procession, and illuminates the ritual significance of this kind of entertainment as part of a memorial service for "ordinary folks." The author is apparently concerned enough about the contemporary interpretation and practice of *zi mingfu* by the general populace to bring it to the attention of the literati. The term *zi mingfu* has usually been understood in modern times to mean "praying for the repose of a soul" in any East Asian funerary discourse. But during the middle period, it was predominantly used in the ritual context after being introduced as a tradition of the Indian Buddhist funeral, as mentioned in a travelogue about the western region written by the eminent Tang dynasty monk Xuanzang (596–664).[39] The *zi mingfu* was often accompanied by the chanting of sutras, an act of "investing" (*zi*), hence literally translated here as "investing in the deceased's welfare in the afterworld."[40] It is difficult to determine which bothered the author Wang more—the "hybrid" form of the funeral, imbued with the foreign, Buddhist practice, or the newer trend of inserting entertainments in the *zi mingfu* ritual. Regardless, it is clear that more elaborate types of entertainment, rather than just striking the cymbals, had become a part of the popular *zi mingfu* ceremony for the common folk.

This account provides a crucial clue for understanding the relationship between the *zaju* performance and the procession, represented separately on each sarcophagus panel. According to the text, this ritual action was intended for and directed toward the deceased in transition; the use of the term *jiu* in *sangjiu*, referring to "the body placed in a coffin" as opposed to the corpse (*shi*) in a context-neutral sense, indicates that the intended recipient of the performance was the dead in the funerary ritual—that is, the ritualized body.[41] While the exact timing of the entertainment (the playing of "drums and flutes") in a memorial service is unstated in

Wang's record, suffice it to say that it was meant to be a part of an extended funerary ritual, albeit an unorthodox one. In fact, the two components—religious service and entertainment—had often been linked as a pair of commemorating rituals for both auspicious events (*ji li*) and inauspicious ones (*xiong li*). For example, one tenth-century account relates that during the Tang dynasty, a certain Chen in Linzi, Shandong Province, would hold an extravagant birthday celebration every year during which he would hire Buddhist and Daoist monks to prepare a vegetarian feast (*zhaiyan*) for which the musicians and miscellaneous entertainments would all be provided.[42] There is a significant link between Chen's birthday feast and the practice of *zi mingfu,* the link being the rite composed of religious services and entertainments—in other words, both auspicious and inauspicious events shared this coupled program. When we think of the time-honored notion of "postmortem immortality" that matured as late as the Eastern Han period (25–220),[43] which conceptually transcended the dichotomy between the earthly world and the afterworld, the seeming conflict in what was to be commemorated—that is, birth and death—would not have troubled the minds of these folks. They probably did not feel obliged to follow strict Confucian ritual codes, nor did they find it problematic to use the same set of the ritual (i.e., religious service and entertainment) performed for the two heterogeneous events in nature.[44] Since this practice was considered incorrect according to Confucian precepts, it could not, of course, be included (and explained) in contemporary manuals on proper mourning practice.[45] Judging from Wang's account and other contemporary criticism, however, in actuality people did conduct this version of funerary ritual quite widely and frequently.

TOWARD THE HEAVENLY GATE

The two components of the *zi mingfu* ceremony mentioned in Wang Yong's account are visible in the panels of the Zhu sarcophagus: the deceased couple are entertained by the *zaju* performance and then leave their home, led by the Buddhist monks. Wang's account mentions only musical performances in the ritual, but the *zaju* performed by the four actors here can be seen as a part of the extensive *zi mingfu* ritual provided for the Zhu couple, as reflected in the strictures from Lu You against the common theatrical performances at funerals—a prototypical form of which can be traced back to the theatrical spectacles in the late Tang funerary procession discussed at the beginning of this chapter. Depicted in the two stone panels, these two scenes also structurally resonate with the twofold *zi mingfu* practice.

Where in the larger funerary program was this twofold ritual located? That this pair of scenes is in fact a segment of a larger narrative is immediately apparent when we resume our examination of all the panels on the sarcophagus, continuing in the direction of the procession shown in the second panel. Carved on the head panel—which is often the most symbolic section of a coffin in the Chinese funerary context—is the facade of an elaborate gate in relief (fig. 1.8). In the middle of this tripartite architectural facade, framed within a solidly tiled roof at the top and the

FIGURE 1.8. Line drawing of the head panel of Zhu Sanweng's sarcophagus.

railings of staircases at the bottom, a figure peeks out from a partially open door. An eleventh-century version of the well-known pictorial motif of a half-open door, which can be traced back to the Han period,[46] this image had been established as an important funerary symbol and may have been understood as such by anyone who saw it; its position within the narrative presented on the sarcophagus (and on other tomb decorations as well) is a crucial determinant of its significance.

Perhaps the earliest and best-known image that can be associated with the door motif on a coffin is the rather abstract rendering of a rectangular opening represented on the head panel of the inner coffin of Marquis Yi of the Zeng state, buried about 433 BCE. The image of an opening on a coffin—though the details may vary from image to image—symbolizes a "path" to the sphere of the dead, whether it suggests the space of death or immortality.[47] This idea endured in funerary decorations of subsequent periods, with new historical and religious connotations and gradually taking a characteristically architectural form. Images of a gate depicted on many Eastern Han sarcophagi panels are reminiscent of the earlier rectangular opening painted on Marquis Yi's coffin. One frequently sees representations of a single *que* tower (or a pair of them) on the surfaces of sarcophagi of the Eastern Han period, either on a side panel or the head panel, especially in Sichuan Province (fig. 1.9). A *que* image on the head panel alluded to the passage through which the soul of the deceased enters the spiritual world, an interpretation that has been confirmed by archaeological discoveries (fig. 1.10).[48] Whether the representation of *que* towers symbolizes a gate to the celestial world or to the terrestrial world might be determined by the particular context of a particular image. But a new type of sarcophagus design hints at a more distinct idea underlying the *que* image. The quintessential form of this type is a double door with or without a standing figure,

FIGURE 1.9. A pair of *que* towers carved on a sarcophagus discovered in Nanxi County, Sichuan Province. Ink rubbing. Eastern Han. 67 × 67 cm.

FIGURE 1.10. Line drawings of copper medals found in Wushan, Sichuan Province. Han. Diameter 25.4 cm.

carved on the head panel of a sarcophagus. One of the earliest and best-known images of this kind is the one on the head panel of the sarcophagus of an Eastern Han man, Wang Hui (212 AD), that was excavated in Lushan, Sichuan Province (fig. 1.11). The head panel shows a gate with a fairylike winged figure that has been interpreted as an immortal welcoming the deceased to paradise.[49]

The continuing practice of representing an opening on the head panel of a sarcophagus—either as a part of a pictorial program or as an independent icon—is visible in several surviving examples from the Southern and Northern dynasties (420–589) and the Sui dynasty (581–618). The door images from this period are highly decorative, resembling an actual gate seen from outside, often with two figures flanking it. Reflecting its popularity, the funerary connotation deeply embedded in this

FIGURE 1.11. Wang Hui's sarcophagus. Lushan County, Sichuan
Province. Eastern Han. H 101
(front)×W 83 (widest)×D 250 cm.

motif was adopted by Buddhist image makers (and their sponsors) during the Tang
and Song periods. Their door images were often affixed to objects with defined ritual
mortuary functions, such as pagodas or reliquaries, sometimes replacing the conventional figure with a monk or a bodhisattva (as in fig. 1.12).[50] The motif of figures flanking doors continued to appear both on reliquaries and sarcophagi during the middle
period and enjoyed great popularity. Furthermore, some door images took a distinctively three-dimensional form, which transformed the entire sarcophagus—not just
the head panel—into a piece of house-like architecture (fig. 1.13).[51]

While some of the earlier scholarship focused on specific meanings of the image
as an isolated icon, often attempting to read its meaning according to fragmentary
textual sources, more extensive studies have demonstrated its complex role in evoking the existence of the space beyond the tomb chamber or coffin.[52] The general idea
underlying the door motif can be understood as a gateway to the unknown world
reserved for the deceased.

CROSSING THE BOUNDARY

This is the context in which the *zaju* performance and the procession that unfolds
on the two side panels of Zhu's coffin function in an extended funerary narrative.
The movement of the funerary procession is clearly indicated by the panels' representation of the forward motion of the deceased couple and their entourage and by
the wide-open doors of the house gate through which the deceased couple has just
emerged. Zhu and his wife are shown taking steps toward the higher end (the head)
of the panel, where the striking image of the gate is located.

How exactly is this twofold funerary narrative connected to—and eventually
subsumed into—the motif of a half-open door? At first sight, the image of the gate
may appear independent of the ongoing funerary events. The ambiguous relation-

FIGURE 1.12. Aśoka stupa. Paint on marble. Found in the front chamber of the relic deposit at Famen Monastery, Fufeng, Shanxi Province. Tang, ca. 8th century. H 78.5 cm.

FIGURE 1.13. House-shaped clay coffin from a tomb discovered in Yueshan, Sichuan Province. Five Dynasties, 10th century. H 40.5 (front) × W 29 (widest) × D 81.5 cm.

ship between the funerary narrative and the iconic gate can be discerned at both the visual and conceptual levels. Besides its larger scale when compared to the buildings and figures on the side panels, the gate is distinctively architectonic, in sharp contrast to the shallowly carved line drawing of the narrative scenes. More fundamentally, the time and space underlying the image of the half-open gate are liminal as well as universal, generally accepted as symbolizing the unknown timeless space (as the brief survey above has shown), whereas the scenes of the *zaju* and funeral procession are anchored in a particular time and place and are hence historical—at least within the pictorial space.

As an attentive observer may notice, however, there is a pictorial element that subtly links these realms of apparently dissimilar nature. A railing with carved balusters, resembling those in the balustrade of the gate facade, encircles the entire coffin—including the foot panel, which also features two pairs of auspicious animals. The balustrade belongs specifically to the grand architecture of that gate whose facade is represented, and the railing—rather than being an organic part of the ritual setting—serves as a conceit that encompasses those scenes of the funeral occurring in the mortal world. On first glance, this continuous railing seems superfluous, as the two sites of the *zi mingfu* events—both outdoors—do not require the kind of handrails that would usually appear only on a balcony of a building or on a bridge in carved or painted scenes from this period.[53] Yet this seemingly arbitrary inclusion of the railing with carved balusters may not be just a simple decorative element, as it corresponds to a spatial and conceptual hierarchical order between the two realms: the narrative scenes are visually connected by a component of the architecture metonymically represented by the heavenly gate. Some of the surviving Buddhist reliquaries of the middle period provide an interesting point of comparison. A silver reliquary in architectural form found in the crypt underneath a pagoda of the Fusheng Monastery (Fusheng si) in Dengzhou, for example, is surrounded by railings placed on a platform (fig. 1.14). If this type of three-dimensional railing in reliquaries or coffins can be considered a possible prototype of the balustrade on Zhu's sarcophagus, why would it have been imitated as a flat representation on the surface of the sarcophagus, at the risk of the awkward and illogical rendering of space?

This choice of inclusion had to do with the effect of creating an ambiguous space within the picture plane. What lies between the balustrade of the heavenly architecture and the pictorial space existing behind it remains undefined. In other words, the overall design denies a single spatial or visual logic that governs all three realms: the historical realm of the funerary narrative, the universal realm symbolized by the semicorporeal presence of the heavenly gate, and the present world in which the sarcophagus as an object (i.e., the bearer of the images) exists. To the coffin designer and Zhu's son (who commissioned this sarcophagus), perhaps this ambiguity was not a problem but instead something that resonated with the liminal status of the deceased in transition at the moment of the funeral. Notably, some of the recent archaeological discoveries echo the discursive way in which such a transitional state was rendered. The walls of several Song tombs found in the Zhengzhou area in Henan Province are opulently painted with various themes,

FIGURE 1.14. Silver reliquary in architectural form. From the crypt under the pagoda at the Fusheng Monastery in Dengzhou, Henan Province. Song, ca. 1032. H 26 (front) × W 20 (widest) × D 40 cm.

including a series of funerary processions similar to that represented on Zhu's coffin. On the upper register of a tomb found in Pingmo in the city of Xinmi dating to 1108, there are three scenes corresponding to the funerary narrative depicted on Zhu's sarcophagus, positioned between the popular images of the children known for their filial piety in history, conventionally called the Twenty-Four Exemplars of Filial Piety (*Er shi si xiao*).[54] Two groups of figures are depicted on the northwest wall. A Buddhist priest stands at the left, wearing a purple headdress and a clerical robe (a typical outfit for a distinguished monk, especially when participating in a funeral),[55] flanked by a female attendant and a monk, and at the right are a man and a woman kneeling on a mat (fig. 1.15a). The excavators of the tomb have identified the object in the priest's hand as a sutra, which indicates that this scene represents the chanting of a sutra for the deceased couple. As mentioned above, the chanting of sutras was a major component of the *zi mingfu* ritual during the Song dynasty, often taking place alongside musical or theatrical performances.[56] Surrounded by thick layers of clouds, the monk and his attendants are looking at the man and woman on the mat, who are clasping their hands in prayer. A cartouche accompanying this scene reads, "The Great Saint of Sizhou [*Sizhou dasheng*] guides the old gentleman and his wife to cross [*du*] [over to the other world]."

It thus identifies the hooded priest as a revered monk from Central Asia, Sengqie (617–710), and the couple as the tomb occupants. Sengqie, who was thought to have become an avatar of the Bodhisattva Avalokiteśvara (Guanyin) after his death, enjoyed wide popularity and became an object of worship in the lower Yangtze River region during the late Tang and Song periods.[57] Given his deified status, it is plausible that the deceased couple were among the enthusiastic worshippers in the local community of Pingmo when they were alive, and that that is why they had the image of Sengqie depicted in their tomb. It is noteworthy that Sengqie appears here as a living monk who conducts a *zi mingfu* ritual for the tomb occupants, as if replacing a regular local cleric; that is to say, Sengqie's anachronistic presence along with the deceased suggests that different types of Buddhist figures—be it anonymous local monks, as in Zhu's sarcophagus, or a celebrated historical cleric, as here—were appropriated to represent the persona of the *zi mingfu* presider in the formulaic funerary narrative.[58] A comparison of this and the Zhu Sanweng sarcophagus thus reveals different degrees of localization of the popular funerary praxis.

Turning to the opposite wall of the Pingmo tomb, we find what seems to be the next scene corresponding to the funerary narrative on Zhu's sarcophagus. Here the deceased, whom we saw kneeling on a mat in the first scene, reappear in the middle of a bridge that is floating on clouds (fig. 1.15b). Their faces are turned to the left, the direction in which they appear to be walking, guided by two women, each of whom holds a light-emitting sutra and a *mingjing* funerary banner; they are followed by an entourage of four more women. A fuller-scale representation of such a procession can be found in a tomb in Nanchui Village in Changzhi, Shanxi Province, dating to 1153; this representation effectively combines the *zi mingfu* ritual and the crossing of the great boundary in a single frame set on a grandiose bridge over a deep blue river (fig. 1.16). While the procession in the Nanchui mural does not reveal the group's destination pictorially, the Pingmo case does. The deceased and their entourage are headed to a majestic architectural complex on the north wall, consisting of four double-roofed buildings, that is painted on the wall between these two scenes (fig. 1.15c). The site is clearly indicated as auspicious and sacred: the lower part of the complex is covered with clusters of clouds, and many rays of light are emitted from the roofs—a common pictorial motif in Buddhist and Daoist paintings for suggesting the spiritual power and sacredness of a particular site.[59] Appearing in all three scenes, the clouds demarcate a realm of transition, just as the continuous railing does in Zhu's sarcophagus.[60] The imposing sight of the heavenly architecture signals that the role of the *zi mingfu* ritual has now been completed: the deceased have crossed (*du*) the boundary between this world and the next.

Both the pictorial details and the narrativity of these scenes are strongly reminiscent of the images represented on Zhu's sarcophagus. Laid out on the walls that flank the central image of the magnificent building, as on Zhu's coffin, the two scenes of the deceased depicted in the Pingmo tomb allude to their procession on a path to the auspicious place existing beyond the world of the living.[61] The formulaic pattern used to depict the funerary narrative in both examples is reaffirmed by murals in another contemporaneous tomb from 1097 in Heishangou in the city of Dengfeng, Henan Province. On the uppermost register of this octagonal tomb are depicted a number of figures who appear to be walking in the same direction. The deceased couple portrayed on the northwest wall are led by their entourage, some of them banging *naobo* cymbals (fig. 1.17a), and some holding *mingjing* banners (fig. 1.17b); again the procession stops at a palatial gate, here painted on the north wall (fig. 1.17c). These contemporaneous examples thus visually annotate how the *zi mingfu* ceremony and the funerary procession depicted on Zhu's coffin are linked to the site of the heavenly gate. Connected to the flow of the foregoing narrative, yet conveying its significance as a sacred destination through its symbolic location and form, the iconic gate in relief on the head panel thus concludes the funerary narrative.

The representational mode of the funerary narrative in the examples presented thus far suggests that the rituals depicted were based more on the existing funerary praxis of that time than on a prescriptive or imaginary vision. These two aspects are interrelated, of course, but there is an undeniable sense of contemporaneity—of how people in that local society carried out an important aspect of their lives at that time—embedded in this series of pictorial narratives. The paired scenes of the *zi mingfu* and the procession represented in the murals discussed above, in contrast to the rest of the images depicted on the same horizontal sections in the tombs, create their own narrative space rooted in the historical time. In the case of the Heishangou tomb, for instance, there is an unmistakable contextual breach between the array of the legendary episodes of the exemplars of filial piety and the continuous scenes in which the tomb occupants appear as the protagonists of the funerary narrative (fig. 1.18). Such a contrast, despite their shared, juxtaposed physical position in the tomb, highlights the distinct temporality underlying the *zi mingfu* and procession scenes. Breaking out of the chain of filial episodes set in the past, each of which constitutes an isolated tableau, the continuous funerary narrative in these scenes evokes a strong sense of the here and now.[62]

Such distinct contemporaneity suggests that the oft-depicted funerary narrative was derived from a funerary praxis common to many members of the local elite during the Song period, especially in the Henan area. Although they obviously deviated from orthodox Confucian practice, both entertainment and the religious ser-

OPPOSITE PAGE
FIGURE. 1.15A. Top, Deceased couple kneeling in front of Sengqie. Mural, upper section of northwest wall. From a tomb discovered in Pingmo, Henan Province. Northern Song, ca. 1108. FIGURE. 1.15B. Middle, Procession of the deceased with their entourage, northeast wall of the Pingmo tomb. FIGURE. 1.15C. Bottom, Palatial architecture, north wall of the Pingmo tomb.

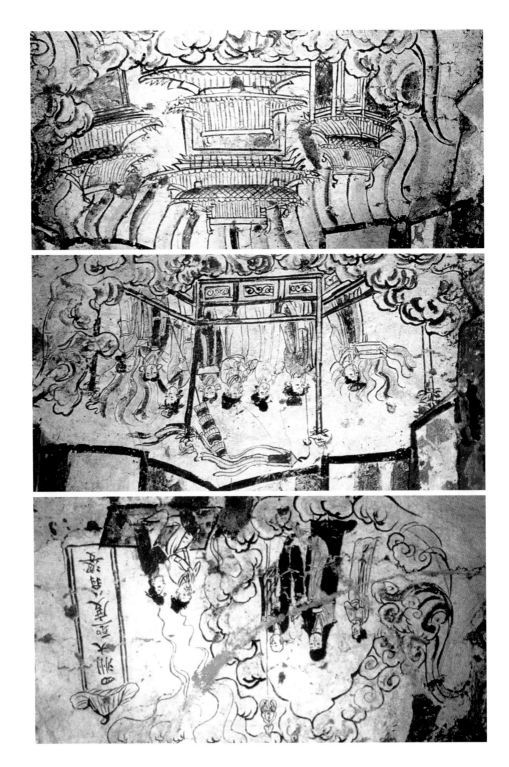

FIGURE 1.16. Procession painted above the tomb gate on the south wall. Nanchui Village, Changzhi, Shanxi Province. Jin, ca. 1153.

vice as the components of the *zi mingfu* were nevertheless conducted widely. The form of action, not the belief itself, thus defined the meaning of the event, which might be characterized as orthopraxy.[63] While these people maintained the largely Confucian ideal of ancestral worship and the promotion of the successive lineage, manifested by the construction of the tomb itself as a part of the ritual action, they incorporated unorthodox components into the funeral as long as these were believed to help the dead pass into the heavenly realm.

THE CELEBRATION OF THE FUNERAL

As one of the earliest known representations of the Song period *zaju*, the performance image carved on Zhu Sanweng's sarcophagus thus allows us a rare glimpse

OPPOSITE PAGE
FIGURE 1.17A. Top, *Naobo* players. Mural, upper section of the east wall, Heishangou tomb.
FIGURE 1.17B. Middle, *Mingjing* carriers on a bridge. Mural, south wall, Heishangou tomb.
FIGURE 1.17C. Bottom, Palatial architecture. Mural, north wall. Heishangou tomb, Dengfeng, Henan Province. Song, ca. 1097.

FIGURE 1.18. Location of funerary narrative (a) and episodes of filial piety (b). Line drawing of murals in Heishangou tomb.

FIGURE 1.19. Dancers performing in front of the deceased. Detail. Ink rubbing of the head panel of a sarcophagus found in a tomb in Luoning, Henan Province. Song, ca. 1117.

into its own funerary context and helps us to better understand other, less clearly defined, contemporaneous images of entertainment performances that are depicted in tomb spaces. A good example is a performance scene incised on the head panel of a sarcophagus found in a tomb in Luoning, Henan Province (ca. 1117; see fig. 1.19).[64] Here, a dancer and musicians are performing in front of the deceased, flanked by servants who prepare tea and food. Although the funerary procession

FIGURE 1.20. Acrobats followed by the deceased walking toward a heavenly gate. Detail. Rubbing from a side panel of a sarcophagus, Changning, Sichuan Province. Eastern Han.

is absent, this entertainment scene could be viewed as a version of the *zi mingfu* ceremony. While the twofold *zi mingfu* ritual featured on Zhu's sarcophagus is stretched out onto the two side panels and merges with the heavenly gate on the head panel, the performance scene here is emphasized as the focal point by its singular position on the head panel, aligned on an axis with the heavenly gate carved on the opposite (foot) panel. With the episodes of the twenty-four filial paragons extensively illustrated on the two side panels forming an independent pictorial space, the images on the head and foot panels would have been regarded as part of the larger funerary "plot," selected as "significant wholes out of scattered events."[65]

This rarely recognized funerary context of the performance image reveals the contemporary desire to capture and imprint funerary experiences pictorially on carved or painted images. The sarcophagus, by permanently bearing representations of highlights of the funeral—events that would have occurred just before the entombment of the coffin itself—thus serves as a medium for commemorating the death ritual for the deceased.

In fact, visually recording funerary events on sarcophagi or tomb walls was itself not a new practice by this time; a few representations of funerary rites at ancestral temples have survived in Han and Eastern Han tombs.[66] What distinguishes Zhu's sarcophagus from the early examples, however, is not only the unsanctioned content of the funerary narrative (based on actual events in addition to, or in place of, established symbolic notions) but also the distinctive mode in which it was portrayed. As a point of comparison, the performance images depicted as a portion of a larger funerary procession or journey in these earlier times are imbued with a heavily symbolic tone. Take, for example, the stone carving from an Eastern Han tomb in Changning, Sichuan Province (fig. 1.20); in this image, the deceased on a horse approaches a heavenly gate, led by a double-headed giant bird, while ahead of the deceased (who has not yet passed through the gate) a pair of juggling acrobats is performing, unambiguously belonging to the afterworld. The otherworldly ambience of the performance space is commonly spotted in other tomb images of the Eastern Han and succeeding time periods.[67]

The overall narrative mode in these early examples is similar to that of Zhu's sarcophagus, but they highlight the whereabouts of the deceased's soul in its transitional status in a clearly symbolic manner, whereas the Song-period images tend to show the practiced ritual firmly embedded in the sense of the present moment and existing place. In the case of Zhu's sarcophagus, as well as in the other contemporaneous examples discussed above, the course of the deceased's symbolic voyage is minimized and only metonymically implied, if present at all: the focus of the events lies in the funerary ritual. In addition, by registering the funerary practice at a discernibly vernacular level and in a distinctively descriptive manner, these eleventh-century images evoke a funerary discourse densely charged with the breath of the everyday world.

Serving to display ritual experiences, this particular mode subtly signals a newly emerging attitude on the part of the people toward mortuary practice: the repositioning of the funerary discourse away from the official and orthodox sphere and toward the lived social world. More precisely, this was the interest of a particular stratum of Song society; as discussed in this volume's prelude, middle period tombs that contained images of performance (or representations of any kind) belonged to members of the local elite such as Zhu Sanweng. In this sense, the reframing of the funerary discourse into the scope of the everyday world can be seen as the local elite's positive expression of its own ritual life and visual culture. By visually registering the events of its funerary experiences—a ritual practice that was never ratified by the imperial court and scholar-officials—this elite actively recognized and celebrated its own cultural standing in society.

The sense of celebration captured in this early image of theatrical performance on Zhu's sarcophagus is consistently present in the examples explored in the following chapters. Whereas this sensibility was imparted by means of the narrative mode in the panels on Zhu's coffin in concretely ritual terms, a new type of theatrical imagery that emerged in the late eleventh century manifested such celebration in intensely visual terms. By bringing the quintessential mechanism of the theater into the space of the dead, this new mode of representation further articulated the socialization of the funerary discourse.

2

THEATER FOR THE DEAD

Around the time Zhu Sanweng's coffin, carved with the commemorative funerary scenes, was laid in his grave, quite a different type of performance image was spreading to the region, conspicuously incorporated into tomb decorations in the increasingly fashionable medium of bas-relief. More than thirty sets of reliefs on brick panels representing actors have been excavated over the past sixty years from tombs in Henan and Shanxi provinces, ranging from the late Northern Song to the early Yuan period (see appendix).[1] In fact, the brick bas-relief of the celebrated actress Ding Dusai, which was discussed in this book's prelude, emerged out of this new trend. Whereas the Ding relief is known to us only as an orphan object, the context of which is completely lost, a set of bas-reliefs found not far from Zhu's tomb provides strong evidence that a new mode of performance image was beginning to appear in local areas of northern China during the late eleventh century, one that illuminates how the performance culture and a new type of image making converged in the funerary context.

In a tomb unearthed in 1958 in Jiuliugou, Yanshi County, Henan Province, less than fifty miles west of Zhu Sanweng's tomb, archaeologists discovered six thin brick panels decorated with figures in bas-relief. A tomb with a single chamber, it included only a few utensils and no image other than these six reliefs.[2] The simplicity of the tomb interior and the interred objects highlights the unusual quality of the bas-reliefs, bearing images of variously dressed male (figs. 2.1a–b) and female figures (2.2a–d). Facing the tomb entrance (which is on the south wall), they occupy the lower half of the north wall, just above the coffin bed where the deceased was placed. The fact that these were the only representations in the tomb points to their significance within the entire burial space and underscores the attention that the tomb

FIGURE 2.1A. Brick reliefs representing actors from a tomb discovered in Yanshi, Henan Province. Northern Song. Left, 43.5×35.8 cm; middle, 43×22 cm; right, 43.8×35.9 cm.

FIGURE 2.1B. Line drawing of figure 2.1a.

FIGURE 2.2A. Above, left, Woman, east side of the north wall. Ink rubbing of a brick relief from the Yanshi tomb. **FIGURE 2.2B.** Above, middle, Woman scooping wine, east side of the north wall, Yanshi tomb. **FIGURE 2.2C.** Above, right, Woman slicing fish, east side of the north wall, Yanshi tomb. **FIGURE 2.2D.** Right, Photograph of figure 2.2c.

FIGURE 2.3. Five actors. Brick relief from a tomb discovered in Luolong, Henan Province. Song.

designer/sponsor paid to the visual effects of these reliefs. Notably, an almost identical set of brick reliefs was discovered in 2009 in Luolong, just twenty-four miles west of Yanshi (fig. 2.3).[3] While this discovery reconfirms the practice of relief making through both molding and carving, which will be discussed in this chapter, the delicate rendering of the theatrical scenes as well as their layout in the tomb space are essentially consistent with the Yanshi case.[4]

Since no epitaph or land-deed (*maidi quan*) was found, the occupant of this tomb remains unknown; however, judging from the interior architectural structure's partially imitating wood architecture, the archaeologists who excavated the tomb dated it from the late eleventh to early twelfth centuries. Conventionally referred to as wood imitation (*fangmu*) by Chinese archaeologists, this interior tomb structure also provides some idea about the social status of the deceased. Wood-imitation brick tombs first appeared in the late Tang period and were then continuously employed for imperial family members and officials until the early Song period.[5] However, from the mid-Song period on, the occupants of this type of tomb began to change drastically from high officials to the elite without office (basically, the local elite defined in this book's prelude). That, together with the fact that the tombs of scholar-officials almost always contained epitaphs describing the offices they had held (epitaphs to which they were entitled), indicates that the occupant of this tomb in Yanshi was a person who did not hold any official title but could afford a decent burial. This is especially pertinent with regard to the rapid development of the public cemetery during the Song period. Contemporaneous examples of the public cemetery (*louzeyuan*) designed by the government for those who had no family or insufficient means to have their bodies properly buried confirm that the occupant of the Yanshi tomb must have been affluent enough to build the relatively elaborate burial chamber.[6]

Having lived in the satellite town (*ji*) that was closest to Luoyang,[7] the west-ern capital of the Song dynasty where "entertainers of every part of the nation flocked,"[8] the deceased during his or her life would have been well exposed to the vibrant performance culture there. Indeed, the tomb occupant must have been particularly enthusiastic about the theatrical performance known as *zaju;* what we see in these reliefs is a troupe of actors. That this set of reliefs was one of just two kinds of images found in the tomb already implies its unusual role in con-structing the burial space with something that only theatrical spectacles could offer.

ACTORS IN ACTION

Placed side by side in a single row, the six bas-reliefs form two visually distinct groups of three, which suggests the two groups' different roles in the tomb space (fig. 2.4). In the panel at the extreme right, the woman stands behind a table, rolling up her right sleeve as if she is about to slice the fish on the plate directly before her; a pot of liquid is boiling on a small brazier in front of the table (figs. 2.2c–d). The panel in the middle shows another woman, who stands between a large basin to the right and a pot of liquid on a round brazier on a table to the left, out of which she is scooping liquid (fig. 2.2b). In the panel to the left of that one, a smaller female is shown carrying a pitcher (fig. 2.2a). This set of images, variations of which are found in other contemporaneous tombs, can be seen as an extension of the traditional representa-tion of "kitchen" motifs in tomb spaces, which had become well established by the eleventh century, just as in the case of the cooking scene on Zhu Sanweng's sarcopha-gus (see fig. 1.2). The forms of the female figures and certain objects, particularly the fish, are reminiscent of an archaic style found in the tombs of the Han and the Six Dynasties periods; they are represented in imitation of that archaic visual mode and the motifs associated with it.[9] For example, descriptions of mincing fish, known as *zhuokuai,* often appear in middle period texts either as a process of preparing for an ideal meal or as a man's snack in daily life, along with heated wine.[10] In this sense, these three women could have been expected to serve the tomb occupant with fish and wine, similar to the role that traditional images of a kitchen in the burial cham-ber were designed to play.[11]

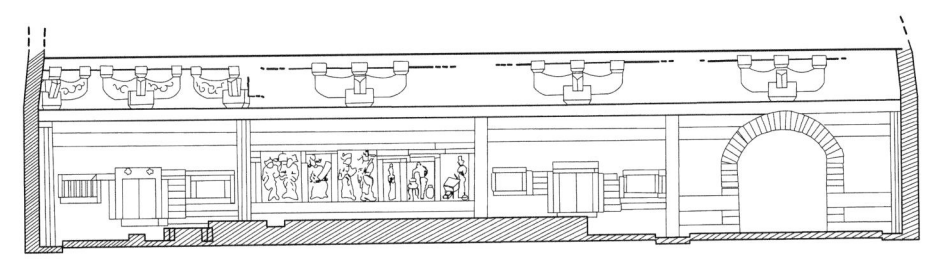

FIGURE 2.4. Placement of six brick reliefs in a tomb found in Yanshi County, Henan Province. Redrawn by Katherine Lester after the original elevation drawing.

The three brick panels at the other end of the north wall, to the left, feature images of five figures whose costumes, gestures, and props help identify them as actors.[12] The costume of the single figure (middle in fig. 2.1a; also see the middle in fig. 2.3)—a distinctive hat and a long robe with a belt—looks like a typical civil official's outfit, but a decorative piece resembling a twig protruding from the back of his or her hat indicates that this is most likely the headgear of an actor or musician (compare figs. 2.6 and 3.4).[13] The gender of this figure is difficult to determine, because in the early stages of theatrical performance, it was not uncommon to have both male and female actors within a troupe.[14] But since the determination of the gender does not affect the content of the ongoing discussion, I am going to assume that this character is male—for the sake of clarity in writing. His torso is bent slightly forward as he unrolls a scroll and shows a painting that includes a simple rendering of what could be a crescent moon at the bottom left. As his posture suggests, an invisible audience is assumed to be looking at him and the picture from outside the pictorial space.

In his pioneering article on this set of reliefs, Xu Pingfang has suggested that this figure could be the sole lead of the introductory segment known as a prelude (*yanduan*) in a Song period *zaju*, a character whose role is briefly mentioned in the late-twelfth-century texts *Mengliang lu* (Record of reminiscing on the past) and *Ducheng jisheng* (Record of the splendors of the capital) and in the fourteenth-century text *Chuogeng lu* (Notes taken while at rest from plowing). According to the two essays written in the twelfth century, the *yanduan* was one of two skits in the early Song dynasty *zaju* in which an actor would present a "common, familiar story," often starting the performance by "making a joke [*dahun*]."[15] The format of this opening segment of the *zaju* seems to have been standardized by the eleventh century, as confirmed by a renowned literatus of the Song dynasty, Huang Tingjian (1045–1105), who described it as follows: "Composing a poem is just like performing a *zaju;* an actor first enters and arranges [the program], after which he makes a joke to start off with, and then finally begins his performance."[16] Whatever scant information exists about the Song dynasty imperial *zaju* has helped scholars to reconstruct a sketchy yet basic structure of the *zaju* in general. The *zaju* at court consisted of two sections (*liang duan*): *yanduan* and *zheng zaju* (the latter being the main *zaju*). Whereas a common, well-known story would be played in the *yanduan* segment, the *zheng zaju* would present more complex stories in two subsections. The contents or formats of the *zheng zaju* are not recorded in *Mengliang lu* or *Ducheng jisheng* as they are for *yanduan,* but these texts do mention five distinctive role types played in the *zheng zaju*.[17]

Although the actual subjects of such performances are not mentioned in any surviving sources, Xu's identification of this figure as *yanduan* is plausible not only in terms of the figure's gesture but also in terms of its central position among the three brick panels. The role of this figure is distinguished from that of the traditional storyteller, or *jiangshi*. A traditional storyteller may have used a visual device such as this scroll, but he would not have needed to wear a costume like the one in this central panel because he was a transparent agent of the narrative, transmitted mainly through voice.[18] While it is not impossible that the format of the kind of performance in the relief image—showing a picture and telling a story simultaneously—bears a clear imprint of its origins, the visual nature of the storytelling "actor" cannot be equated with the role of a traditional storyteller. The actor in this relief presents himself as a visible narrator whose monologue, act of showing a picture, voice, and gesture become incarnated with his face, costume, and prop. The effect of such visual personification would have been one of the new and most attractive elements of the theatrical performance. In the relief, the passage of time was effectively visualized in the act of rolling open the scroll, which unmistakably signals that a performance has just begun. The initial moment of a *zaju* was thus conveyed, enveloping the entire set of three relief panels within what might be called "theatrical time."

The two pairs of actors depicted in the slightly wider brick panels that flank the single-actor panel are contrasting types, the pair at the left appearing to be from a much lower social stratum than the pair at the right. The panel at the far left shows two large men wearing rather crude clothes (left in fig. 2.1; compare fig. 2.3).[19] The man at the extreme left is holding a cage containing a bird, and lifts it toward the man next to him while pointing at the cage with his right index finger, as if saying something about the bird to the other man. Unusual attention was paid in rendering the details of his facial features, such as the deep wrinkles on his forehead, the fleshy area just below each eye, the natural contrast between his high cheekbones and indented cheeks, or even the thin line of teeth and the tip of tongue seen through his gaping mouth. The front of his robe hangs open, exposing his bare chest and protruding belly. The other man is wearing a headscarf with flowers attached at the back, and although his tightly closed robe covers his torso, it reveals his lower legs, which are slightly twisted—almost as if he is pirouetting. He is looking directly at his companion and whistling through his thumb and index finger held at his lips, most likely as a way of taunting him. The gesture of whistling is abundantly found in later representations of actors (see figs. 3.2 and 3.8).

The broad faces of these two men, with their rugged features, wide noses, high cheekbones, thick eyebrows, and playful expressions are quite similar to each other, and quite different from the smooth, oval face and generic features of the figure holding the scroll, which by the Song period had been visually codified as the ideal characteristic of noble or educated men. Any paintings that depict educated men (e.g., literati or royal figures) as well as religious figures (e.g., Buddhist or Daoist deities) from this time period demonstrate that such facial characteristics were firmly stereotyped.[20] The similar faces of the jocular pair, which are in distinct contrast to the polite neutrality of the man holding the scroll, suggest that the pair of figures were also pictorialized as a type, and their role is implied through specific visual codes of facial and bodily features that undeniably evoke a sense of humor.

Unsurprisingly, this "type" was an effective representation of comic roles in the world of the theater, bridging classical images of acrobats in the pre-Song periods and "modern" images of actors in subsequent centuries. For example, the ponderous body of the figure on the left is similar to the images of entertainers in tomb spaces developed in the much earlier periods of the Qin and Han dynasties

FIGURE 2.5A. An acrobat. Painted clay sculpture from the mausoleum of the first emperor of the Qin dynasty, 3rd century BCE. 171 cm. Shanxi Provincial Museum.

(figs. 2.5a–b). It seems that artisans have traditionally favored this particular body type as a stereotypical visual marker of such entertainers as acrobats and comic actors. If such images constituted a model for representing a generic image of entertainers, later depictions of two particular role types in theatrical performance would be the descendants of these Yanshi tomb figures. Several brick reliefs found in tombs of the Jin dynasty bear images of actors whose role types are identified as the second male lead (*fumo*) and the second clown (*fujing*) in quite similar fashion, with each usually represented in one brick panel (fig. 2.6).[21]

The social one-upmanship of the comic actors and their performances was also referred to in near-contemporary essays on life in the capital cities during the Song and Southern Song dynasties. When performing a comic skit, these actors would mimic "village yokels and country bumpkins"—especially those from Shandong or Hebei province—who would "rarely venture into the city."[22] Apparently their comic perfor-

FIGURE 2.5B. Detail of an acrobat. Brick relief from a tomb in Xinye, Henan Province. Eastern Han. National Museum of China.

FIGURE 2.6. *Fumo* and *fujing* (two figures in the middle). Brick reliefs found in a tomb in Yima, Henan Province. Jin.

mances were accompanied by "beating drums" or "blowing whistles."[23] Though random and anecdotal, these accounts give us some sense of what such role types as *fujing* or *fumo* might have actually performed on stage. It is also notable that their performances were imbued with an attitude of proud urbanism, exemplified by their exulting in the city dwellers' cultural superiority over that of the rural people, especially those outside the metropolitan Hedong area in Shanxi Province. Notably, the sense of superiority as a member of an urban community is also echoed in an oft-cited work by Du Renjie, the song "Country Bumpkin Knows Nothing of Theater" (Zhuangjia bushi goulan). The narrator is a country yokel who goes into a large commercial theater in the city and witnesses a performance there. Minute details of the theater, as well as a series of segments performed on the stage, are described via his perspective as he marvels at what he sees.[24] The sense of urban pride is thus conveyed through these brief yet telling descriptions of the theatrical skits and the image of the comic duo carved on the clay relief.[25]

The panel immediately to the right of the single-figure panel shows a pair of formally dressed figures (right in fig. 2.1; compare fig. 2.3).[26] The figure at the left is wearing a cylindrical hat in the Su Shi style (*Zizhan yang*) and holding a wrapped object in one hand while reaching out to his companion with the other, as if talking about the package he is holding. His companion is wearing a standard civil official's outfit and hat, and is holding a *hu* tablet. As in the case with the whistling actor in the previous group, the manner in which this figure is consistent with later depictions of actors, when it became a visual tradition of representing a particular role type—that of the costumed official (*guzhuang* or *zhuanggu*) in the Jin and Yuan theaters (see figs. 3.2 and figs. 4.4a–b). *Guzhuang* is one of five role types mentioned in *Mengliang lu* and *Ducheng jisheng;* the actors performing this role usually dressed like officials, as do the figures in this brick relief. Originally a peripheral role type, at least according to Southern Song accounts, by the early Yuan period *guzhuang* seems to have become a particular role for ridiculing venal officials.[27]

Like the comic duo in the panel at the far left, the specificity of the actions and props in this scene at the far right is remarkable. The small package held by the figure at the left appears to be a precious object wrapped in cloth, perhaps an official's seal,[28] and is certainly not a generic prop commonly found in representations of actors such as a bamboo stick (*zhu ganzi*), a fan, or a *hu* tablet. Whether or not this represents a scene from an actual play of the time (which is difficult to ascertain, given the lack of extant play scripts from this period), such particularity demonstrates the interest of the relief designer (and/or the patron) in evoking an authentic looking tableau.[29]

Although this pictorial mode is in some ways close to that of the image of the *zaju* on Zhu's sarcophagus (see chapter 1), it is distinctly different in its lack of any spatial context: the backgrounds for the three reliefs are all simply empty—no stage set or any other figures are depicted. Thus, it does not seem to have been the intention of the relief makers or sponsors to reconstruct and commemorate a theatrical performance in the midst of a funerary ritual, as was the case in Zhu's sarcophagus.

What was the expected role of these depictions of actors in the tomb space? The overall structure of the three panels and the relationship among them gives us an initial clue. The central position and singular nature of the middle figure, occupying the panel's full pictorial plane in a solo performance, confirms the actor's role as an introducer of the entire performance. As mentioned above, the skillfully drawn gesture of unrolling the scroll (middle in fig. 2.1a) suggests that the figure is performing for a viewer who is outside the picture frame. While this pose is neither iconic nor self-contained,[30] the actor's body, turned partway toward the imaginary spectator, creates a visual "suturing" of the pictorial plane and the world of the viewer,[31] implying an interactive relationship: through the gesture of showing the picture, the viewer is first invited to hear the introductory monologue or joke, and then to choose to watch either the comic duo at the left or the drama at the right. This is not to propose a prescriptive sequence for viewing the three panels; rather, it is one reasonable way of viewing these images together, which may correspond to the contemporary practice of watching a dramatic performance. In this way—regardless of the sequence of the other two relief images—a new space can be formed in which the assumed viewer will be drawn in as a spectator of the performances. The engine of this active interaction is the unique materiality and optical play of the brick relief, which at once participated in and reflected the dynamic practice of seeing in the eleventh century.

THE MATERIALITY OF THE BRICK RELIEF

Brick reliefs in the late Song period were largely categorized as *zhuan* (tile or brick), but the particular medium of clay bricks decorated with images in relief did not have an official term of its own. Although one could refer specifically to the method of carving various materials by the term *shizao wanzao* under the category of *zhuoshi* (cutting) in the government-issued *Yingzao fashi* (Treatise on architectural methods), it does not encompass the distinctive medium of brick carved in relief. This contrasts greatly with the abundant archaeological finds of brick reliefs in the late Song period tombs of the local elite, which suggests that this medium was popular for residences and/or tombs exclusively among people without official titles.[32] It is also likely, judging from the absence of any specific mention of the term "brick relief" in the *Yingzao fashi,* that brick reliefs were not commonly used in official or imperial architecture. This is not surprising, because the basic material for functional buildings during that period was wood, and tomb architecture was not included in the manual (probably due to the fact that construction of elaborate burials was never officially encouraged anyway).

Regardless of the lack of any special terminology, brick reliefs were in widespread use. On the one hand, the particular technique of relief carving seems to have already been popularly practiced in architectural decoration aboveground. The *Yingzao fashi* introduces and explains in detail various patterns of flowers used for adorning architectural elements using relief carving, although it does not specify the material.[33] On the other hand, clay brick had been used in tomb construction since the Han period, and bricks with images—either stamped or molded—also appeared during that time. Although the technique of relief carving involved in making the ancient bricks and the resulting visual effect were quite different from that of Song-period brick reliefs, decorative brick panels were frequently used by Song artisans in the creation of burial chambers. Accordingly, the genesis of the particular medium for the actor images in the Yanshi tomb can be traced in the historical trajectory of tomb making and interior decoration as well as in the contemporary technique of sophisticated relief carving applied to the dwellings of the living.

The basic mechanism of making brick reliefs—embossing, which involves carving or molding a decoration or design on a surface so that it is raised above the surface in bas-relief—is the same for the two sets of reliefs in the Yanshi tomb, the actor images and the female servant images: the main silhouette of the figures is shaped by removing clay from the background of a rectangular brick panel and carving the outer and inner lines of the figures with knives.[34] The first stage is traditionally known as subtracting earth (*jiandi*), in which the outlines of figures are shaped on raw clay tiles through the subtraction of clay from the background. In the second stage, such details as facial expressions, posture, and patterns on clothing or objects take shape through line carving.[35] Reliefs made by this method are usually of shallow depth, with only a slight projection from the surrounding surface, giving a slight convexity to the contours of the figures depicted.

Judging from brick reliefs excavated in tombs built slightly later than the Yanshi tomb, as well as from the method of making clay figurines during this period, these two stages would sometimes have involved using molds.[36] Archaeological finds in the past six decades from the areas surrounding Yanshi indicate that molds were used in duplicating brick reliefs, or at least that models were used for copying them by sight. In addition to the aforementioned actor reliefs from Luolong that are almost identical to the Yanshi reliefs, five brick-relief panels representing actors of each role type excavated in Wen County, about thirty-five miles northeast of Yanshi, show a striking resemblance to the ones from the twelfth or early thirteenth centuries excavated in 1982 in the same area.[37] Molds could be used in one of two ways. The first method was to use a mold in the making of a relief or a figurine with a relatively simple silhouette and a shallow mass that could be fully expressed with limited contouring, such as the five bricks found in Baisha Song tomb and the numerous individual brick reliefs found in Jin tombs in the northern Henan and southern Shanxi areas.[38] Here it is important to make a distinction between duplicability and mass production. The use of molds does not necessarily mean that the molded brick reliefs were produced in a large number and sold to wide audiences; the limited evidence available through excavations so far points to a small number of production and regional circulation.

The second method required the partial use of a mold, involving both mold pressing and hand carving, by which rather complicated outlines and details of a figure could be effectively executed.[39] This method would have been suitable for making the Yanshi reliefs, especially some of the extremely refined lines such as the bars on the birdcage. The extraordinary shallowness of the embossed plane, and the subtle depths between numerous layers through refined carving, suggest that it would have been difficult to mass-produce these reliefs even if molds were used. A mold could reproduce the original design with precision only a limited number of times, as it was usually made of baked clay or of plaster, which is equally or just slightly less fragile than brick. In addition, if hand carving was involved, the completed works would not have been identical. Therefore, refined reliefs like the Yanshi bricks, even if they went through a molding process, would have had some degree of singularity produced by the final touch of hand carving. A good example is the image of *yanduan* in the set of the Luolong reliefs; in contrast to the simply carved form resembling a crescent moon depicted in the scroll painting in the Yanshi case, there is a figure who appears to be a bodhisattva—probably Avalokiteśvara—seated in front of a large tree carved on the surface of the scroll in the Luolong relief (fig. 2.7).

The last stage of making the relief consisted of coloring and baking it. After the figures were carved they were usually coated with white pigment, and then sometimes colors were added; these colors are no longer visible in the Yanshi examples, probably due to the natural erosion of the pigments before or after excavation.[40] According to the seventeenth-century encyclopedia *Tiangong kaiwu* (The works of heaven and inception of things) by Song Yingxing (b. 1587), baking was an essential part of the process of producing bricks of all kinds, but the bricks listed in this text were all standard ones used for practical purposes such as constructing houses, city walls, or bridge pavements, all of which required extreme durability. The art of brick relief might have taken a less functional approach, in which case the process of baking might have been unnecessary.[41]

FIGURE 2.7. Ink rubbing of an actor (the middle figure shown in fig. 2.3) taken from a brick relief in a tomb discovered in Luolong, Henan Province. Song.

INCARNATED THROUGH CLAY RELIEFS: ACTORS ON STAGE

Although the Yanshi tomb's relief panels of the actors and those of the women servants seem to have been made by essentially the same production process, these two groups of works create very different overall impressions. The reliefs of the three servants, despite the dynamic poses that convey the tasks they perform, seem flat and unnatural. For example, the woman at the right (fig. 2.2d) appears to recede into the background as part of the flat pictorial space surrounding her. The stiffness of her posture is accentuated by the mechanically carved lines of her collar, the wrinkles on her arms, and the patterns on her skirt—lines that all look "starchy," as if executed by woodblock. The patterns on her skirt—the pictorial mode of which is common in paintings of women from the Tang and Song periods—seem detached from the surface of the clothing, as if floating on their own; they make her entire body appear flat, like that of a paper doll. Here the effect of the molding and carving technique to make a low relief clearly shows the potential limitations of the medium: the figure's body is distinguished from the background only by the leveled surface, presenting the figure itself as merely another flat surface. As a result, the variation in depth on the embossed surface is barely perceptible. The only part of this relief that shares a sense of deceptive depth with the actor panels is the furniture: every edge of the tables' thin front legs is emphasized by the steep angles of foreshortening that add dimensionality and convey a sense that the tables are projecting forward from the figure. Ironically, this partial emphasis on spatial depth only creates a greater contrast between the furniture and the figure, thus making the figure look even flatter and more static.

In this respect, the contrast with the three actor panels is evident. The single figure in the middle panel of actors stands out from the empty background by his rhythmically forward-leaning posture and by the carved lines that create a sense of depth, conveying the volume of the billowing sleeve and lower panels of his robe, the three-dimensionality of his hat (visible as front, middle, and rear planes), and the subtle spatial hierarchy apparent in his right hand and the unfurled scroll. The sense of depth and movement in the other two panels is even more pronounced, especially in the pair of figures with the birdcage. There the layers of space are succinctly conveyed in less than a quarter inch of depth, from the birdcage at the rear to the actors' gesticulating hands projecting forward (which, on the second-highest plane, recede only slightly from the front plane); the layers of space are further emphasized by both actors' left legs being partly hidden behind their right legs. The relative depth is underscored by details in the depiction of the figures, including their highly natural bodily contours (such as the protruding belly of the actor on the left) and the folds and curved contours of their clothes.

Placed side by side with the three servant panels, as in their original position on the north wall of the tomb, the three actor reliefs stand out as an independent set of images. While the women appear fixed in their brick frames, the images of the actors, endowed with rich spatial layers in the pictorial plane, create a sense of animation that visually frees them from the material medium and enhances the interactive quality established by the inviting gesture of the actor in the middle panel.

One might be tempted to see this distinction as an accident, but a few remarkable tomb reliefs that were made about a century earlier than the Yanshi panels indicate otherwise. These examples confirm that the visual effect of the actor panels would have been used as a means of signifying performative movements. Cases in point are a pair of reliefs installed in the tomb of a military governor, Wang Chuzhi, in Hebei Province (ca. 924),[42] and a set of relief panels in the tomb of another military official, Feng Hui, in Shanxi Province (ca. 958).[43] Seen together, these two cases shed light on the trajectory in which a rather "hybrid" medium such as the Yanshi reliefs came into being in the following century. Furthermore, they illuminate how the particular optical interest in representing entertainments in the funerary setting continued to develop in the eleventh century, marking the close connection between the specific motif and the mode of representation. In the two-chamber tomb of Wang Chuzhi, a pair of large relief panels made of stone were installed on the east and west walls of the rear chamber, toward the back (north) wall, representing a group of musicians on the west wall and a group of female attendants on the east wall (fig. 2.8). These standing figures, almost all shown in three-quarter profile, were exquisitely carved. The carver achieved a strong sense of three-dimensionality by sculpting them in relatively high relief and by rendering the folds of their robes so naturally. Although the composition of these relief panels— rows of figures standing in three-quarter view—is clearly not new, their sculptural quality and the close connection between that three-dimensionality and the motif depicted here (i.e., entertainers) signify a new visual tradition formed during this period.[44] The physical and visual distance between the relief's highest and lowest planes emphasizes this semisculptural quality, exemplified by the figure standing second to the left in the first row and especially the bottom of the wooden clapper (*paiban*) she is holding (fig. 2.9). Rendered with depth to the extent that it even casts a shadow, it seems almost as if she has the actual instrument in her hands.

Notably, the performance images in Wang Chuzhi's tomb are the only bas-reliefs in the entire tomb chamber; all the other images were painted on the walls. The vividly projected figures in this set of reliefs seem to occupy that part of the space and distinguish it from the innermost part of the chamber, which is enveloped by a painted screen (fig. 2.10). Judging from the location of the bodily remains of the tomb's occupant and the coffin beds in front of this painted screen, this space is considered the "spirit seat" (*lingwei* or *lingzuo*) of the deceased.[45] The painted screen and the carved stone reliefs depicting musical performance are both oriented toward the spirit seat, encroaching the physical space as if filling it with live music played for the deceased, whose presence is only implied by the image of his spirit seat confined in the pictorial space.

This strategy is echoed in Feng Hui's tomb. Consisting of one main chamber and three side chambers, the tomb is decorated with brick reliefs depicting a troupe of musicians and dancers on the east and west walls of the corridor leading to the main chamber.[46] The row of figures on the west wall represents female performers, and the row on the east wall male performers; each performer has a matching figure on the opposite wall, holding a matching instrument (figs. 2.11, 2.12). Each performer's face is given definition not only through simple carving but also through a high degree of actual depth between the face and the contiguous surface of the picture plane. Although these are of low relief in all respects, the three-dimensional effect of these figures in this set of reliefs rests more on the physical—rather than optical—contrast between the highest and lowest points on the picture plane. For example, the way the protruding flares in the clothing of the male musicians' suits are carved (fig. 2.13) is strikingly similar to the semisculptural quality of the wooden clapper in Wang's tomb.

Note again that these are the only relief images in the entire tomb, just as in Wang Chuzhi's tomb. All the walls of the main chamber are covered with murals of floral patterns and figures, mostly female attendants, and the interiors of the side chambers are adorned with murals of various other motifs such as coiled bunches of coins and food and tea utensils on a table.[47] That the designers of both tombs consistently chose only the medium of bas-relief for rendering scenes of entertainment while executing all the other motifs in a two-dimensional, painterly medium

FIGURE 2.8. Musicians. Painted marble reliefs. West (left) and east (right) walls in rear chamber of Wang Chuzhi's tomb, Hebei Province. Five Dynasties, ca. 924. H 82×W 136×D 17–23 cm. Hebei Provincial Museum.

points to their unspoken recognition of the special visual characteristics innate to the medium of bas-relief.

What was the particular appeal of bas-relief for depicting entertainment scenes? More precisely, what kind of visual impression produced by reliefs would have been considered especially effective for portraying performance images? All such performances involve movements and gestures by the performers in an interactive context—that is, performing for the audience, which in turn reacts to the performers' onstage actions—and it is therefore reasonable to think that the images depicting the performers would show them making those movements and gestures. However, the choice of bas-relief for these images can be explained only by examining the optical effects of such reliefs as perceived by viewers of the time period, which involves a particular kind of illusionism that appealed to their sensibilities.

THE PERFORMANCE OF THE SURFACE: *YING* ILLUSIONISM

Reliefs such as the two examples from the tenth century just discussed, which were originally adopted for depicting music or dance performances, began to be applied in making images of theatrical performance once the *zaju* became popularized as a fashionable entertainment. While the set of Yanshi actor images was thus related to the earlier reliefs made for a tomb space in terms of the basic carving technique and the arrangement of pictorial space, it was not a mere extension of such prototypes.

As is evident from the subtle yet telling visual differences between the two groups of reliefs in the Yanshi tomb, the actor reliefs were distinguished from their precedents through an intensification and reinvention of the medium, developing a new mode that we now refer to as illusionism. Manipulating the space on the bricks' shallow surface, the carver of these reliefs overcame the physical limitation of the thin bricks by creating visual effects of the richest spatial dimensions compressed upon their surface. As a result, the actor reliefs would have engaged viewers with the unexpected visual effects achieved through the interplay between the limitations of the medium and the carver's technical ability, not just how lifelike they were. In other words, what was attractive about the Yanshi reliefs did not lie on a purely optical level but was located midway between the subtle visual effect and the materiality of the medium. The intense interplay between the optical and the spatial dimensions manifested on the Yanshi reliefs embodied a particular kind of illusionism that appealed to the eye in China during that period—a vehicle suitable for transferring theatrical spectacles to the place for the dead.

The concept of illusionism in traditional Chinese art is as complex as that in other cultures, if not more so. Wu Hung has defined the notion of illusionism by classifying the concept of *huan* in traditional Chinese literature into three groups: "illusion/illusionary," "illusionism/illusionistic," and "magical transformation/conjuration." The "illusionism" refers to a state in which the dualism of the real/realness (*zhen*) and illusion (*huan*) is confused, and the artist of such image deceives "not only the viewer's eye but also his mind, at least temporarily."[48] As is implied in Wu's suggestion, however, the distinctions between these categories are often themselves unclear and the concept of *huan* pertains to rather broader historical phenomena of

FIGURE 2.9. *Paiban* player in Wang Chuzhi's tomb. Detail of figure 2.8.

illusionism throughout the history of Chinese art. Moreover, one must bear in mind that multiple notions of illusionism could always coexist in a single given time and space. The specific kind of illusionism apparent in the Yanshi reliefs is one of several possible practices of seeing during the eleventh and twelfth centuries.

Where in the visual field of the eleventh century should we locate the conspicuous optical interest encapsulated in the Yanshi actor reliefs? Referring to the term "carved painting," coined by Gustave Ecke to describe the well-known stone reliefs of the Twin Pagodas (Shuang ta) in Quanzhou, Robert Maeda has suggested that the visual sensibility evoked by the Yanshi reliefs could be derived from the medium of painting,[49] noting that "the three-dimensional effects [were] obtainable from the painter's brush."[50]

Maeda's recognition of the reliefs' painterly character is visually insightful, but it should be noted that the practices of seeing and image making during the middle period were far more complex than what is implied by these two dichotomous terms. First, the division between artistic mediums during this time period was more fluid than what modern viewers might assume. Although there certainly was a formal categorical distinction between painting and sculpture, several accounts from the Tang and Song periods note that exchangeable and overlapping agendas in appreci-

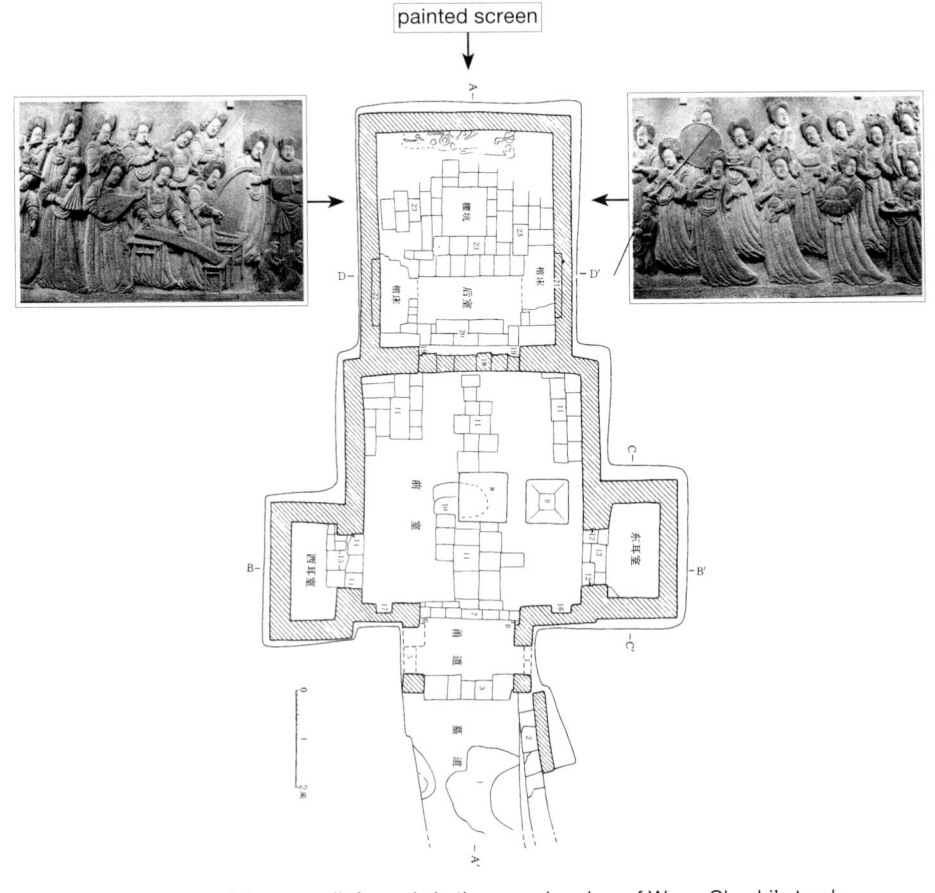

FIGURE 2.10. Layout of the two relief panels in the rear chamber of Wang Chuzhi's tomb.

ating paintings and sculptures existed. Oft-cited painter Wu Daozi (fl. 710–760) of the Tang period is a good example. In his painting catalogue, the early Song author Guo Ruoxu (fl. 1070–1075) writes, "The paintings from this period that use light coloring are called 'Wu embellishment [*wu zhuang*]'; the sculptures [that use light coloring] are also called 'Wu embellishment.'"[51] From a different angle, Dong You (fl. 1127) of the Southern Song period, evaluating Wu's painting, makes an even more direct analogy between painting and sculpture: "The figures in Wu Daozi's painting are like sculptures [*suo*], both from side and full views; four sides all meet as they should."[52] Notably, in evaluating an artist's talent in traditional China, it was usually the painter who earned credits for making his work resemble a sculpture, not vice versa; a sculptor was evaluated not for the picture-like quality of his work but for how lifelike it might be. In short, the seemingly painterly effect of the actor reliefs would have derived from multiple visual traditions that were already hybridized rather than pure painting techniques or a pictorial sensibility.[53]

FIGURE 2.11. Female musicians playing flute (left) and drum (right). Painted brick reliefs from west wall in corridor, Feng Hui's tomb, Shanxi Province. Five Dynasties, ca. 958. H 60–77 cm.

Second, as touched upon above, the category of brick relief itself should be taken into account as an existing genre of art during the middle period despite the fact that it never officially entered the vocabulary of art criticism. After emerging in the visual field during the Han period, brick reliefs had developed in their own way, even though they were rarely recognized (as painting or sculpture were) as a clear artistic category in the received texts. Following that line of artistic trajectory (i.e., bas-relief) is certainly

FIGURE 2.12. Male musicians playing drum (left) and flute (right). Painted brick reliefs from east wall in corridor, Feng Hui's tomb. H 60–74 cm.

one way of tracing the multiple visual sources for the Yanshi actor panels, as demonstrated by the reliefs from the tenth-century tombs. Rather than emphasizing the painterly character of the Yanshi actor reliefs as the outcome of a merging of the genres of painting and sculpture, it is more productive and essential to uncover what sorts of preexisting discourses and practices of illusionism before and during the middle period laid the groundwork for the emergence of such a complex visual invention.

FIGURE 2.13. *Paiban* player, Feng Hui's tomb.

Amid the dearth of sources on relief making an unusually rich twelfth-century episode, from *Hua ji* (The lineage of painting) by Deng Chun (fl. 1127–1167), reveals how the bas-relief as an artistic medium appealed to contemporary viewers as creating a particular kind of illusionism. Through this account of the rare "collaboration" between a sculptor and a painter that had been executed over three centuries we learn the tangible materiality of clay relief as well as its multifaceted optical effects as perceived by the viewers of the middle period:

> In the Central Plain, there are many "landscape walls" [*shanshui bi*] modeled by Yang Huizhi. Once Guo Xi saw one, and was inspired, he accordingly kept a plasterer from using the trowel and [he himself] rapidly applied clay to the wall using only his hands. As the overall image emerged, [some areas of the surface were] concave [*ao*] and others were convex [*tu*], no matter where it was forming. When [the clay surface was] dry, [Guo] went over the outlines [of the relief] with ink, which brought forth dizzying mountain peaks and lush valleys; then [he] added to it elements such as architecture and human figures. [This was] completely naturally formed, and was called *Yingbi*. Afterward, those who executed [this kind of work] became extremely numerous. This is what remains of Song Di's intention when he "spread the white silk on the ruined wall [*zhang su bai bi*]."[54]

This deceptively short episode contains references to several significant visual phenomena colored through the agency of renowned artists from the late Tang to the Song periods. The main subject of the relief landscape was originally executed by the Tang sculptor Yang Huizhi (fl. early eighth century), who was celebrated as mastering, together with Wu Daozi, the style of the well-known sixth-century painter Zhang Sengyou.[55] Although a description of Yang's original "landscape walls" is absent here, it is worth noting that clay reliefs on walls were already commonplace throughout the lower Yellow River regions in the north—that is, pictorial reliefs were made and placed not only in tomb spaces but also in the realm of the living and thus displayed publicly.

The focus of this passage, however, is the extraordinary transformation of Yang's relief landscape into something new by Guo Xi (ca. 1011–1090), one of the most distinguished painters of the Academy of Painting (Hanlin shuhua yuan) at the Song court.[56] In fact, some of the visual sensations described by Deng Chun are quite familiar to scholars of Chinese art. The notion of concave and convex (*aotu*) inevitably evokes the classical account of pictorial illusionism credited to Zhang Sengyou, the artistic model for Yang Huizhi. It is said that Zhang painted flowers on the doors of the Temple of the Single Vehicle (Yicheng si) in Moling, Zhejiang Province, using red and blue-green in the Indic style, and that they were greatly marveled at by visitors: "viewed from a distance, they appeared to be concave and convex [*aotu*], but when closely viewed, they seemed flat."[57] Now reconceived as a clay relief, the purely pictorial illusionism introduced through Zhang's painting was translated into something tactile, carrying out the connotations of the term *aotu* in a quite literal fashion. The court painter's impulsive refashioning of the relief wall and the enthusiastic response by contemporary image makers reflect the interest of middle period artists and viewers in seeking new illusionary effects.

The vivid description of the process of creating this painted relief reveals the ways in which different mediums coalesced and articulates a multifaceted visual sensibility involved in every stage of the representation. The quintessential characteristic of

the newly recognized illusionism is captured by the evocation of "dizzying mountain peaks and lush valleys" in the quoted passage. Referring to a specific visual
sensation, the concept of *ying* in *Yingbi* connotes a complex optical phenomenon.[58]
The meanings of the word *ying* appearing in traditional Chinese texts fall mostly
into two categories: a dark area formed by an object placed between light rays and a
surface (shadow or shade), and a reflected or mirrored image (reflection). Although
these two meanings were not always clearly distinguishable in the use of the word
ying (especially in some texts of Buddhist discourse), the term generally signified
either of the two meanings. In the case of Guo's clay wall, the presence of physical
shadows as the sole meaning of *ying* is unlikely, because if it was actual shadows
formed by the relief that defined this particular visual sensation, all of Yang Huizhi's
"landscape walls"—as reliefs that had existed through the centuries—would have
been referred to by the same term before Guo renewed the tradition. In addition,
although there had been some pictorial rendering of shading in painting,[59] the term
ying had rarely been used for characterizing the kind of representational shading
that had developed by the Song dynasty. For example, the essay "Record on painting
Cloud Terrace Mountain" (Hua Yuntai shan ji) by Gu Kaizhi (ca. 345–406) provides
a concise pair of good examples for the common use of the term *ying* in pictorial
terms. While Gu uses *ying* to refer to actual shadows in mountains, and *jing* (exchangeable with *ying*) for the reflection of the mountains on the surface of water,
the term is never used to refer to shaded areas in a painting.[60] For this other terms
were used, such as *ming'an* (brightness and darkness) or *yinyang* (darkness and
brightness).[61]

    The second concept of the word (as reflection) centers on the mirroring relation-
ship between the object of representation and the represented. A literal application
of this concept to painting can be succinctly illustrated in the paintings of buffalo by
Tang dynasty painter Dai Song (fl. eighth century), in which "a reflection [*ying*] [of
the water-drinking buffalo] on the water is seen" in one painting, and "a herd-boy [is
reflected] in the eyes of the buffalo" in another.[62] A less pictorial and more conceptual
use of *ying* as "reflection" is mentioned in an older Buddhist discourse on the so-
called *foying,* "Buddha's shadow" or "Buddha's reflection." Originating from a tale in
which Sakyamuni Buddha, seated in a dark cave, was only visible to those who looked
at him from afar, this "image" of the Buddha—referred to as *ying*—preached the law
and was admired by later Chinese for evoking the Buddha in contemplative visualization.[63] This notion of *ying*, despite the conventional translation of it as "shadow," is in
fact closer to a simulacrum or reflection of the original.[64] Heightening the typical
Buddhist emphasis on "the formless real" over its physical form, the painter Zong
Bing (375–443) adopted the tale of this religious vision and translated it into pictorial
terms, if not practice, in his theory of landscape painting.[65] Further analyses of this
extremely rich discourse go beyond the scope of the present discussion, but it should
be noted that a robust phenomenological connection between the notion of *ying* as
reflection and the viewer's perception of a represented image was already established in the pictorial field by the fourth century.

    This particular concept of *ying* as "reflection" has greater potential to articulate
the optical sensation engendered by the *Yingbi*. The dense visual analogy packed in

the last line of the passage quoted above from Deng Chun's *Lineage of Painting*—summarized as "zhang su bai bi"—is particularly illuminating and reveals a distinct meaning of *ying*. Here, Deng relates Guo Xi's *Yingbi* to a well-known story featuring the painter Song Di (fl. early eleventh century) in which Song gives advice to another painter, Chen Yongzhi (fl. 1024–1031), on how to improve his painting. This anecdote within the anecdote begins with Song's criticism of Chen's painting as bearing verisimilitude (*xin gong*) yet lacking natural flavor (*tian qu*), and then proceeds to relate Song's suggestions for Chen:

> First you go find a deserted wall and a piece of white silk. Then hang the silk over the wall and stare at it every morning and evening. After looking at it for a long time, [you will] begin to see on the surface of the white screen projections and curves all appearing, forming an image of a landscape, as it existed in your mind and configured in your eyes: the high becoming mountains, the low becoming water, the indented becoming valleys, the clear forming the close, and the vague forming the remote. As [your] spirit leads and creates, in a trance, [you will] see there are images of people, birds, grass, and trees, formed as flying and moving, coming and going, which clearly exists in your eyes. That is to say, in accordance with your mind, drive your brush.[66]

Regardless of the concluding line, embellished with the rather generic concept of using the mind's image or idea to paint (which was especially familiar to the literati painters of the Song period),[67] what is most relevant here is the fact that Deng found a fundamental connection between the images projected on the white silk and on the clay wall in terms of their parallel manner of materialization despite their clear difference in medium. In other words, it was in this visualizing process that Deng saw the shared effect of rhythmic animation registered on the two mediums. The concept of *ying* in the *Yingbi* in this context thus emphasized less the resulting image than the process in which the representation took shape, in which every step involved in formulating the natural world would be unfolded and reenacted on the surface of the medium. This interest in visually expressing the order of natural growth and movement in representations was something that other painters of the time also eagerly pursued. The eleventh-century author Liu Daochun, for example, describes the way that the renowned painter of bamboos, Xu Xi (fl. late tenth century), would work: "[Xu] first used ink to establish the branches, leaves, pistils, petals, and such, and would then go back over them with colors," which resulted in a remarkable sense of vitality that was "not very far removed from the process of creation itself."[68]

Seen in this light, the concept of *ying* in *Yingbi* extended beyond the basic definition of "reflection" and embraced a sense of emanation, connoting a generative force in the process of representation rather than something static or passive. This newly defined notion of *ying* helps to situate the specific illusionism evoked by the Yanshi actor reliefs in a larger visual field during the middle period. As in the case of the *Yingbi*, the visual effect produced by the actor reliefs is shaped by the interaction between the optical and the tactile rather than by purely pictorial illusionism. In particular, the sense of an animated surface created by these reliefs, through the intense contrast between their lack of actual physical depth and the great pictorial depths that they appear to convey, echoes the sense of emanating imagery in the creation of the *Yingbi*. An equivalent to the formulating process of the *Yingbi*—the even, malleable clay surface gradually forming into a landscape with various heights and spatial depths, as if miniaturizing the real landscape onto the wall—is visible in the Yanshi reliefs, but in the reverse direction: layers of spatial depths were compressed onto (or carved out of) the surface of thin, flat, clay bricks, evoking a seemingly limitless extension of space. Constituting two sides of the same coin, these two examples of clay reliefs manifest contemporary viewers' strong attraction to the sense of organic surface that could effectively animate the depicted image by densely registering multilayered space.

The shared way of seeing and artistic practice centering around these two types of reliefs—one by an anonymous artisan and the other by a renowned court painter—may come as a surprise to those who are used to a strictly hierarchical understanding of traditional Chinese art. But one must not forget the public nature of the medium as well as the contemporaneous interest in the optical wonders that cut across social boundaries. For example, the transmission and propagation of Guo Xi's relief landscape, as mentioned at the end of the quoted passage, suggest that regardless of Guo's association with the imperial court, this new type of relief would have reached audiences of various social strata in the extended arena of the visual arts, including relief makers in their workshops and in the marketplace. The open accessibility of the medium, compared to paintings on scrolls or in any other format that allows physically limited viewership, would have facilitated just such a wide range of viewers. While this is not to assume any one-directional dissemination of an individual style among artisans working at the popular or commercial level, it is worth noting that the spheres of image making during this time, particularly that of the clay relief, were not necessarily confined by the divisions according to social strata that are evident in other spheres of life and art.

LAUGHTER IN THE TOMB SPACE: IMAGINARY PERFORMANCE FOR THE DEAD

What made it appealing for the tomb designer and/or his patrons to place the actor reliefs in a dark underground chamber in which no living eye would enjoy such visual play? While this question is generally valid for any kinds of images furnished or painted in a tomb space, it applies here even more because of its vibrant illusionism, which suggests the assumed gaze of a viewer. The issue of the assumed gaze in a tomb space is a complex one, and no single premise can be applied to what in fact comprises a variety of situations, conditioned by many different components, including motif, medium, ritual use, and so on. For example, potential viewers of the image(s) of the deceased are generally considered to be the worshipers of the dead in imagined—if not physical—form, whereas the viewer of the scenes of entertainment is usually thought to be the deceased person who is entombed there. As to the possibility of the living as the intended audience, it is not impossible that such images could be seen before or during the burial, but the meaning of this category of gaze should be distinguished from the "ideal gaze" that was imagined to be present in the burial chamber.[69]

An immediate answer to the question raised above might lie in the common idea that any images of entertainment in a tomb space would have been prepared for the tomb occupant alone to view. Yet without considering the specific mode of representation and its relationship to its surroundings (i.e., other images and objects in the same burial space), such an assumption should remain only as a working hypothesis. If the *zaju* performance represented on the Yanshi reliefs was to be seen by the tomb occupant, in what form was it imagined for the deceased to see—as a representation, or as a real performance? More important, in the space where the gaze of the deceased was not represented and where there was no image of the deceased, what did it mean to install these vivid theatrical images? In fact, the position of the actor reliefs provides the first clue. As pointed out above, the reliefs were installed on the lower left part of the north wall, in front of which lay the deceased's coffin bed;[70] their close proximity to the body of the tomb occupant thus implies the existence of the deceased's gaze.[71] Unlike the representation of the *zaju* on Zhu Sanweng's sarcophagus discussed in chapter 1, where the image of the deceased was included, there is no indication of the performance here as a part of the funerary ritual. The nature of the gaze assumed here is thus physical rather than pictorial: it is the presence—not the representation—of the deceased that is imagined to play the role of spectator.

The presence of the symbolic gaze implied by the reliefs' particular location within the burial space suggests that the designer and/or sponsor took no issue with envisioning the tomb as an eclectic spatial setting in which ontologically heterogeneous beings could coexist and interact. In some contemporaneous tombs in which the deceased were represented, the pictorial space was shared with images of different motifs and could potentially form a self-contained sphere of its own. But in the Yanshi tomb, which has no spectators depicted—and thus assumes a viewer outside the image world—the actors' performances are not confined within the pictorial world but are meant to be engaged and activated by the imagined viewer positioned in the physical space of the tomb.

What facilitated the interaction between the represented actors and the virtual spectator was the vivid sense of animation embedded in the reliefs. Just as the *ying* illusionism in the clay landscape astonished the viewer by evoking images of mountains and waters cast onto a surface, the Yanshi reliefs, through the intense interplay between their material and visual sensibilities, had the capacity to conjure up lively theatrical spectacles that would have captured the gaze of the living. Given the implied spectatorship of the deceased, it was only the tomb occupant who could trigger the theatrical spectacles immanent in the representation of the actors in the brick relief panels.

What, then, were the deceased's eyes supposed to see? Perhaps the actor reliefs were intended to evoke the tomb occupant's experience in the public theaters known as *washe* (literally, tile markets) in daily life, where he or she could sit and watch a segment or two.[72] Or perhaps the reliefs were presumed to show the tomb occupant a private *zaju* performance that used to be held in his or her own house.[73]

Either way, what seems common to these performances in different venues is their humor. Whenever there was a *zaju* performance there was to be laughter, wherever it occurred and no matter who the audience might be. Indeed it is remarkable that for audiences ranging from emperors to anonymous commoners, the overriding response to a *zaju* performance was always laughter.[74] This feature of early *zaju* performances in the Song period, seemingly taken for granted, was such an essential element that it was sometimes considered the most important agenda for evaluating the success of a performance—so much so that if there was even a single audience member who was not laughing, actors found that fact shameful and tried their best to make that last audience member laugh. An amusing eleventh-century anecdote reveals how indispensable laughter was in a *zaju* performance, both to actors and audiences. In this account, when Su Shi was the one audience member who was still not laughing, an actor jumped into a performance that another actor had been leading, and scolded him: "If our scholar guest is not laughing, how can you be called a decent actor?"[75] He then took over the show and finally succeeded in inducing Su's laughter by uttering the following witty phrase: "It is not that Su Shi is not laughing; rather, his not laughing is because he finds it truly laughable."[76] Su finally bursts out laughing, recognizing this ad-lib as a clever parody of his own famous line about how to govern barbarians (*zhi yidi*),[77] here turned into perhaps the most playful subject of all—laughter itself. This self-reflective moment in which laughter becomes the main subject of the supposedly comic performance illuminates the significance of humor as an essential component of the *zaju*. The ceaseless laughter flowing throughout an arena of a *zaju* performance was thus what characterized the atmosphere of performance, regardless of the themes of the particular performance.

Relocated to the space of the dead and oriented toward the deceased, the imaginary performance projected through the actor reliefs would not only have conveyed the laughter of anonymous audiences but would also have induced laughter from the tomb's occupant. Introduced by the central lead actor's unrolling of the hanging scroll, the two segments of the *zaju* would have been imagined as being witnessed by the deceased. In particular, the comic duo's playful facial expressions, gestures, and costumes were the most likely laugh inducer, with the joyous atmosphere heightened even further by the sound of "beating drums, blowing whistles." In such a way, this imaginary performance reveals the shared memory of many contemporary spectators' lived experiences. The actor reliefs thus created a theatrical space in which the experience of *zaju* performances in the realm of the living was brought to life in the tomb and, in turn, would become an imaginary performance triggered by the single spectator—the deceased. This twofold performance—experiential and imaginary—would have filled the theatrical space enclosing the deceased's coffin bed with laughter. Through such an imaginary performance saturated with the jolly sound of laughter, the conceptual distance between the earthly dwelling and the afterworld was thus narrowed.

3

THEATER
OF THE
DEAD

The growing popularity of theatrical performances in northern China during the eleventh century was never interrupted by the major political turmoil caused by the Jurchen Jin dynasty's invasion of the northern half of the Song dynasty in 1126. On the contrary, it formed an unprecedentedly vital hub of theatrical performance in the Pingyang area, the middle and the southwest part of Shanxi Province, within the territory of the conquering Jin dynasty. Apparently, when the Jin troops stormed through the metropolitan area around the Song capital Bianjing, 375 miles southwest of Beijing, they actively sought not only artisans, doctors, and eunuchs who served at the Song court but also actors and other entertainers for a new court.[1] Theater culture, apart from its imperial incarnation, was becoming deeply embedded in the lives of regular folk. As poignantly featured in a few Yuan dynasty plays such as *A Playboy from a Noble House Opts for the Wrong Career (Huanmen zidi cuo lishen)*, in which a Jurchen nobleman chooses an acting job and rehearses farces and plays with his actress lover, theatergoing was no doubt a popular leisure activity.[2]

With this theatrical culture flourishing, modes of representing and reproducing theatrical spectacles grew more diversified. Coexisting with the once innovative medium of the illusionary bas-relief, yet another new type of actor image began to occupy tomb spaces; it manifested the local people's deeper involvement with the world of theater, while revealing their attitude toward death and the afterworld. The remarkable discovery of an early thirteenth-century tomb in the city of Houma in Shanxi Province richly showcases this new development. In the winter of 1959, in the southern part of an ancient city wall at Niucun in Houma, archaeologists unearthed an elaborate brick tomb, now officially called Houma Tomb No. 1. The interior walls were entirely covered with exquisitely molded brick reliefs simulating wooden architectural structures (fig. 3.1). Stepping inside the burial chamber after passing through the low and narrow entrance corridor, where only one person at a time could reasonably pass, the archaeologists were dazzled by the sight of a row of five sculpted and richly colored figurines standing within a miniature stage built into the north wall (fig. 3.2). The figurines depicted a troupe of actors, representative players of *yuanben* in the Jin dynasty theater. They might have seemed at first sight to be a simple decoration embedded in the brick replica of the wooden architecture, but the figurines—and their relationship to the tomb space—marked a new phase in the making of a performance image by embodying a particular conception of the afterworld.

A dated land deed revealed that the tomb belonged to a local man named Dong Qijian and his wife, who were buried in 1210.[3] Since the content of the land deed is formulaic, generally following a template recorded in the popular geomancy manual *Dili xinshu* (New book of earth patterns), printed in the twelfth century in this area,[4] the only personal information inscribed was Dong Qijian's name and that of his younger brother, Dong Ming (d. 1210), whose tomb was found about thirty-three feet southwest of Dong Qijian's.[5] Given the absence of a formal epitaph, Dong Qijian probably did not hold any offices at the Jin court, yet the extraordinary lavishness of the tomb interior clearly indicates the couple's affluence: at a time when cremation had become popular for those who could not afford proper burials, being able to construct such a luxurious tomb as this signals a relatively high level of wealth.[6]

The miniature stage and exquisite interior of Dong's tomb are an extension of the wood-imitation (*fangmu*) brick tombs derived from those of the late Tang through Song periods such as the Yanshi tomb examined in chapter 2; Dong's tomb is far more elaborate, however, as can be seen in an elevation drawing (fig. 3.3).[7] Only a few comparable Song tombs have been found in this area, and therefore we do not know much about the direct predecessors of the elaborate tombs in and around Houma; besides the possibility of cremation, an earthquake that hit this area in 1144 might have destroyed many architectural structures and brick tombs.[8] Yet

OPPOSITE PAGE

Top, **FIGURE 3.1.** Interior view of Houma Tomb No. 1. Shanxi province. Jin, ca. 1210. App. 254×221 cm. Bottom, **FIGURE 3.2.** Five figurines. Painted earthenware. North wall in Houma Tomb No. 1. H 20-22 cm.

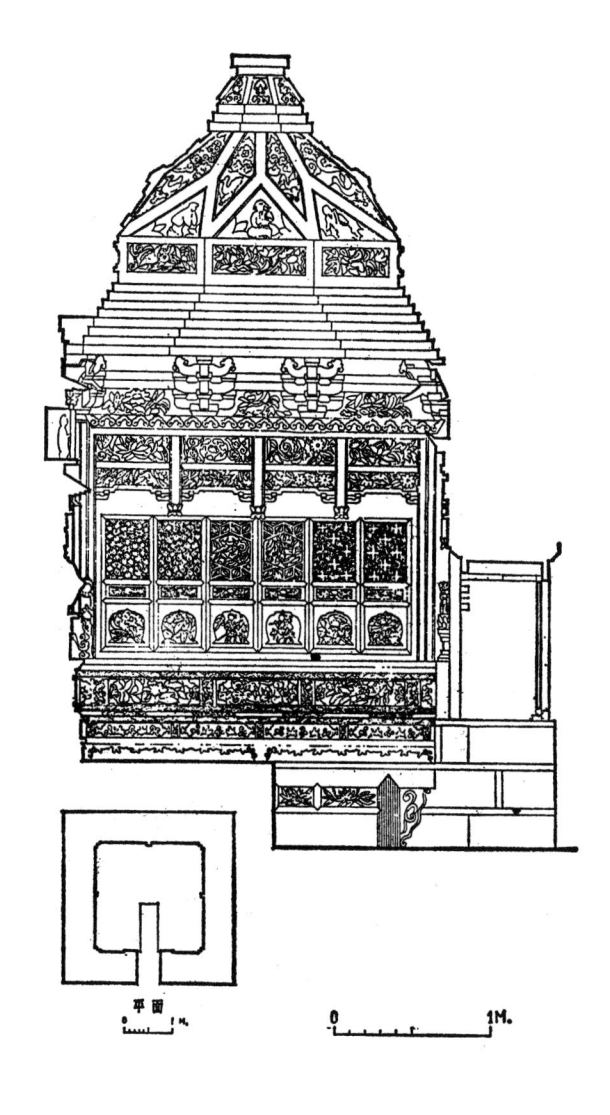

FIGURE 3.3. Elevation of
Houma Tomb No. 1.

平 图

0   1M.

there is no doubt that the basic design and structure of the wood-imitation brick
tombs are similar to the popular methods of tomb making during the pre-Song and
Song periods in Henan, Shanxi, Shandong, Shanxi, and Hebei Provinces. Again, a
strong cultural continuity is evident here despite the political ferment that was occurring; reflecting the general picture of the cultural field of the Jin, this region retained strongly Song cultural and demographic elements.[9]

In fact, the entire area of Jiangzhou, within which the city of Houma was located, was a significant economic and cultural center during the Jin dynasty, and it
would have provided the Dong family with easy access to advanced technology and
artistic practices. It is no coincidence that the most elaborately decorated wood-
imitation brick tombs of the Jin period were all excavated in this area: besides Dong

Qijian's and his brother's burial spaces, a tomb that belonged to a certain Dong Hai (d. 1196) and another tomb that bears a striking resemblance to the Dong brothers' tombs (Houma Tomb No. 104 and Houma Tomb No. 102) were both unearthed in Houma.[10] In addition, nine tombs of the Duan family cemetery with extravagant interior wall reliefs, known as the Macun Tombs, were found in the village of Macun in Jishan County, forty-five miles west of Houma.[11] That almost all of these tombs included images of theatrical performance corresponds to the cultural vibrancy of the middle and southern parts of Shanxi Province in general. This region produced some of the most prominent dramatists of the time, and during the thirteenth century it was also one of China's largest printing centers, which would have facilitated the dissemination of theater culture through the publication of inexpensive books.[12]

STEREOTYPED ACTOR IMAGES

By the thirteenth century, theatrical spectacles were nearly ubiquitous in urban areas, and they were prominently represented in underground spaces designed for the dead. In the Dong couple's tomb, the richly colored actor figurines stand out among the meticulously carved relief panels simulating louvered doors, columns, and brackets. The miniature stage on which they are ensconced is in the middle of the higher part of the north wall, above a carved representation of the couple sitting in what appears to be a mansion hall, which stretches across the entire width of the lower part of the wall. A close look at the figurines reveals a high level of detailing, which indicates the maker's interest in visually registering the actors' role types.[13] In addition to the grouping of five—making them easily recognizable as the familiar group of Five Actors of the Yuanben (*yuanben wu ren*)—certain theatrical characteristics given to each figurine help narrow down the range of possible role types while recalling many of the physical features of role types discussed in previous chapters.[14] The figure at the far left wears an official's headgear and yellow robe and holds an object in his right hand that resembles a wooden clapper. There are black circular patterns painted on his chest and shoulders, as if he were tattooed, as well as black streaks painted on his face.[15] Judging from his hat and makeup, this figure can be identified as a costumed official (*guzhuang*).[16] The figure standing second from left wears a blue suit and black hat in the so-called Su Shi style (*Zizhan yang*), and part of his outer garment is tucked into his belt. As discussed in previous chapters, this costume is associated with a second male lead (*fumo*). The middle figurine among the five is wearing an official's black headgear and a red robe with wide sleeves and is holding a *hu* tablet; given his central position, this figure may be identified as a male lead (*moni*).[17] The next figure to the right is wearing another black official's hat and a long red robe over white pants, and is holding a round yellow fan in his right hand. Zhou Yibai has identified this figure as the introducer of the play (*yinxi*) based solely on later textual sources; contemporary sources do not provide detailed roles for this particular actor type, and therefore the identification is less certain than that of the other figures.[18] The costume of the figure at the far right is the most elaborate of the group: his head is covered with a piece of cloth gathered at the top, and he wears a short yellow robe with tiger skin patterns on it, exposing his chest, which is painted (or tattooed) with cloud patterns. Above (and on either side of) his eyes and eyebrows are diagonally painted ink lines, in the shape of 八. He is whistling, while holding a short stick in his left hand. The gesture, makeup, and costume of this figure are most frequently seen in other representations of actors from the late Song through the Jin to the Yuan periods, and are easily identified as belonging to a second clown (*fujing*).

The figures, conspicuously dressed and posed, evoke playful descriptions of *yuanben* actors by the contemporary poet Du Renjie. Written as if seen through the marveling eye of a country bumpkin who stumbles into a swanky commercial theater in the city, this song suite (*sanqu;* literally, "independent songs") provides rare visual details about the actor and conveys the fascination that people had with the world of theater during the Jin period:

> Dressed in a black kerchief, with a brush stuck through the top,
> His whole face was limed white, and then brushed with ink-black lines.
> I know how he probably got along!
> His whole body
> Head to toe was covered in a flowered cassock.[19]

The congruence between the *fujing* figurine and the actor described in Du's song suggests that the visual codification of actors' role types was firmly established by the thirteenth century, and that contemporary theatergoers would have been able to easily recognize each role type through its makeup, costumes, and props. In fact, most of the visual features that I have described here had been "stereotyped" by the time these five figurines were made. An attentive reader might have noticed that many of the traits of their theatrical attributes recall a handful of earlier representations of the *zaju* actors of the Song times: the hat in "Su Shi's style" and the tucked-in clothes of the *fumo;* the official's headgear and *hu* tablet of the *moni;* and the wrapped head with a topknot and the whistling gesture of the *fujing.* It is also notable that a relatively new element in theatrics—makeup—seems to have become more popular around the time these Houma figurines were made. Several examples of representations of actors from this period and slightly later, such as the *guzhuang* and the *fujing,* have faces bearing makeup identical to that of the Houma figurines (fig. 3.4).

Underlying this visual stereotyping was the five figurines' particular roles in the tomb space. These highly detailed figurines call the viewer's attention to their existence per se rather than suggesting that they were meant to depict a specific theatrical spectacle through a composite performance. Three factors point to this "nonperformance." First, instead of engaging with one another, each figure is posed as an individual actor. None of the figurines gazes at, or turn his body to, his neighbor: each figurine stands at the front of the stage with his own distinctive posture, looking out at the empty space of the tomb. This contrasts starkly with some of the earlier and contemporaneous images of actors who are shown engaged with one another as if in the midst of performances (fig. 3.5). Although this performative

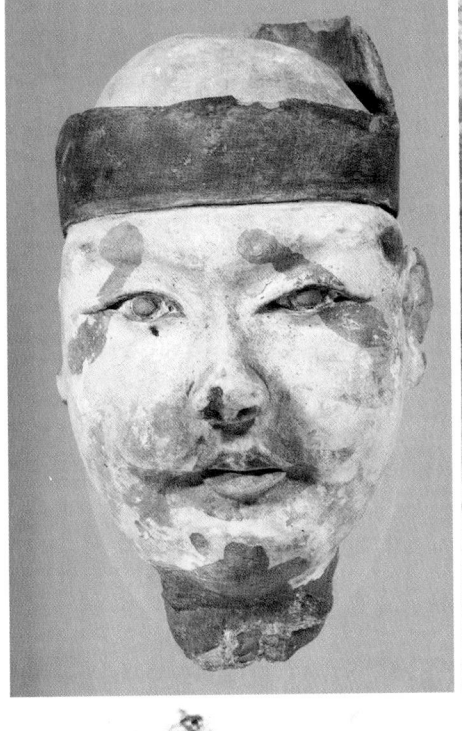 

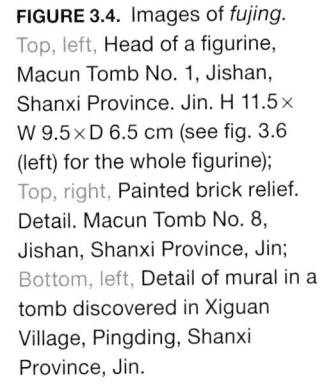

FIGURE 3.4. Images of *fujing*. Top, left, Head of a figurine, Macun Tomb No. 1, Jishan, Shanxi Province. Jin. H 11.5 × W 9.5 × D 6.5 cm (see fig. 3.6 (left) for the whole figurine); Top, right, Painted brick relief. Detail. Macun Tomb No. 8, Jishan, Shanxi Province, Jin; Bottom, left, Detail of mural in a tomb discovered in Xiguan Village, Pingding, Shanxi Province, Jin.

FIGURE 3.5. Tableau of *zaju*. Mural on the west wall of a tomb discovered in Hancheng, Shanxi Province. Northern Song. App. W 7.4 m.

mode could have been an option for the artisans of the Houma actors, they chose to depict the actors so that each would stand out as an individual player. Second, judging from the norms of a *yuanben* traceable through Yuan and Ming theatrical performance, all five role types can never be simultaneously present on the same stage except during the roll call; each segment is performed in sequence by a different role type, and all five never appear on one stage at the same time.[20] The roll call might seem a possibility as the subject of this arrangement of figures on the miniature stage, but the nature of the performance for the roll call is fundamentally different from acting a fictional persona in a play in progress: during the roll call, they are present onstage only as individual actors, and not as characters. Thus represented, the five actor figurines would not have triggered a vision of an actual performance onstage.

This nonperformative nature is reaffirmed by the distinctive location of the miniature stage just above the image of the mansion hall, where the actors would be invisible to the deceased. Most scholars have concluded that the location of this stage is exceptional only in comparison with other contemporaneous tombs in which the representation of a stage appears on the wall opposite the deceased's image. This conclusion is based on the assumption that theatrical images in tomb spaces were meant to be viewed only by the deceased interred there.[21]

While this idea of the deceased viewing entertaining performances certainly runs through the convention of image making for tombs in general, it should be noted that the tomb space was never governed by a single, consistent perspective. As briefly touched on in chapter 2, tomb occupants were not the only potential viewers of images represented in the tomb space. Some representations were designed to induce a particular visual effect that would operate on the viewing habits of the living,

FIGURE 3.6. Left, Reconstructed figurines representing actors (two of four), Macun Tomb No. 1, Jishan, Shanxi Province; Jin; Right, Empty space on a ledge in a miniature theater, Macun Tomb No. 1, Jishan, Shanxi Province; Jin.

and some assumed the gaze of living worshipers, albeit imagined ones, such as portrait images.[22] The complexity of this issue is clearly demonstrated by the actor figurines excavated from Macun Tomb No. 1 in the Duan family cemetery at Jishan, one of the most important examples of actor figurines found in Song, Jin, and Yuan tombs.[23] During excavation, archaeologists found broken pieces of four actor figurines lying on the ledge that represents the stage of a miniature theater on the south wall; these figurines most likely stood on that now-empty stage (fig. 3.6).[24] As in the case of the Dong couple's burial chamber, only actors are represented in figurine form, while all the other images in the tomb appear in bas-relief. It is noteworthy that the actors, in such outstandingly three-dimensional form, have no visible spectator in the tomb: there is no image of the tomb's occupants. Of course, by this time, the absence of the deceased's image in a burial space was not unusual,[25] but with the common assumption that images of actors there were intended to be viewed by the deceased, this absence has a particular meaning: the deceased as spectator was not a required component in the imaginary performance of the actor figurines within the representational space. This point is confirmed by a more recent discovery in a contemporaneous tomb in the same region. In that tomb, in which four prominently executed high reliefs of actors were found, there is no representation of the deceased, nor did the bodies of the deceased couple face the images of actors (fig. 3.7); the bodies were placed just below the actor reliefs installed on the south wall, with their heads abutting that wall.[26] Thus, the absence of the deceased's image in this tomb and the negation of the expectation of spectators for the five actor figurines in the Houma tomb are two sides of the same coin: in both cases, actor figurines and their performance required no spectatorship on the part of the deceased.

Instead of entertaining the tomb occupants, the actor figurines had symbolic roles and meanings in the burial chamber, manifested through their ontological status. To put it simply, they cut across two separate but not mutually exclusive lines of image making for a tomb space. On the one hand, the motif of actor figurines was relatively new: although the representations of more traditional entertainers such as dancers or musicians continued to be made, representations of drama in the form of actor figurines were a cutting-edge development in the realm of entertainment at that time and were also starting to be used as tomb furnishings. On the other hand, they take the generalized form of the tomb figurine (*yong*), a particular kind of burial object that traditionally accompanied the deceased as early as the sixth century BCE.[27] It is in the nexus of these two contexts of image making that the roles and meanings of the five actor figurines in the tomb are defined. The impetus for this convergence was the fully three-dimensional and portable medium of the figurine—it was not painting, not stone engraving, not bas-relief.

BETWEEN SPIRIT ARTICLE AND DOMESTIC DOLL

The choice to use figurines in Houma Tomb No. 1 is a curious one, as it is a departure from contemporary funerary practice and all the other representations in the tomb, which are bas-reliefs. Judging from archaeological reports, excavated tombs of northern and central China that were made from the tenth to the fourteenth century included few tomb figurines, though even fewer in human form.[28] Generally speaking, the most frequently found grave figurines have been imaginary ani-

OPPOSITE PAGE
FIGURE 3.7. Top, Actors (south wall); Bottom, Door flanked by servants (north wall). Painted brick reliefs, Huafeichang Jin tomb, Jishan, Shanxi Province. Jin.

mals and zoomorphic images of various calendrical phases rather than figurines of humans related to the deceased in their expected roles as attendants. The Dong couple's tomb did not include any figurines except those of the five actors. Considering the precedents during the three centuries before that tomb was made, it seems unusual for the representations of actors to take the form of figurines and to occupy a miniature stage that was designed exclusively for them.

The status and roles of tomb figurines in human form inside and outside tombs were colorfully recounted in pre-Song stories, especially from the late Tang period. Many episodes concerning ghosts and tomb figurines were both written and orally circulated, and by the early Song period they had become widespread.[29] Most stories from this period treat figurines as potentially supernatural beings who can transform themselves into real humans or ghosts and then typically occupy a burial space. Jessica Rawson, citing such stories from the eighth-century text *Guang yi ji* (Extensive records of marvels), by Dai Fu (fl. 757), has pointed out that grave figurines were viewed as both inert and alive, which makes them notably ambiguous.[30] In two of these stories, the tomb figurines' animated bodies demonstrate uncanny abilities: in one episode a seemingly friendly ghost turns out to be a tomb figurine, and in another a group of tomb figurines are accused by a ghost, the occupant of his own tomb, of rebelling against him. This seemingly generic characteristic of "animation" given to tomb figurines in such literature is indicative of the medieval imagination—in contrast to the classical conception of tomb figurines. Although all figurative tomb items made since the Warring States period were given human likenesses in one way or another, by the late Tang period, animation became the quintessential characteristic of grave figurines as they were envisaged in the popular imagination.

If these episodes underline the figurines' identity as *yong*, exclusively associated with the funerary context, other stories illustrate their emancipation from this original context. In a seventh-century story collected in the early Song imperial compendium *Taiping guangji* (Extensive records of the Taiping era), two wooden female figurines are picked up by the military officer Cao Hui from a Buddha hall attached to his office compound. When he brings them home and gives them to his little son as toys, the figurines begin talking to the boy and moving around. When the boy mentions their unusual behavior, Cao interrogates them. The figurines explain that they were initially made about a hundred years earlier by a talented servant of Shen Yue (441–513), who had named them Humble White (Qingsu) and Humble Red (Qinghong), and that Shen had ordered the servant to sculpt them so that he could mourn the death of his dear friend Xie Tiao (464–499). The figurines were buried in Xie's tomb, but tomb robbers broke in some time later and removed them, along with other objects, thinking that they would make good toys for children. Since then they had been moved from one house to another by different owners before finally ending up in Cao's Buddha hall. Impressed by their supernatural character, Cao decides to grant their request and orders an artisan to repaint them, dress them in silk dresses, and release them. Later, Cao hears that they have become wives of the deity of Mount Lu.[31]

The journey of the two tomb figurines adds another layer to the aspects of pre-Song concepts and images of *yong* featured in the previous narratives. First, as a *yong*, a figurine could still retain its supernatural abilities, even outside the funerary realm. A *yong*'s power to animate itself came from the experience of passing through the mortuary sphere with the dead. Second, as an artifact, a *yong*'s identity was fluid; depending on the intention of an owner, it could be a tomb figurine at one time or a doll or toy at another. Humble White and Humble Red experienced such transitional moments four times: they were taken out of the tomb by the tomb raiders and became toys for children; they were somehow left in a Buddha hall as wooden dolls (*mu ouren*); they were collected by Cao and became toys again; and finally, released from this mundane domain with new adornment, they became new beings who belonged to the realm of a deity. Thus, while a *yong*'s association with the burial space was a crucial condition for its body becoming animated, once it was removed from its original context it could become many things. Third, a tomb figurine could easily oscillate between categorically heterogeneous realms, such as those of the netherworld and of worldly entertainment. The tomb robber first recognizes them as spirit articles (*mingqi*) and then decides to turn them into toys (*xiju*) for children,[32] after which, in theory, the tomb figurines had no problem crossing the border between the two realms.

That story reveals a specific relationship between the tomb figurine (*yong*) and the spirit article (*mingqi*). Although the *yong* were clearly designated in the story as *mingqi*, reflecting the ways that most medieval Chinese would have categorized this kind of figurine, it was not the most orthodox practice to do so. The *yong* was a problematic ritual object since its inception, and had never been officially accepted as *mingqi*. Confucius criticized everyone who made the humanlike *yong* for burial instead of nonfigurative straw figures (*chuling*).[33] After that time, the status of *yong* as *mingqi* had not always been positive and was often referred to indirectly. For example, a rather abstract account of *mingqi* reported in the Han text *Yantie lun* (Debate on salt and iron) characterizes *mingqi* as something "with form but without substance," though it does not provide any list of appropriate items to use as *mingqi*.[34] Applying this description to the general definition presented in the Han lexicon *Shi ming* (Explication of names), it seems as if any paraphernalia used for sending off the dead could be called *mingqi*.[35]

By the Song period, the praxis of entombing funerary goods had never been officially standardized, but in reality *yong* had clearly entered the category of *mingqi*, as indicated by the observation of twelfth-century author Ren Guang that *mingqi* refers to "figurines, carts and horses."[36] In the preceding century, writer Gao Cheng had noted that "nowadays [people] refer to *yong* as *mingqi*"—thus acknowledging that the notion of *yong* as *mingqi*, which he considered a vulgar practice, was already widespread—but, after mentioning in *Li ji* (Book of rites) that *mingqi* are objects that superficially resemble the originals but, unlike them, are unusable, he concluded that "using *yong* as *mingqi* is erroneous."[37] Thus, during the Song period, even though the old guard still maintained the orthodox view, *yong* did actually constitute one important item that entered graves as *mingqi*. It is this tension between the ideal and reality that gave *yong* an ambiguous quality. Such fluidity of identity is further complicated in an arena of consumption and circulation, the marketplace, as is apparent from this sentence from a twelfth-century description of Bianjing, *Dongjing menghua lu:* "At Ghost Festival [Zhongyuan jie], the fifteenth of July, for the first couple of days, [merchants] in marketplaces sell spirit articles, shoes, hoods, hats."[38] Thus, by the early twelfth century, spirit articles were sold in marketplaces along with other sundry articles for daily use. Some sellers of such spirit articles also made the goods themselves. These craftsmen-merchants were called *mingqi fenzuo* (artisans who specialize in making spirit articles), a category of *tuanhang* (itinerant group merchants).[39] Moreover, judging from the existence of the itinerant group of merchants who exclusively sold such objects, it is clear that people could purchase *mingqi* in a regular market at any time, not only on a festive occasion such as the Ghost Festival.

In tandem with this vigorous commodification, the materiality of *mingqi* was also changing. While the craftsmen still retained the traditional clay, ceramic, and wood, paper became a major material for spirit articles. Most contemporary texts on the functions and treatment of *mingqi,* due to their emphasis on ritual process, are silent on the specific materials from which *mingqi* were made. For example, a section on spirit articles in the Tang dynasty geomancy text *Da Han yuanling mizang jing* (Secret burial classic of the original sepulchres of the Great Han) provides full details of how to locate a tomb site, as well as what and how to furnish it for burials, but no information on the materials of spirit articles.[40] Furthermore, there are relatively few archaeological finds that can be examined along with any relevant texts, because of the perishable nature of the favored materials of the time, such as wood and paper. The observation by Neo-Confucian scholar Chen Chun (1159–1223) on contemporary *mingqi* practice is particularly to the point: "The custom of our age is to use paper to form humans and make houses and the like; though different in size, [they are] still remnants of the *mingqi* [tradition]."[41] By the time of the late Ming (1368–1644) and early Qing (1644–1911) dynasties, the replacement of clay or wooden figurines with paper ones seems to have been commonplace. According to Gu Yanwu (1613–1682), clay or wooden figurines of humans or horses had mostly been replaced with paper figurines by his time.[42]

Paper *mingqi* were destined to perish shortly after entombment due to the nature of the material—if they had not already been burned at the time of burial, as Su Bai has suggested.[43] While this helps explain why there are only a few *mingqi* found in tombs built during and after the Song period,[44] another question arises: What happened to nonpaper *mingqi* such as clay or wooden *yong*?[45] It should be remembered that some clay figurines were still being buried with the deceased.[46] Even though, during the Song period, paper *mingqi* began to replace clay or wooden *mingqi,* of which there were only a relatively few being made by then, this did not mean that the more traditional versions lost their ritual and visual significance. On the contrary, their enduring presence suggests potential meanings underlying the persistent choice of such traditional materials by contemporaries.

The ways in which the five actor figurines in this tomb would have been perceived and identified by contemporaries before and after burial provide an essential clue for understanding the meanings and functions of the few *yong* still found in tombs. Removed from their funerary context, the five actors could be neutrally identified as clay figurines. Originally they could have been produced as either tomb figurines or decorative dolls that sat in the house of the deceased when the couple was living. Small clay figurines as domestic decorations or dolls had become extremely popular since the Song period among ordinary people and scholar-officials alike, as well as at court; and in Bianjing, for example, they were displayed for sale on the corners of all the main streets.[47] Some of the figurines were so finely made that even "nobles and court dwellers competed to purchase them for a high price."[48] Among those who appreciated such figurines was the renowned scholar Lu You (1125–1210), who enthusiastically described a clay figurine of a child, made by the famous figurine maker surnamed Tian, that he had acquired for his own collection.[49]

Numerous ceramic figurines representing actors have been unearthed in the past two decades, demonstrating that actor figurines were certainly a major part of this trend. A series of excavations since 1990 has revealed some hundred polychrome ceramic figurines of children, scholars, women, and actors datable to a period spanning the late twelfth and the thirteenth centuries.[50] Among the actor figurines found at one of these sites is that of a *fujing* (fig. 3.8) whose hairstyle, painted mouth, and gesture of whistling closely resemble those of the *fujing* figurine in the Dong couple's tomb. Furthermore, among the very few figurines found or excavated in residential sites, three colorful ceramic ones found in a dwelling foundation in Chengwu, Shandong Province, illuminate the multiple uses of figurines during the Jin period.[51] The location of this find is particularly pertinent here: they were unearthed in a section of a side room in a residential foundation rather than in a tomb or a kiln.

Tellingly, the same type of figurines were found in a tomb site. According to the report on the Chengwu figurines, they are identical to the ceramic figurines excavated in a tomb at Yangjiayuan Village in Qufu, Shandong Province, in 1954. These archaeological finds prove that the same type of figurines produced in a single kiln that sometimes occupied a domestic space were at times placed in a tomb with the deceased. In other words, there would have been no ritual taboo or restriction in the choice of figurines as *mingqi,* which were essentially the same as the decorative objects for a domestic space. The boundary between ordinary dolls and tomb figurines was thus often ambiguous.

Given both possibilities, the set of five actor figurines in the Houma tomb does not belong exclusively to either the category of *mingqi* or that of decorative domestic figurine. If the first possibility were the case, their relationship to other *mingqi* made of paper or wood should be examined. There were only practical objects excavated inside the Houma tomb: no *mingqi* were found. Since contemporary texts mention the popular practice of putting paper *mingqi* in tombs, it is likely that the tomb would have originally included paper *mingqi*. Therefore, the question of why only the five actors were made in the traditional form and material of *mingqi* remains unanswered. If the second possibility was the case—that the five actor figurines were domestic dolls—their meaning and status would be proximate to those of the functional articles found in the tomb, such as ceramic bowls, a wooden comb, or bamboo chopsticks—household

FIGURE 3.8. Fragment
of a *fujing* figurine.
Painted earthenware.
Unearthed in Henan
Province. Song to Jin.

objects that had possibly been used by the deceased couple during their lives[52]; in
ritual terms, this type of object could be categorized as *shengqi* (used or "lived" articles).[53] But the actor figurines do not easily fit in this group, either, due to their
conspicuous location in the tomb. All the personal goods mentioned above were
placed just above the heads of the bodies on the coffin bed, but the five actor figurines occupy the most prominent part of the tomb walls, more than four feet away
from the bodies. Even if they might have been used as home decoration during the
deceased's lifetime, the transformation of their identity from domestic dolls to tomb
figurines changed their status in the new environment of the tomb space. Thus, in
either case, a single prescriptive category of *mingqi* or *yong* cannot fully delineate
the ontological status of the five actor figurines. The literary definitions of such
terms in orthodox ritual texts do not immediately translate into historical reality;

rather, a more concrete picture can be drawn by focusing on the actor figurines' ambiguous status itself.

The figurines' undefinable status turns our attention to the convergence of the two visual contexts mentioned above—that is, their being the representation of actors and their form as figurines, a convergence that can be best characterized as a theatrical image "becoming" *yong*. Seen in the continuum of categories of performance image making for a tomb space, the actor figurines clearly mark a moment of new representation; these images, completely separate from the stone or clay surface to which they were applied, emerge from the pictorial plane and fully occupy the space. Their ontological meaning is intrinsically linked to their form as figurines, distinguishing them from the traditional figurines of dancers, acrobats, or musical performers in tombs of earlier times. Traditional figurines of entertainers were not the only three-dimensional form in the tombs in which they were buried; they were often accompanied by other human or animal figurines or architectural models. By "becoming" *yong*, the actor figurines' indexical relationship to the relatively new tradition—the representation of theatrical performance—thus merged into another visual context of figurative *yong*. At the same time, while deviating from any single category of *yong, mingqi,* or domestic doll, the five actor figurines carry traces of these categories within their bodies.

SOCIAL TYPES OF LIVING SOCIETY

Underlying the transformation of the actor figurines into *yong* was their socialization on two levels. Above I have discussed the figurines' potential exposure to the everyday world before their burial; figurines, initially commodified and displayed in the hustle and bustle of the marketplace, were fully connected with the everyday world until the moment of burial. Their densely socialized nature is embedded in their bodies not only ontologically but also visually. Given their "nonperformative" character, it may seem unnecessary that the figurines were presented with such articulated postures, distinctive costumes, and props, all of which give them a high degree of individuality as actors of varied role types. Furthermore, each face and body form differs from the others: from modeling to coloring, each figurine is endowed with unique facial and bodily characteristics. To be sure, this does not indicate that each figure "has a singularity" in ontological terms; we cannot know if any of these actors would have had his individual prototype outside of the tomb space.[54] In other words, each of these figurines is equipped with an anonymous individuality as a type,[55] succinctly portraying one of the role types of the *yuanben* theater with a fictional but singular identity.

That each of these five actors represents a type has a twofold meaning. On the surface, they are actors whose identities are to be recognized by their "role types" onstage. But they may also represent imagined individuals who, beyond the theater stage, would have had their own social lives. The individuality rendered in the characterization of each figurine through varied facial and bodily traits would have been unnecessary if each one was only intended to represent one actor's role type; distinguishing one from another with different costumes, props, makeup, and gestures would have been sufficient. As such, the five actors exhibit their double identities by possessing both external and innate singularities—distinct theatrical regalia and physical singularity—in a single body.

Their twofold visual identity inevitably draws our attention to the world outside the tomb. Whereas a regular, traditional *yong* in a tomb usually represents a type of individual in living society, each actor figurine represents a type of component of society in double form: beyond his identity as an actor with theatrical regalia, he is an acting individual who has a role in society.[56] Thus, a more accurate characterization of this ostensibly simple layer of the five figurines' identity as "actors as individuals" is in fact "actors (onstage) as individuals as actors (in society)."[57]

Such layering of the actor figurines' identities has a comparable discourse in contemporaneous spectators' experience of theatrical performance. To the spectators living in China from the eleventh to the thirteenth centuries, as in other cultures, actors and their performances were certainly a powerful reminder of the world in which they were dwelling, and this fact endowed spectators with a theatrical lens through which to look at their own lives. One of few accounts of this shows how deeply the view of their world was imbued with the theatrics of their time: "In the literati's dealings with the world, his looking for wealth, honor, and a profitable salary is exactly like an actor enacting the role of official [*canjun se*]; seated properly with an armrest under his arm, [he] sighs, scolds and thrashes [others]; a group of such actors clasp their hands in veneration and listen to edicts; [but when] the play is over, that's it."[58] In this satirical view of the literati's vain effort to seek wealth and fame through officialdom, Hong Mai (1123–1202) draws analogies between literati and actors who enact the role of officials, as well as their "dealing with the world" (*chu shi*) and theatrical performance.[59] Behind these analogies is the structural pairing of literati/actors and world/theater. While generally resonating with the cross-cultural notion of *theatrum mundi* (theater as world), this pair of analogies has yet another dimension. By choosing the specific role type of official—that is, *canjun se* (or *guzhuang se*)—Hong likens officials to actors impersonating officials. Provided that the role type of official would always enact anything related to officialdom, this may seem tautological. Nevertheless, none of the subjects of the analogy is in fact conceptually identical to any other: "officials (in society) as actors as officials (onstage)." Thus, genuine officials are represented through the act of disguised officials who are in fact actors, which alters the usual order of prototype and theatrical representation, blurring the boundary between the self-contained realms of theater and society.

The characterization of officials in Hong's satire structurally resembles the ways in which the five actor figurines' complex identities were visualized. Most salient is the synecdoche of the two realms—theater and society. While each figurine was presented within the whole troupe as an actor in his own theater, each was also a part of another entity outside the tomb as a type of social individual. Seen in this synecdochic scope, the aforementioned anomaly of the simultaneous presence of the five actors onstage makes more sense. Displayed as a complete troupe, the five actor figurines speak to a larger whole in which their seemingly unnecessary individuality finds its proper place: society. In other words, the troupe of actors, through their placement, materiality, and articulated individuality, metonymically alludes to society outside the tomb.

REORDERING THE TOMB SPACE

The actor figurines' deep connection to society brings up a fundamental question: What were their roles in the space prepared for the dead? A key to answering this question lies in the relationship between the actor images and the other representations of the tomb, including the images of the tomb occupants.

One of the important factors that define the actor figurines' relationship to the other images and to the entire space is the contrast in scale. Being about one-third the size of the figures of standing servants carved at both corners of the north wall (fig. 3.9), the five actor figurines appear tiny in the tomb space. The relationship of their size to the tomb space differs from some other cases in which *all* the figurative representations in the same tomb are of uniformly miniature size, such as the oft-cited example of those from a tomb in Shaogou, Henan Province (see fig. Pr.2). As Wu Hung has argued, a consistent scale of figurines is necessary for a coherent visual display in a tomb space, which constitutes the metaphoric world of the miniature that skews the temporal and spatial relations of the everyday world.[60] Viewed in this way, the size of the five actor figurines in the Houma tomb, uniformly scaled down as a group, breaks the visual harmony of the entire tomb interior; they thereby inhabit their own world, separate from that of the other representations in the tomb.

The resulting effect of this deviation in scale is not just a simple "break" from an otherwise coherently represented space, however. It is the Houma actor figurines' tiny size relative to that of the other tomb figures that alters the order of the dichotomous worlds of the real and the fictional. All the other human forms in the tomb, such as the images of the tomb occupants seated below the stage and those of the servants standing at the corners of the north wall (all visible in fig. 3.1), are already scaled down to one-third life size, and they form the baseline measurement for the rest of the tomb space; that is, the entire simulated architecture covering the tomb walls, including brackets, columns, and louvered doors, is adjusted to the size of these figures, not to the five actor figurines.[61] The reduced size of these human figures thus serves as visual testimony that the entire tomb space forms its own realm, separate from the outside world.

Within this consciously reconfigured world, how should we understand the miniature stage set in the context of tomb space architecture that is already reduced in size? The verisimilitude of the architectural detail has led some scholars to suggest that the tomb represents an actual house. Ellen Laing has argued that the structure of this simulated architecture represents a mansion's courtyard, and that it literally duplicates a house, creating an abode for the deceased.[62] Laing suggests that when standing in the tomb chamber one is standing not inside a hall but in the courtyard, and that the walls of the tomb represent the architecture surrounding that courtyard. Although Laing's study of the "organizational principle" of Song and Jin tombs is helpful as a systematic analysis of the patterns and structure of the

FIGURE 3.9. Contrasts in the sizes of figurines, image of the deceased, and viewer. Houma Tomb No. 1. Houma, Shanxi Province.

tombs, this particular suggestion calls for further reconsideration of the Houma tomb space on both the visual and conceptual levels.

On the visual level, even though each part of the walls emulates an actual piece of architecture, these parts do not constitute the composite whole of a mansion. For instance, the facade of the "mansion" looks plausible at first sight, but its component, such as the columns and screens, do not fit into a unified architectural system, which makes the "interior" space on the facade visually ambiguous. More important, the "mansion courtyard" scheme cannot explain the presence of the miniature theater stage on the roof of the hall. Laing, following J. I. Crump's suggestion, argues that this is a temple stage type, opening on the courtyard and facing the temple altar directly across the courtyard on the north.[63] Crump's suggestion seems to have derived from the assumption that the miniature theater and the architecture below it are the representation of a single building. But the way in which the two buildings are connected cannot be reduced to a faithful portrayal of a single prototypical model.[64] On the conceptual level, the problem with the "mansion courtyard" scheme is obvious when one takes into account the observations made above: the simulated architecture does not have to have just one single model. In other words, the realistic details of the architectural surface in this tomb do not necessarily indicate that they were meant to be a copy of an actual house; indeed, the simulated architecture may well have been the result of selectively chosen parts of different types of buildings.[65]

Instead of attempting to assemble haphazardly surviving prototypes of such variegated architectural parts, my discussion here deals with why the two structures had to be different sizes and different types of representation while sharing the same level of consistently meticulous detail. Despite its direct connection to the rooftop of the deceased's hall, the miniature theater, supposedly being part of an organic building, exhibits a number of nonsensical architectural elements. When viewed apart from the couple's mansion, the theater stage appears at first sight to be a generic pavilion that faithfully represents a standard architectural structure; for example, two octagonal pillars support a lintel with three sets of brackets (puzuo) that follow the contemporary architectural principle of yidou sansheng (one support and three brackets).[66] In addition to such plausible details, the theater's loose connection to the mansion highlights its independence; the two columns in the theater pavilion are simply inserted into holes in the rooftop, which makes a sharp contrast to the meticulous execution of all the joints connecting the brackets and columns to the rest of the simulated architecture. Most obviously, the overall size of the theater is drastically disproportionate to the mansion's facade.

From this analytical angle, the theater stage might be considered as a structure entirely independent from the mansion. In the larger visual context, however, the theater reveals its multifaceted relationship to the mansion as well as to the entire tomb space. The most relevant contradiction is observable in the form of the roof. The roof of the theater facade encloses a triangular area, a xieshan (or shan-hua). The orientation of the xieshan is puzzling, for a xieshan of a one-story building is usually visible on the two sides of a building rather than its front and back, and therefore should not be able to be seen on the facade (top in fig. 3.10).[67] Seeing the miniature theater as an independent structure, Liao Ben has suggested that it could represent a type of temple stage in which the xieshan faces front.[68] But this particular style of xieshan, the cross-shaped xieshan (shizi xieshan; see fig. 3.11), is not apparent in the miniature theater here, which shows only the front xieshan of the roof. A more fundamental problem with this suggestion is that the example that Liao discusses—the stage in Dongyue Temple—is most likely a Yuan or post-Yuan structure,[69] and none of the other similar extant stages can be safely dated to Jin or pre-Jin times. In fact, surviving temple stages from the Jin period went through multiple renovations over time and often no longer exist in their original form.[70] Unlike the core components such as brackets or external columns, roofs had to go through multiple renovations, and therefore the current form of a roof should not automatically be considered contemporaneous to the main architecture.

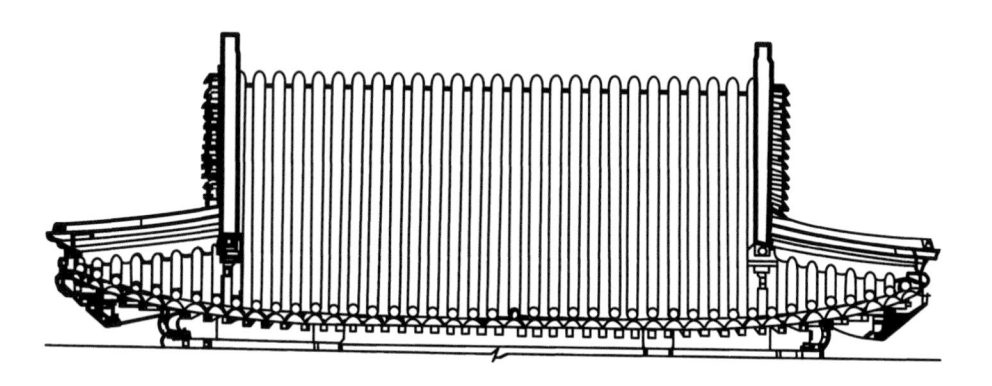

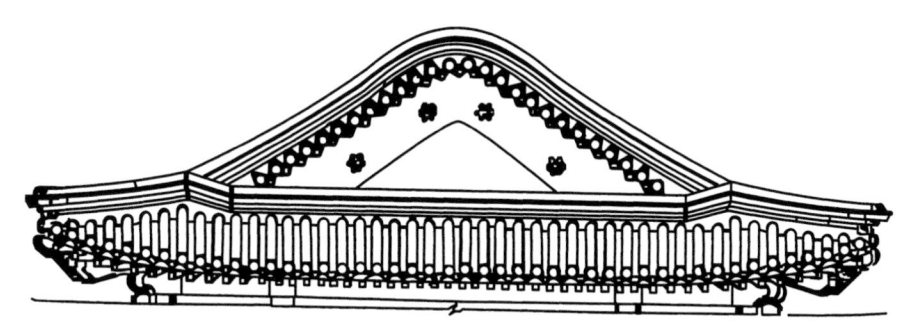

FIGURE 3.10. Structure of *xieshan*. Top, Frontal view; Bottom, Side view. Drawing by Katherine Lester.

FIGURE 3.11. "Cross-shaped" *xieshan* of a stage in Dongyue Temple, Linfen, Shanxi Province, Yuan, ca. 1345.

Liao's suggestion, based on the premise that the miniature theater represents a prototype of the single-story structure as an independent building, overlooks the theater's relationship to the larger mansion in which the deceased couple is seated. Taking this into account, I relocate the question within a broader visual field of architecture and focus on the facade of the simulated architecture in the tomb as a whole—especially the visual resonance between the miniature theater and the simulated hall. Doing so does not presuppose yet another single, composite prototype that may have existed outside the tomb; rather, it helps to expose newly configured visual and ritual contexts that dynamic relations between the miniature theater and the hall create within the tomb space.

Normally constituting a triangular section between two sides of a sloped roof, the body of a building below the *xieshan* is supposed to be a sealed wall. It is composed of a *shanqiang* (mountain-shaped wall) rather than an open space, as seen in the facade of the miniature theater, which led some scholars to consider its particular location in the tomb an error.[71] Yet this seeming error in the architectural simulation carries its own visual logic. With the *xieshan* relocated, so to speak, to the facade of the building, the pavilion now looks as if it were the second floor of a building. This visual plausibility derives from certain types of contemporaneous multistory buildings (such as *ge* or *lou*) in which the *xieshan* is designed to face the front. Buildings with rather complicated roof types emerged during the Sui and Tang periods and continued to appear in the Song and Jin periods.[72] Some of them structurally echo this two-story architecture in which the second floor is open to four sides, with its *xieshan* facing front, as depicted in a twelfth-century mural in Yanshan Monastery, Shanxi Province (fig. 3.12).

For contemporary viewers who were probably familiar with such an architectural structure in their built environment, the effect of this appropriated theater roof of the Houma tomb would have made the mansion look as if it were an architecturally connected first floor, thus causing the two buildings to look like one. Moreover, the unified forms and sizes of architectural components shared by the theater and the mansion, such as brackets and columns, enliven the effect of visual consonance. Underlying this uniformity was a negotiation between visual plausibility and conceptual need. Given the highly skillful craftsmanship of the small building blocks, the artisans of this brick structure must have been capable of making even smaller pieces of the components that would proportionally fit into the size of the theater. But they chose not to further downscale the parts and instead to leave it half miniature, half "real,"—that is, the already downscaled "real." The theater was thus designed as a model of the second floor of the mansion, only partially conforming to the "real" world in the tomb space.

THE MINIATURE THEATER: INTERFACING TWO WORLDS

The tension between the theater's visual plausibility as part of the larger architecture and its still conspicuous distinction from the mansion articulates its ambiguous status. While the theater with a "relocated" *xieshan* was designed as visually incomplete, without the first floor of a building, the building did not have to be

FIGURE 3.12. Detail of
mural at Yanshan
Monastery, Shanxi
Province. Jin.

structurally and proportionally consonant with the miniature theater as long as it
existed as the ground floor. Why was the miniature theater designed to require a
structure below it, and what could it gain in effectiveness by looking like the second
floor of a larger architectural entity?

An examination of miniature theaters in other contemporaneous tombs reveals
significant spatial logic that helps provide a possible answer to these questions.
Even though the miniature theaters that have been found are not all located on the
same wall as the one at Houma Tomb No. 1 (some are on the south wall—i.e., the
wall opposite the deceased's image—and others are on the north wall), all of them
are placed on what is meant to look like the second floor of an architectural structure.[73] One particularly relevant example is the miniature theater in Houma Tomb
No. 104. Constructed around the same year as Houma Tomb No. 1, it includes actor
figurines and a miniature theater as well as a relief interior similar to those in the
Dong couple's tomb.[74] The only notable difference is the location of the miniature

FIGURE 3.13. Reliefs representing actors placed above tomb gate, south wall of Macun Tomb No. 3, Jishan, Shanxi Province. Jin.

theater above the tomb gate on the south wall, combined as if part of the facade of a uniform architecture, with its *xieshan* facing front. Tomb No. 3 of the Duan family cemetery in Macun is another good example of a miniature theater building above the tomb entrance on the south wall (fig. 3.13).[75]

These theaters' particular association with a gate below them has not drawn much attention from scholars because most scholarship has concentrated on their presumed relationship to the images of tomb occupants as spectators. Yang Fudou's observation in his excavation report on Houma Tomb No. 104 constitutes the sole discussion regarding this issue. Yang points out a resemblance between the position of the miniature theater in the tomb and the second floor of a temple gate (*shanmen*) and suggests the former as the representation of the latter.[76] Though this suggestion is visually insightful, the miniature theater's partially independent status from the larger wall surface in the tomb makes it difficult to follow the view that the theater was a faithful representation of the upper floor of a *shanmen*. Rather, it is the *structural* resemblance between the tomb entrance wall and *shanmen* that hints at particular visual and spatial experiences shared by people who would have developed and appreciated this architecture over many generations. Several later temples with a similar structure confirm that the idea of placing a performance space above a gate or an open space—if not yet its actual practice—became firmly established by the late imperial period as a particular architectural type (fig. 3.14).[77]

At the core of the resemblance between the miniature theater and the *shanmen* is the theater's organic relationship to its ground structure, particularly the gate. As

FIGURE 3.14. Stage above the entrance of the Dongyue shrine in Jinyuanzhen, Taiyuan, Shanxi Province. Qing.

in the case of the Dong couple's tomb, the theaters in the aforementioned tombs are not architecturally self-contained but constitute cohesive structures when viewed together with the gates of the tombs below them. Although they belong to distinct ritual contexts—one funerary and the other religious—the miniature theater and the *shanmen* share a spatial principle: underneath the theater is an open space that connects inside and outside. Regardless of its intended use, the second-floor architecture in both cases thus stands at the boundary of the two spaces. The space below the stage is physically manifested in Houma Tomb No. 104 and Macun Tomb No. 3 of the Duan family cemetery by the presence of a gate that serves as an actual entrance passage, whereas it is only pictorially expressed in the Dong couple's tomb, signifying the "inside" and "outside" of the deceased couple's hall. Seated in this ambiguous space, where they are flanked by a column and a freestanding screen on either side, the deceased couple seems to rest in an amorphous realm beyond the surface of the architecture that is represented.

It is noteworthy that an open space of a hall such as the one depicted in the Dong couple's tomb was sometimes rendered differently in other contemporaneous tombs. In many cases, the main wall of a tomb that faces the tomb entrance—often called the back wall (*houbi*) by Chinese archaeologists—is where an image of doors appears, implying that an open space exists on the other side.[78] Such doors are in some cases painted and in others carved in relief, with or without a figure, but they nearly always occupy the main wall of a tomb.[79]

As was discussed in chapter 1, previous studies generally share the idea that regardless of the medium (coffin surface or tomb wall), such doors symbolize a liminal path for the deceased to move from one space to another, from this world to the next. The image's symbolic role can be largely understood as such, but how to define the represented "space" implied as existing beyond the surface remains a question.

FIGURE 3.15. Sculptures of the deceased placed in front of a gate. Macun Tomb No. 8, Jishan, Shanxi Province. Jin.

Why would it have been depicted at all, when the sight of the doors was already firmly established as a sign to evoke the liminality of the tomb space? My foregoing discussion of the relationship between the image of doors and that of the deceased on the main wall is one way of addressing this question, which will help define the nature of the open space represented in the Dong couple's hall. In most cases, the image of the deceased and the image of doors do not appear simultaneously on the main wall. Where there is an image of tomb occupants, there is usually no image of doors in the tomb, and vice versa. However, in two rare examples from the Macun Tombs of the Duan family cemetery, these motifs are both present on the main wall. Macun Tomb No. 8 has an image of the tomb occupants in a niche on the main (north) wall (fig. 3.15), as in most other Jin tombs with images of the deceased. What is unusual in this setting, though, is the simultaneous presence of partially open doors behind them. The right-hand panel of the door is ajar, pushed slightly inward toward the other side from where the couple is seated. The space to which the deceased couple belongs is thus clearly rendered as "outside" the building, and the inner space beyond the doors is hidden.

The conspicuous demarcation of the deceased's place through the image of doors is further articulated in another tomb in the same cemetery, Macun Tomb No. 4. In this burial chamber the deceased couple, along with their servants, appears in a niche on the main wall (fig. 3.16). As in the case of Macun Tomb No. 8, the niche is

FIGURE 3.16. Sculptures of the deceased seated on the threshold of a gate. Macun Tomb No. 4, Jishan, Shanxi Province. Jin.

constructed as the facade of an independent building with doors, but this time the doors behind the couple are wide open, pushed inward toward the "inside." Precisely where in the building the couple was meant to be seated is unclear, as they occupy a space neither inside nor outside the doors but exactly between the two. Furthermore, the presence of a screen—placed just behind the doors, blocking any view of the inside—implies that the openness of the doors was designed to delineate the deceased's particular realm in the liminal space rather than to expose the inner space of the building. Such a subtle strategy of spatial demarcation visually describes how the border of the earthly world was perceived in the contemporary imagination: the boundary between this world and the afterworld formed its own space, facing both realms yet only accessible to the deceased.

The spatial layers revealed through the position of the deceased in Macun Tomb No. 8 help define the ambiguous pictorial space in which the Dong couple is represented in the Houma tomb. The background of the deceased couple in the Houma tomb appears spatially vague, especially when compared to the rest of the simulated architecture. We cannot ascertain whether the blank background was the relief maker's practical choice to emphasize the silhouettes of the figures or the deliberate representation of a space, but the couple's specific position framed within an architectural structure precisely echoes what we see in the Macun Tombs of the Duan family, which display a shared characteristic of an undefined background: a veiled, inaccessible space behind the couple. In other words, the hidden space signified with the dummy doors in the Macun tombs is only implied by the emptiness in the Houma tomb. The couple is seated at the margin of unknown yet continuous space, beyond which nothing can be seen, but only imagined, by the living.

The symbolic distinction among these three elements—the space alluded to as existing behind the represented hall, the architectural surface, and the physical space in the tomb—is made more pronounced by the intense visual effects conveyed by the surface representations. Some parts of the furniture and architecture on the Houma tomb's north wall, such as the legs of the screen, the tabletop, and the elaborate brackets in the corners, are represented in high relief, whereas the other decorations on that wall, and all the decorations on the other three walls, are bas-reliefs and remain comparatively flat.[80] Though anchored firmly at the surface, the images in high relief seem to be exaggerated three-dimensional entities that jut out from the walls, almost as if they extend outward from the space beyond the surface. These sculptural elements possess an anomalous sense of depth and volume that complicates the binary spatial division in the tomb, breaking the conceptual distance between pictorial and real spaces. They are projected into the real space to an extreme degree, as if they could transcend the border between the two spaces and eventually belong to both.

This sense of growth and animation engendered by the surface representations reorders the physical space with which they make direct contact. As the counterpart of the hidden realm of the dead existing beyond the architectural surface, this tomb space is redefined as a realm still conceptually accessible to the living. *Wai zhai* (outer abode), one of several contemporary terms that refer to a tomb, reasserts this observation. In the epitaph found in another tomb excavated in Houma and dated 1212 (Houma Tomb No. 31), for example, the tomb is referred to as *wai zhai*.[81] Yet the *nei* (in)/*wai* (out) dualism during the middle period, especially in the theatrical context,[82] carried substantial slippage in terms of its referent; rather than definitely signifying a fixed place, the meaning of *nei* or *wai* was often contingent on the perspective of the subject. From the vantage point of the living, *wai* could be understood as a conceptual counterpart of anything living, and hence outside the world of the living. But from the deceased's point of view, it could mean the tomb space itself that existed outside his or her own mansion, in which case the exterior (*wai*) of the architectural surface is metonymically redefined as the sphere of the living. In fact, the idea of shifting perspectives between the living and the dead in funerary art had been manifested in different ways since the Han period, if not earlier. One of the most distinctive practices was the so-called *dao shu* (reverse writing) in epitaphs. A good example is a pair of stone pillars in the funerary park of the Liang dynasty (502–557), commemorating Emperor Wen, erected in the spirit way (*shendao*); the one on the right shows the graphs identical to the one on the left, yet in reversed (mirrored) form.[83] Wu Hung has suggested that in reading/viewing the pillars, a visitor relocates him- or herself to the other side of the gate and therefore identifies with the dead, assuming the dead's viewpoint.[84] Wei-cheng Lin's recent discussion of the change of perspective in conceiving the tomb space during the middle period further articulates this issue.[85] Extending the central idea of the shifting perspective to the visual role of the architectural surface in the tomb, I suggest that such terms as *wai zhai* or *nei zhai* may not always have referred to a single, specific place such as a tomb or a house. In the larger scheme of the discourse of reversal between the worlds of the living and the dead during the middle period, the *nei/wai* dualism is better understood as a mode itself through which a perspective could shift in either direction, rather than as defining a fixed location—an observation fully discussed in chapter 4. That the architectural surface in Houma Tomb No. 1 is charged with the dense sense of emergence and movement that allude to the existence of the world on the other side resonates with this discourse; the wall surface is thus defined as a fundamentally marginal border from which the two realms respectively extend their space limitlessly inward and outward.

The miniature theater and actor figurines, set directly above the edge of the deceased's mansion hall but appearing to jut out further into the tomb space, share the skin of the architectural surface but remain ambiguous by traversing the worlds of the dead and the living. On the one hand, the actor figurines display a remarkable corporality that exclusively belongs to the world of the living, outside the deceased's mansion. By "emerging" from the shared representational ground and being completely detached from the surface level of the simulated architecture, the actor figurines insert themselves into the space of the living. On the other hand, the theater's physical attachment to the architectural surface connotes its symbolic position as the organic extension of the liminal space. In other words, while the actor figurines take the form that is perhaps closest to that of living humans among all the images in the tomb, the theater itself is still rooted in the fluid architectural surface. The theater thus serves as a "third space," a site in which variously represented and imagined layers of different realms intricately merge, and acts as a mediator between the earthly world and the afterworld. This concrete visualization of the third space in material form reveals an important postmedieval mode of conceiving the binary spheres—be it the afterworld versus the earthly world or the realms of the numinous versus the mundane.[86]

STAGING THE DEAD WITHIN A VIRTUAL THEATER

The recognition of the miniature theater as a realm midway between the two worlds not only reaffirms that the actors' performance required no spectatorship from the deceased but further hints at what constituted the unusual nature of such performance. I have emphasized the actor figurines' pronounced three-dimensionality and individuality that denote the synecdochic relationship between the theater and living society. When recontextualizing this metaphoric connotation within the spectrum of spaces discussed so far, we begin to see a visual and conceptual tension created between the images of the actors and those of the deceased. The tension derives from the simultaneous presence of the images of the dead and the living—that is, the deceased couple and the actor figurines as a version of variegated types of the living.

But the juxtaposition of the two worlds registers their relationship in a hierarchy. The presence of the actor figurines ties together the entire architectural surface and the space implied beneath it, not the reverse. When they become detached from the shared representational ground (i.e., when they "became *yong*," as discussed above), the actor figurines break the equilibrium of the fictional reality painstakingly formulated through the illusory architectural surface. In so doing they frame the image of the deceased, and their space implied underneath the simulated surface, as a setting to behold. Notably, such a bracketing effect echoes the basic mechanism of configuring different versions of reality in the world of theater: while coexisting in the physical space of a theater, the social reality constantly brackets the fictional reality, which then turns into an alternative reality in the new theatrical space.[87] The entire architectural setting simulated within the fictional space thus becomes a plausible stage set in which the deceased couple become actors. Rather than simply being a portrait of the deceased, the image of the tomb occupants thus presents them as impersonators.

This impersonation is, of course, anomalous to the conventional pairing of an inner self and a persona, for the image of the deceased couple was meant to represent who they were and therefore the self and persona were, for them, ontologically one and the same. But it is this seemingly nonsensical impersonation that shapes the doubly theatrical nature of the deceased's image: the figures impersonate themselves as if they were alive. By the same token, the architecture housing them is presented as if it were their house. In this sense, the image of the deceased is an enactment of themselves in living form rather than a portrait or documentary representation of their former lives. In contrast, the five actors, occupying the "real" space, deviate from the fictional realm of this virtual theater. Located outside the virtual theater, the image of the actors presents the *mise-en-scène* of the deceased couple and their current abode. Thus, while occupying the symbolic theater that interlaces the worlds of the dead and the living, the five actor figurines yield the task of giving an actual performance to the virtual actors—that is, the tomb occupants.

The reversal of the roles between the actors and the deceased raises the question of spectatorship. Was there an implied audience for the virtual performance of the deceased? In principle, any underground tomb space in any time period in East Asia was to be inaccessible to the living after entombment, except if the tomb occupant were reburied or if there was an additional entombment of a family member. And yet, the contemporaries of the Dong couple did not exclude the possibility of their presence in their ancestors' tomb space, as demonstrated by an inscription composed by the tomb occupant Duan Ji in the Duan family cemetery (Macun Tomb No. 7, ca. 1181) expressing the wish to be present in the burial chamber for a worshiping ceremony: "There are the noble and base, the wise and foolish, and thus people are all different. But in the circle of life and death, they end in one. I realized myself that my life is drawing to a close, to the eternal night, and therefore make this burial chamber in advance in preparation for taking in my coffin. . . . I prepare this tomb as a space for later descendants to worship [their deceased ancestors]."[88] After giving the date of the composition, the inscription on the stone panel ends with a list of names in their genealogical order, albeit modest in its scale as a descent group: from Duan Ji's great-grandfather through the fifth (and last) granduncle to his grandchildren.[89] We simply do not know whether this worshiping ceremony actually took place in the tomb space;[90] even if it did, it would have been a one-time event rather than something repeated by generations of offspring, because the tomb was eventually closed. At a practical level, the compact size of the tomb as well as the narrow corridor in which not more than two or three persons could barely stand and move around would also have made it difficult to hold any rituals inside the burial chamber. However, at a conceptual level, it is clear that people of that time did consider the tomb space as a place for worshiping the deceased, and they therefore had no qualms about visualizing their presence in the deceased's space. In this context, future tomb occupants could have, when preparing their tombs, imagined their descendants worshiping in front of their images. By the same token, if it were the children of the deceased who sponsored the tomb construction, the imagined worshipers would have been the offspring, including the children themselves.

In this sense the implied audience is further characterized as all living descendants. Note that the ideal picture of ancestral worship described by Duan Ji operates on the genealogical framework in which the subject and object of worship were to be renewed by upcoming generations. In other words, it was expected that the ones doing the worshiping would become the worshiped at some point, and therefore all later descendants (*houdai zisun*) were the potential ancestors in the future. It is remarkable that Duan Ji, as the maker of his own burial chamber, embraced this open-ended framework in his conception of worshiping, which went beyond a scope limited to himself and his immediate ancestors.[91] This expanded vision of a "lineage" as the object of the imagined worship,[92] which gives us an indication of the conceptual scale of the ritual practiced by the local elite, was also visually imprinted in the "portraits" of the deceased in contemporaneous tombs. When seen through this expanded scope of genealogy, the images of the tomb occupants in these burial chambers can be more accurately defined as a visual agency of the collective ancestors and not necessarily of individuals. Indeed, it is misleading to call them portraits if by this term we assume the intrinsic connection between the ontological singularity of the deceased and his or her visual individuality. This point is illuminated by the representation of the tomb occupants on the north wall of Houma Tomb No. 104 (fig. 3.17): the image of the deceased in this tomb is identical to that of the Dong couple.[93] It was thus acceptable to duplicate the images of the dead—just as any other motifs—for tombs of different individuals. This is not to argue that the sponsors of these tombs were not interested in seeking individuality of the deceased in such representations; the visual individuality was a nonissue. Rather, it is to suggest that they cared more about the presence of the portrait-like images in the tomb space as a focal point of worship (albeit imaginary) than about how such images should carry the personal characteristics of the individual ancestors or, in some cases, the preparers themselves as future ancestors.[94]

FIGURE 3.17. Tomb occupants. Brick reliefs. Houma Tomb No. 104, Houma, Shanxi Province. Jin.

It is in this infinitely regenerating scheme of ancestor and offspring that the audience for the virtual performance of the deceased can be best defined. The implied audience was not simply limited to the sponsors of Dong couple's tomb but may well have included all the descendants of the Dong lineage collectively. Just as the "portraits" of the deceased were prepared as an agency of the ancestor, it is likely that the envisioned audience of their performance was the offspring as a collective whole. The virtual performance of the deceased was thus to be viewed by the living descendants, the people who would eventually replace the performers' position at some point in the future. This answers the question of why the actors and their theater, among many other entertaining motifs available, would have been chosen and conspicuously displayed in such a symbolic mode. The sense of theatricality constructed through the particular representational mode was probably the most powerful way to remind the living of their shifting position from that of worshiper to that of the worshiped—hence, the virtually endless lineage.

Guided by the actor troupe's implicit presentation of the scene of "theater" below them, the gaze of the living encountered the realm of the dead. The sight of the actor figurines, while reminding the living of themselves, served as a deictic sign pointing to what was unfolding below their own stage. Within the virtual theater of the dead, the world of the deceased was thus framed as something to be looked at through a theatrical lens. The underlying logic of this framing differs from the generic notion of *theatrum mundi;* while *theatrum mundi* operates on the idea of the mirroring of two worlds, mutually blurring the boundary, what the actor image presents here is the theatricalization of the unknown afterworld through the agency of the living.

In accordance with the existing understanding of Song and post-Song religiosity, this observation conforms to the view that the world of the dead was generally
conceived as a realm that shared a similar world order with living society.[95] Rather
than merely mirroring the living world, however, the funerary realm configured in
people's minds was enveloped by the vision derived from their own society as a cognitive frame. In the juxtaposed sight of the realms of the dead and the living, the
content of the afterworld was not the focal point. What was emphasized was the
mode of objectifying the sphere of the dead through the intense theatricality, a sensibility originating from the characteristically mundane activity. Born out of the
deeply ripening performance culture, this theatricality thus served as a medium
through which members of a local elite such as the Dong couple reflected on death
and life. This particular visual mode became further intensified in the subsequent
period, profoundly incorporating the funerary world into the social sphere.

4

THEATER,
BODY, AND
PASSAGE

The Pingyang area was firmly established as a vibrant center of theatrical performance by the mid-thirteenth century. As with the invasion of northern China by the
Jurchen-based Jin dynasty in the early twelfth century, the new dynastic shift from
the Jin to the Mongol Yuan in the late thirteenth century did not inhibit the thriving
cultural scene. While China's new capital Dadu (in present-day Beijing) was crowded
with celebrated playwrights such as Guan Hanqing and Ma Zhiyuan, the south-
western Shanxi and northern Henan regions also continued to foster a sophisticated
theatrical culture.[1]

   There are a number of extant textual sources that provide us with written accounts of the exuberance of the performance culture in the capital,[2] but most of the
visual representations have been discovered in the Pingyang area, especially at
tomb sites. Furthermore, the cultural vitality of Pingyang, unlike that of the newly
established capital city, was something that had been inherited from previous time
periods. Even Puzhou—the southernmost part of Pingyang that was subjected to a
series of intense battles between Jin and Yuan troops in the early thirteenth

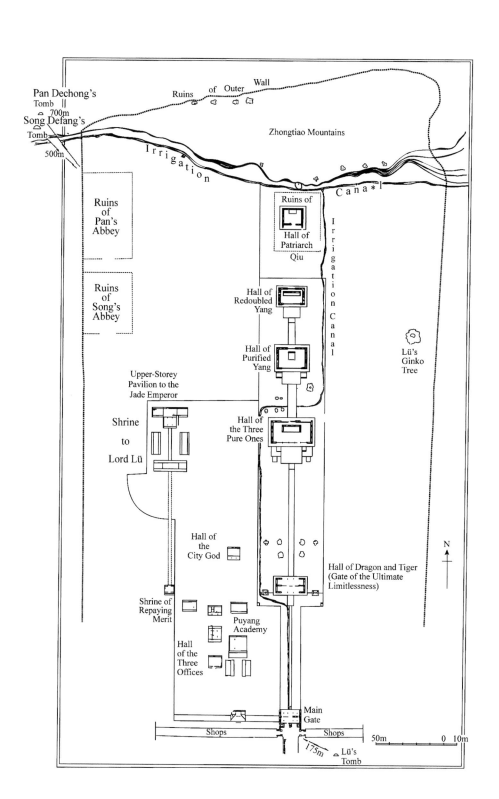

Pan Dechong's
Tomb
700m
Song Defang's
Tomb
500m

Ruins of Outer Wall

Zhongtiao Mountains

I r r i g a t i o n

C a n a *l

Ruins
of
Pan's
Abbey

Ruins
of
Song's
Abbey

Ruins of
Hall of
Patriarch
Qiu

I
r
r
i
g
a
t
i
o
n

C
a
n
a
l

Hall of
Redoubled
Yang

Hall of
Purified
Yang

Lü's
Ginko
Tree

Upper-Storey
Pavilion to the
Jade Emperor

Shrine

to

Lord Lü

Hall of
the Three
Pure Ones

Hall of
the
City God

Hall of Dragon and Tiger
(Gate of the Ultimate
Limitlessness)

N

Shrine of
Repaying
Merit

Puyang
Academy

Hall
of the
Three
Offices

Main
Gate

Shops

Shops

50m

0   10m

175m   Lü's
Tomb

century—persistently maintained its status as a cultural, intellectual, and religious hub throughout the Yuan and Ming periods.[3]

It is not surprising, then, to find a most intriguing image of theatrical performance in this area. In the winter of 1959, a sarcophagus with an incised image of a troupe of actors and their stage was found in a tomb located at the northwest corner of a renowned Daoist monastery, the Palace of Eternal Joy (Yongle gong), now in Ruicheng, Shanxi Province (fig. 4.1).[4] This tomb belonged to an abbot of the monastery, Pan Dechong (1191–1256), one of several people who played crucial roles in the founding of the monastery as a ritual center for the increasingly influential sect of Daoism, the Complete Perfection (Quanzhen), an eclectic collection of aspects of Buddhism, Daoism, and Confucianism.[5] We know some facts about Pan's life based on a memorial stele dedicated to him that is written in a manner that focuses only on his career trajectory as a priest. Originally from Qidong, Shandong Province, Pan was active on both the north and south roads of the Hedong area. After becoming an abbot at the Palace of Eternal Joy around 1245, he worked on rebuilding the abbey until his death in 1256. The original abbey had been destroyed during the war between the Mongols and Jin in the 1230s, and the rebuilding had been initiated by the previous abbot, Song Defang (1183–1252), another key Quanzhen priest.[6] Pan's and Song's tombs were discovered at the same time,[7] Although the identity of the tomb occupant Pan as a priest of this new Daoist sect provides hardly any specific context that might explain why the theatrical motif was chosen for the design of the sarcophagus,[8] it helps us firmly locate the material within the local environment as a center of festivals and performances both secular and religious.[9]

LOCATING THE PAN DECHONG SARCOPHAGUS

Pan Dechong's tomb opens to the south, and has a single hexagonal chamber with a tomb corridor. The interior is largely undecorated; only a few items were found in the tomb. The sarcophagus was found on a coffin bed at the north side of the chamber, its head panel facing east.[10] Inside the sarcophagus was a wooden inner coffin in which a skeleton was discovered, clad in a robe.[11]

The sides of the sarcophagus, consisting of four trapezoidal panels, are covered by a lid that is not flat but arch-shaped, with an overhang that extends past the front panel; it rests on a base composed of three pieces of flat stone (fig. 4.2). The side panels are decorated with finely incised line drawings, and each of the two longer side panels shows dozens of figures within twelve sections arranged in two rows, with an incised cartouche containing the names of historical personages famous for their filial piety (fig. 4.3).[12] Xu Pingfang was the first to identify the subject as a so-called picture of the Twenty-Four Exemplars of Filial Piety (*Er shi si xiao*), a motif

OPPOSITE PAGE

FIGURE 4.1. Plan of the Palace of Eternal Joy, Ruicheng, Shanxi Province, in 1958. Yuan, late 13th century. Redrawn by Katherine Lester after Shanxisheng wenwu guanli gongzuo weiyuanhui, *Yongle gong* (1964).

ubiquitous in Song and Jin tombs in central and northern China.[13] This motif was often used to decorate tomb walls or sarcophagus panels, in pictorial or sculpted form, to express the tomb sponsors' own feelings of filial piety toward their deceased ancestors. In light of that convention, the engraving on Pan's coffin seems to be out of place—that is, the surface of the coffin is not exactly an appropriate place for motifs on this theme. Pan seems to have had no spouse or descendants who could express such filial feelings for him, at least officially; for married couples, sharing a single tomb was the norm in the central and northern regions during this time period, but Pan was buried alone. It is likely that the extreme popularity of the filial piety theme encouraged the workshops and/or patrons to choose it even when its symbolic meaning would have no direct relevance.

Above, **FIGURE 4.2.** Pan Dechong's limestone sarcophagus. H 103 (front) × W 86 (widest) × D 222 cm. Palace of Eternal Joy. Below, **FIGURE 4.3.** Lao Laizi (one of the Twenty-Four Exemplars of Filial Piety). Detail of the images carved on a side panel of Pan Dechong's sarcophagus.

The head panel of the sarcophagus bears a representation of a motif that is strikingly original, completely different from these images of filial devotion in a formulaic "catalogue" style in which an image in each section of the grid is accompanied by a brief cartouche identifying each figure. The panel's entire pictorial space is framed by the facade of a two-story, three-bay building, the middle bay of which projects forward on both floors and constitutes, visually, the main body of the building (figs. 4.4a–b).[14] On the ground floor, two figures stand on either side of a large, square opening carved out of the center of the stone panel; this square opening is congruent with the upper three quarters of a rectangular void depicted in the ground floor portion of the central bay. Framing (and obscuring the corners of) the lower part of this rectangular void in the panel's foreground are two railings on either side of barely visible stairs that lead up to the ground floor. The rendering of these railings (in slightly foreshortened perspective, thus showing depth) clarifies the somewhat ambiguously rendered structure of the building. Seen within the convention of the images of paired attendants flanking representations of tomb occupants, the two figures standing on either side of the opening most likely represent female and male attendants. The absence of the representation of the deceased in this same pictorial space is understandable: the attendants are facing toward the square opening, beyond which the body of the deceased lies; the presence of the body thus replaces a representation of the body. The meaning and role of this replacement can best be explained in the context of what is depicted on the stone surface.

On a small balcony that projects out from the central bay just above the square opening are four figures in dynamic poses. Flanked by columns, the four figures stand in front of a screen decorated with pseudo-calligraphy. Thanks to their stereotypical costumes and gestures, it is immediately apparent that they represent actors. The figure at the far left wears a hood with what seems to be a bundle strapped to the top left part of his head, and his eyes are painted with lines in the shape of 八—makeup that by this point should be familiar to readers of the present volume. He is whistling, which closely resembles the second clown (*fujing*) figurine in Houma Tomb No. 1 and other images representing *fujing* found in pre-Yuan tombs (see figs. 2.6 and 3.4). The figure second from the left wears a literary official's robe and headgear, and is holding a *hu* tablet. The clothing and the prop explicitly indicate that he represents a male lead (*moni*). The figure standing second from the right wears a loosely open jacket with his protruding belly exposed, and a hat with a pointed top; on his left arm is hung an object that looks like a wooden clapper. The comic effect evoked by his twisted gesture and exposed belly suggests that he represents a second male lead (*fumo*). The figure at the far right wears a long robe with a scarf around his neck and a butterfly-shaped hat. He is politely gathering his hands at the center of his chest, posing in the so-called *chashou* gesture, slightly turning his body toward the center, as if responding to the other actors. His marginal position and relatively nondescript costume suggest that he represents either a costumed official (*guzhuang*) or introducer of the play (*yinxi*).[15] Regardless of this particular figure's role type, however, there is no doubt that the four figures as a group represent a troupe of actors. The image's overall theatrical atmosphere resembles the well-known

Above, **FIGURE 4.4A.** Rubbing of the head panel of Pan Dechong's sarcophagus.
Below, **FIGURE 4.4B.** Line drawing of figure 4.4a.

FIGURE 4.5. Mural of actors in Mingyingwang Hall, Guangsheng Monastery. Hongdong, Shanxi Province. Yuan.

mural depicting a theatrical performance in the Mingyingwang Hall at Guangsheng Monastery in Hongdong, Shanxi Province (ca. 1324; see fig. 4.5).[16]

The four figures' distinctive costumes, props, makeup, and gestures signify that what we are looking at is a troupe of actors shown as collective *dramatis personae* rather than a representation of a tableau in a play in performance.[17] In fact, they retain legacies from the Jin-dynasty *yuanben* (scripts from actors' guilds) rather than the norms of the *zaju* of the Yuan period, insofar as there are fewer characters, and they portray comic role types (*fujing* and *fumo*). In the Yuan dramatic tradition, roles were categorized into four types: male (*mo*), female (*dan*), antagonist (*jing*), and miscellaneous roles (*za*), and each type was again subdivided into a few roles (fig. 4.6).[18] By combining an image suggesting a hint of tableau vivant (through some actors' interactive gestures and poses) with a non-

FIGURE 4.6. Actresses. Ink and colors on silk, album leaf. Southern Song, 13th century. 24 cm×24.3 cm. Palace Museum, Beijing.

performative setting that could be seen only before or after a performance (through the actors' lining up, as if for a curtain call), this representation of the four actors sets the level of theatricality perceivable to viewers of that time as an effective indicator of the *idea* of theater. Such a visual mode, far from implying a portrayal of a particular drama, presents the pictorial plane as an abstract sphere existing outside any sort of coherent narrative or historical time. The depiction of the actors thus functions as a void sign, lacking a specific context either real or fictional.

In contrast to the actors' formulaic gestures, the enclosed space they occupy is far more distinctively rendered. At first glance, the large screen covered with pseudo-calligraphy that serves as a backdrop for the actors is reminiscent of the typical background for images of the deceased that is often found in tombs of the Song, Jin, and Yuan periods (fig. 4.7). In fact, because no examples of an outdoor screen used for a stage setting have survived, it is difficult to determine if this screen was meant to be the representation of an actual backdrop used on a stage or if it borrows its form from a commonplace domestic screen that was used in households as a do-mestic decoration or demarcation of a seat that signifies the importance of the per-son who would occupy it (in everyday, ritual, or social occasions). Regardless of the prototype of the backdrop, however, the ways in which the architectural facade is structured suggest that the entire second floor was specifically designed for the ac-tivities of this troupe of actors and marks their own space.

FIGURE 4.7. Tomb occupants and servants. Mural in Baisha Song Tomb No. 2, Henan Province. Song.

FIGURE 4.8. Architectural compound. Line drawing of a side panel of Song Defang's sarcophagus, Palace of Eternal Joy. 68 (front) × 183 cm. Yuan. Redrawn by Katherine Lester based on images in Gao Wen and Gao Chenggang, *Zhongguo huaxiang shiguan yishu* (1996).

The balcony on the second floor of the central bay is spatially linked to the side porches flanking it, even though they are recessed in relation to the central bay and its balcony; thus, the flow of movement between these different spaces is assumed to be continuous. A similar type of building is depicted on one of the longer panels of the aforementioned sarcophagus of Song Defang (fig. 4.8).[19] In the center of a group of buildings in a courtyard complex that occupies the entire left part of the panel is a two-story pavilion that has an elaborately layered roof. Closely resembling the architectural facade carved on Pan Dechong's sarcophagus, the central section of this three-bay building projects forward from the two side porches that flank it. The highly detailed, meticulous style of the representation points to its emphasis on faithful rendering of ideal architecture. This attention to pictorial plausibility—what might be called the ruled-line painting (*jiehua*) effect—demonstrates the carver's interest in depicting the building in a way that would have been most convincing to viewers of the time.[20] In that sense, the balcony in the three-bay building engraved on the Pan sarcophagus was probably meant to be seen as a real, functional space, specifically designated for actors to use, on a building that actually existed in the local area.

The second floor of such a building was most likely used as a space for performances. My discussion about the miniature stage in the Dong couple's tomb at Houma in chapter 3 explains the particular spatial logic underlying this kind of two-story building, with its ground floor functioning as a passage between two spaces. Representing more of an appropriated structure that combines two separate architectural entities (slightly downsized mansion and further miniaturized theater) than a whole building, the case of the miniature theater opened up the possibility that the second floor would have been conceived as a performance space during the early twelfth century.

The balcony depicted on Pan's sarcophagus is clearly presented as an organic part of a single building, the use of which is explicitly associated with theatrical performance. This point is reaffirmed by other contemporaneous images of a similar architectural setting. For example, the facade of the entrance to a tomb found in

Wulingzhuang, Shanxi Province (ca. 1276), is composed of two parts: a balcony with a simulated roof in the upper part and a gate in the lower part, functioning as an actual tomb gate. A set of brick reliefs placed below the roof bears images of actors and musicians in costume (fig. 4.9).[21]

While the Wulingzhuang facade demonstrates the convention of using a second-floor balcony as a performance space during that period, a ceramic model of a building from a tomb in Fengcheng County, Jiangxi Province (ca. 1338), points to a

Above, **FIGURE 4.9.** Painted reliefs of actors and musicians placed above the entrance to the rear chamber. Tomb found in Wuling-zhuang, Shanxi Province. Yuan.
Left, **FIGURE 4.10.** Epitaph in the shape of a two-story building. Painted earthenware. From a tomb in Fengcheng, Jiangxi Province. Yuan, ca. 1338. H 29.5 × W 20.5 × D 10 cm.

firmer association between this architectural form and its use in the late Yuan period (fig. 4.10).[22] The overall shape of the building represented by the model resembles that of the actors' pavilion depicted on the Pan sarcophagus, with the tripartite
facade and a balcony above the entrance. The ground floor is identified as a granary,
as the inscription on the facade of the side porch at the left indicates: "Storage area
for the five kinds of grains" [*Wugu cangsuo*]. Representations of granaries in tomb
spaces, in pictorial or sculptural form, had been common since the Han period,[23]
and usually symbolized the welfare of the deceased in the afterworld. Nonetheless,
the fact that the ritual functionality of such an object is designated as a granary
does not determine that the object's *form* matched that of an existing granary of the
time. The surface of the entire middle section of the model's ground floor bears an
epitaph, the centrality of which indicates that the primary purpose of this object
was to function as a place to hold such an inscription. More pertinent to our discussion, several tiny modeled figures placed on the second-floor balcony are playing
musical instruments, which has little to do with the potential uses of the object
either as a symbolic granary or as a place for an epitaph. This example suggests that
there was a built environment common to both the southern and northern regions
of China during the early fourteenth century and also reflects the familiarity with
the practice of using the upstairs balcony of a pavilion as a performance space.[24]

   This way of looking at such a structure challenges the dominant method of identifying represented theaters by comparing them only with surviving architecture
aboveground. For example, Liao Ben has argued that the actor image on Pan
Dechong's sarcophagus symbolizes a performance taking place inside a residential
building. This argument is based on the fact that there is no extant two-story theater built during the Yuan period, and that screens decorated with calligraphy are
generally believed to have been used only in domestic spaces.[25] Given the limited
number of surviving theater buildings to begin with, however, this interpretation
excludes the possibility that a greater variety of theater spaces may have existed
(as discussed in the prelude to the present volume). Moreover, it dismisses the spatial logic of the stage image on the Pan sarcophagus that would have appealed to
viewers of the time. As was emphasized in chapter 3, a representation does not necessarily reflect the structural accuracy of its prototype, but it often requires visual
plausibility. The cases of Wulingzhuang tomb and Fengcheng granary-shaped epitaph not only reassert the specific relationship between the miniature stage and the
deceased's hall in the Dong couple's tomb at Houma but also demonstrate that by
the early fourteenth century such positioning would have become a visual norm for
representing a performance space.

   With the second-floor balcony on the Pan sarcophagus secured for their performance, the actors' space was also extended to the second floor's interior space, designed to enable continuous movement between all the second-floor spaces, just as
the railings on the balcony are continuous with the railings on the side porches
flanking the central bay. All we can see of these porches is their front facade, each of
which features a pair of louvered doors with an opening in between, and each opening occupied by a panel with pseudo-calligraphy on it. These calligraphy panels,
though not entirely legible due to damage on the surface of the sarcophagus, seem

to represent the interior space of the porches, seen through the opening between each pair of louvered doors. Unlike the screen behind the actors, only a vertical two-column "slice" of these calligraphy panels is visible; and the edges of the panel appear truncated, without the proper amount of marginal space that a work of calligraphy would typically have. This implies that their frames may well exist but are hidden by the louvered doors. Therefore, regardless of the possible form of the frames, these calligraphy panels—whether they are screens or hanging scrolls—are depicted as objects placed inside the chambers. Indeed, the louvered doors are shown partially open, displaying only the far right and far left leaves of a standard four-leaf louvered door, folded back against their adjacent leaves, as exemplified in the *Yingzao fashi* (Treatise on architectural methods) and many other near-contemporary examples from tombs (fig. 4.11).[26]

The subtle indication of the side chambers' interiors was not an accidental representation but suggests the coffin designer's special interest in emphasizing the relationship between the stage on view and the spaces hidden behind the doors. The pictorial elaborateness of the auxiliary rooms hints at their nature as a contingent space: they are linked to the stage, as the connectedness of the railings and of the second-floor spaces through the partly open doors suggests; yet the fact that the louvered doors, shown folded back, could be opened fully to close off the interiors from view, which would also prevent access from the balcony, means that those spaces have the potential of being either connected *or* disconnected from the stage. This spatial contingency becomes significant when we think of the potential users of the interior spaces—that is, the actors, whom we can imagine are able to freely move into the rooms in the side porches by entering and exiting through the louvered doors. This implied mobility of the actors within and beyond the balcony space through the louvered doors suggests not only an extended space existing behind what is represented on the panel but that they are connected simultaneously to the (visible) ground floor of the building and to that (implied) actual space behind the surface of the sarcophagus. While the actors' connectedness to two spaces is conveyed by pictorial means, it is the presence of the actual opening in the stone that makes clear the unusual nature of such linkage. A symbolic sign of the channel between two ontologically heterogeneous spheres, the square opening evokes the represented actors' accessibility to a new realm beyond their image world. This new sphere was inevitably a mortuary one, conditioned by the very medium of both pictorial and physical form—the coffin.

THE SARCOPHAGUS, THE BODY, AND THE PATH

Although the origins of representing an opening or "gate" on a coffin panel can be traced back to as early as the fifth century BCE (as was discussed in chapter 1), extant archaeological evidence suggests that making an actual opening on the head panel of a sarcophagus did not begin until the middle period. The long-standing representation of doors, while continuing to adorn funerary monuments as a classical icon, spawned a visually striking form of an opening that was accordingly imbued with new mortuary connotations.

From a purely formal perspective, some of the Buddhist stone pagodas that began to be constructed during the sixth century can be seen as the antecedents of such form. Several surviving monuments of this kind have a square opening on the surface of a stone pagoda within which a statue of the Buddha was enshrined (fig. 4.12). Although this has some structural components in common with some later sarcophagi, there is a fundamental distinction between the sarcophagi with an opening and these medieval Buddhist pagodas. The quintessential role of the opening in the pagodas was to create a particular condition for *viewing* the icon inside;[27] this was not so in the coffins, however, where the occupant of the interior space was never intended to be revealed. The body itself was cased in an inner coffin, which corresponds to the basic idea of burial (*zang*), in the sense of "to hide" (*cang*), as defined in *Li ji* (Book of rites). The role of the opening was conceived of quite differently according to this core principle.

A few sarcophagi found in the southern Shanxi area, made during the Jin period, bear actual openings in their head panels. The earliest known example is a stone coffin of a certain Yao (ca. 1153) found in a single-chambered brick tomb in Yongji County (fig. 4.13). Its head panel has a square opening, flanked by the carved images of a female and male attendant on either side. When the sarcophagus was excavated, there were wooden dummy doors attached to the left and right edges of the square opening—swinging doors that were designed to open and close freely, and were thus "functional"; they were even colored with vermilion pigment and adorned with three rows of decorative door nails.[28] Since nothing could be seen through the opening but darkness surrounding the inner coffin, why did the sarcophagus designer not just carve an image of doors on the panel, which had become the norm for representing a gate on a coffin by this time period (as exemplified in fig. 1.8)? What were the conceptual impetuses and visual effects desired in making an actual opening and incorporating it into the pictorial space? A sarcophagus made half a century later provides some clues. This sarcophagus (ca. 1212) unearthed in Yonghe County, Shanxi Province, was for a local landowner named Feng Rong and has an opening in the head panel, but its shape does not resemble a standard gate and there is no trace of door leaves attached to it (fig. 4.14a). The opening is skillfully cut in the form of a gourd, positioned within a rectangular frame in the center (fig. 4.14b). A thin vertical line runs through the axis of the gourd, a pictorially rendered gap between door leaves commonly seen in the images of a gate on the surface of coffins made in earlier periods. Here the entire surface outside the frame is covered with incised texts that list the names of three generations of Feng Rong's patrilineal ancestors as well as his wives and sons, composing a kind of abbreviated, informal genealogical epitaph.[29] It is noteworthy that Feng's sons, the sponsors of the coffin, chose this specific location on the sarcophagus for presenting the genealogical account; while it reaffirms the symbolic economy of the head panel in

OPPOSITE PAGE
FIGURE 4.11. Louvered doors on painted brick reliefs installed in Fenyang Tomb No. 5, Shanxi Province. Jin.

FIGURE 4.12. Sculpted pagoda sanctuary, limestone with pigment. Probably from Shandong Province. Late Northern Qi to Sui, ca. 570–600. H 241.3 × W 171.5 cm. Image © Metropolitan Museum of Art. Source: Art Resource, New York.

the funerary context, the text as a background image highlights the gourd-shaped opening as the focal point.

The centrality of the opening and its striking optical contrast with the flat, even surface ground, as well as with the rather formulaic decorative patterns on the other panels,[30] emphasize its supremacy in the overall design of the sarcophagus. With the gourd-shaped form defined by the absence of its own physical ground, the wholeness of the surface as the enclosed pictorial world is broken. In

FIGURE 4.13. Ink rubbing of the head panel of the Yongji sarcophagus, Shanxi Province. Jin, ca. 1153.

other words, the equilibrium between the positive and negative spaces surrounding the form is altered by the perforated shape, which points to another dimension that exists beyond the image world. A reminder of the image as an object, the gourd on the stone surface was thus given a new ontology of the invigorated *thingness*.[31] When contextualized within the established tradition of the door motif on sarcophagi, this particular ontology, fashioned through the new practice of the perforation, is further articulated: the actual opening without door leaves replaced a represented gate, which spatially connected the realms inside and outside the sarcophagus.

When making an opening was unnecessary—because a simple line engraving of the image would have been readily recognized as a gourd—the reasoning behind the perforation must be understood in terms of its efficacy in invoking the spatial linkage between the image and object worlds. The prototypes of this gourd-shaped opening could have been an actual gourd or a type of gate in the shape of a gourd, as seen in extant examples from the late imperial period, but we simply do not know whether this kind of gate already existed in the middle period. Regardless, the distinctive silhouette of a gourd unmistakably evokes the fruit's historical and conceptual significance as a cosmological symbol, a significance that had been fully developed as late as the third century in China. One of earliest and best-known legends, concerning the adventure of Fei Changfang, characteristically captures the traditional Chinese conceit of the world of immortals that exists within a gourd. One day in a marketplace, after the market has closed and nobody else is in the street, Fei witnesses an old man who sells medicine disappearing into a gourd jar hung in the shop. Puzzled by what he has seen, Fei visits the man the next day. Reading Fei's mind, the old man leads Fei into the gourd with him, where Fei sees dazzling palaces made of jade and finds fragrant food and wine. It turns out that the old man is an immortal, living in the gourd.[32] Terms such as *hu zhong riyue* (the sun and the moon within a gourd) or more simply and commonly *hutian* (the heaven within a gourd, or "gourd heaven," used as a metaphor[33]) arose out of such folklore and became common terms by the middle period, referring to heavenly sites in general or a Daoist immortal's dwelling in particular. As Rolf Stein has convincingly

Above, **FIGURE 4.14A.** Limestone Yonghe sarcophagus. Shanxi Province. Jin, ca. 1212. H 90 (front)×W 74 (widest)×D 197 cm. Below, **FIGURE 4.14B.** Ink rubbing of the head panel of the Yonghe sarcophagus.

demonstrated, the origins of the association of a gourd with an ideal realm outside the world of mortals—be it a paradisiacal site or an immortal's abode—are too complex to be reduced to a linear historical development.[34] And yet, the oft-cited Fei Changfang story confirms that by the fourth to the fifth centuries, when the legend was recorded by Ge Hong (284–364) and Fan Ye (398–445), the notion of "a world in a gourd" evoking a magical vision of an ideal abode had already been well established.[35]

It is possible that as the sponsors of this sarcophagus Feng Rong's sons envisioned the coffin as a paradisiacal site in which, by transforming the interior of the sarcophagus into a gourd heaven (*hutian*), their deceased father would rest eternally.[36] Making the opening in the shape of a gourd as a kind of passageway would have thus been essential in this desired transformation. Notably, the choice of this motif also resonates with what that "universe" contains: the body. As Fei Changfang's legend reappears in the seventh-century Daoist text "Jinsuo liuzhu yin" (Guide to the golden lock and the moving pearls),[37] we learn that the idea of a gourd as an idealized world entered the Daoist canon as a practice of inner cultivation (*neidan*).[38] Furthermore, the term "gourd" (*hu*) itself extended its signifying content to the notion of the body during the twelfth and thirteenth centuries. In *Wuzhen pian* (Essay on the immediate awakening to truth)—a treatise on alchemic principles by Northern Song Daoist master Zhang Boduan (987–1082) that was one of the most popular texts dealing with inner cultivation from the eleventh century on—the word *hu* is consistently used to refer to a body.[39] The compound word formed by combining *nei* (interior) with *hu* indicates the lower abdomen as a part of the body that is vital for inner cultivation.[40] The extended use of *hu* as referring to the body is evident in other Daoist texts as well. For example, the heart, considered the most important organ of the body, is called the *yu hu* (jade gourd).[41] Finally, it is noteworthy that by the eleventh century the word *hu* in Daoist usage referred not merely to an analogy to or metaphor for the body but also to the body itself as a microcosm of the universe.[42]

One can hardly miss the overarching characteristic of the gourd in these cases as containing something inconceivably larger than its mere physical capacity would indicate. Unsurprisingly, the spatialization of such transcendent nature accompanied the shift in the ontological status of the occupier of the space—that is, the body. According to the contemporaneous connotations of the gourd, the interior of the sarcophagus—designed to be occupied by the body—could be equated with either an immortal's paradise (gourd heaven) or a bodily microcosm (gourd body) where a *living* person is supposed to dwell. Therefore this Daoist concept underlying the design of the gourd gate as an icon reveals an idealized paradigm in which the dead body could turn into a living body—or, more precisely, an immortal.[43] In this respect, such a discourse revolving around the gourd-shaped opening reaffirms the oxymoronic concept of "postmortem immortality" deeply rooted in the traditional Daoist desire for an afterlife.[44] Leaving a physical opening in the sarcophagus thus would have satisfied the sponsors' wish for immortality in symbolic form.

The open gate as a tangible marker of the transitional status of the dead also configures and defines the relationship between the spaces within and outside the sarcophagus. The ideas of the gourd heaven and gourd body make clear that the interior space of the sarcophagus would be viewed, metaphorically, as the inner microcosm or as the dwelling for an immortal. Both terms—"gourd heaven" and "gourd body"—utilize the gourd as an infinitely and inwardly spatializing mechanism. Here the actual opening, as opposed to a representation of a door, was not designed to highlight the separation of such a metaphysical realm, formed inside the coffin, from the outside. Rather, it served as a powerful sign alluding to the threshold that would convert the defined interior space into an open-ended universe. From this point of view, the act of making an opening on the stone panel not only invigorated the physicality of the medium but also created an access to the otherwise unreachable universe. In so doing, the basic functionality of the sarcophagus as the receptacle of the body was negotiated: the stone panel came to simultaneously divide and connect the worlds of the deceased and the living.

The examples of the Yongji and Yonghe coffins help us to recognize the visual and conceptual appeal of the new practice in sarcophagus design that emerged during the twelfth and thirteenth centuries. Deviating from the traditional roles and connotations of the door image on the head panel, this new form of the open gate registers a spatial relationship between what is seen on the coffin surface and what lies behind it. While the peculiar shape of the gourd in the Yonghe example was imbued with a Daoist flavor, it is likely that most residents in middle and southern Shanxi, where the presence of Daoist temples was ubiquitous by the early twelfth century, would have been exposed to basic Daoist ideas and images.[45] Given the eclectic and popular nature of the Daoist practice, the ideas alluded in the gourd shape would not have remained esoteric, only accessible by priests or scholars, but shared in a wider range of community in the region. More important in visual and material perspectives, the *modality* underlying the opening itself is shared among all the examples discussed herein and the Pan Dechong coffin: it redefines the connection between the stone panel's interior and exterior. In all cases, the quintessential efficacy of the perforation was to "open up" the gate on the coffin surface toward the unknown, infinite realm inside.

There is, however, a fundamental difference between these antecedents and the Pan sarcophagus: there is no representation of space on the pictorial plane in these earlier examples. Unlike them, the opening on the Pan sarcophagus seamlessly incorporates itself into the image represented on the pictorial plane and actively takes part in the picture as a whole. Combined with an incised image of the two-story building and actors deployed in the pictorial space, the opening becomes an organic component of the image, carrying the iconic weight of its presence as a reminder of the actual space existing behind the surface. The opening as an image thus calls for a separate inquiry.

DOORWAYS AND THE PLAY ROOM

Seen within the overall frame of the entire head panel of the Pan sarcophagus, the square opening readily fits in on the ground floor as an open space underneath the balcony in which the actors stand. The opening, with its richly constructed connotations as a threshold through which the physical space of the coffin interior is transformed into the infinite universe of the deceased, accordingly characterizes the actors' space in the image world.

Indeed, the delicate connection between the two worlds was delineated by means of visual cues saturated with contemporary experiences of the theater. As has been mentioned, the first and second floors of the building are organically connected through the unshown areas behind the two pairs of narrow louvered doors flanking

the section where the actors are posed. Although we lack any contemporaneous account of the details of stage structure or actual architecture built during the late
thirteenth century, it is likely that this pair of doorways represents a stage entrance
and exit for the actors' performance. Liao Ben has argued that stages of the Yuan period only had a backdrop with no openings in it, and Che Wenming has suggested that
it was probably not until the early sixteenth century that doorways for actors' entrances and exits became popular in theater architecture.[46] Yet given that the few extant stages of this time are limited to the ones remaining in temples, which were
mostly renovated over time, this suggestion excludes other forms of theater architecture that may have existed at the time. By the same token, there is no counterevidence
that the flanking doors on the second floor depicted on the Pan sarcophagus were
structurally unable to function as actors' doorways. In fact, the three-bay structure
with two flanking doorways represented on the sarcophagus would have been familiar to viewers during that period as a kind of performance space, as discussed above.

The issue then becomes why this specific part of the building was selected in
this representation for hosting the troupe of actors rather than whether this type of
architecture was actually used as a stage. Critical for our inquiry is understanding
the spatial logic and meaning behind the representational process. In this light, the
structure of the second floor space needs to be examined in relation to the expected
movement of its occupiers: the actors who were supposed to perform there.

The actors' movement is implied in the ways in which the louvered doors are
depicted. The careful representation of both the continuous space that runs across
the entire balcony and the doors rendered to suggest an interior and exterior indicates the designer's intention to reveal the use of the doors for the actors' entrances
and exits. Especially noteworthy is the way that the two doorways are portrayed,
with the interior of the rooms subtly exposed. Why did the designer include such
details as the wooden bars and patterns on the doors, or the pseudo-calligraphy
screens or wall hangings beyond the doors, which are visually convincing yet unnecessary for a background setting?

In the context of the significance of entrances and exits for actors in Chinese
theater, the examination of doorways on this sarcophagus requires a delicate interpretation. According to Judith Zeitlin, expounding on Zhou Yibai's insightful characterization of the role of entrances and exits in Chinese drama,[47] the control of such
openings is of paramount importance in Chinese traditional drama (as opposed to
modern theater), which was performed on a stage devoid of scenery, and thus lacking
visually cued scene changes, and without front curtains or modern lighting.[48] More
sophisticated forms of entrances and exits appear in later times,[49] and judging from
Yuan period dramatic scripts, there is reason to believe that at least some sort of
measured and stylized movement accompanied those entrances and exits.[50]

In this regard, recognizing the depiction of the two doorways on the Pan sarcophagus as part of the performance space is crucial. Specifying where the actors
entered and exited, they transform the actors' space into a "living" theater. Unlike
previous performance images, such as the actor figurines and their stage in Houma
Tomb No. 1, here the stage constitutes an organic part of the actors' performance by
implying the actors' potential movement through the doors. Without the doorways,

the performance scene carved on this coffin would be just another formulaic sign of a theatrical performance, conveyed mainly through the ostentatious theatrical regalia and gestures of the actors.

What went on in the space behind the doors? An early term referring to this particular space behind the stage was *xifang* (play room), which came into use sometime in the twelfth to thirteenth centuries.[51] The role of this space was versatile. While the terminology itself appears in the fourteenth-century essay *Chuogeng lu* (Notes taken while at rest from plowing),[52] the existence of such a room and its function can be inferred from an early thirteenth-century text of southern drama (*xiwen*), given that certain structures of southern and northern dramas had already begun to overlap before the Yuan period.[53] One of the earliest surviving texts of southern drama, *The Top Graduate Zhang Xie (Zhang Xie zhuangyuan)*, written in the early thirteenth century,[54] provides a glimpse of the versatility of the play room actively used as a secondary stage:

> SECOND MALE LEAD: *(Makes barking sound in play room, and then speaks.)* Kid, go check out the wall. I am afraid that someone is coming to steal chickens!
> MALE LEAD: *(Yells out from play room.)* What kind of woman comes through the main hall? Guards, why aren't you beating her?
> MALE LEAD: *(Shouts in play room.)* What a commotion! How can I not go out?[55]

In this scene two characters offstage make sounds or narrate dialogue as part of the performance on the stage. The play room is thus sometimes used simply as a device that hides an actor from the audience, and sometimes as another fictional space existing beyond the stage (effects that in later theaters would be produced by actors moving behind a backdrop or into the wings). Such spatial separation and distinctive deployment of actors enlivens the performance by slightly breaking the spatial frame of the stage and expanding the potential arena of performance into the play room. At the same time, this sense of the expanded performing space that is created by the interaction between the stage and the play room is eventually blurred by the invisibility of the actors performing in the hidden area beyond the doors. What lies there is unknown to the audience and is only suggested by disembodied voices. The audience, which is supposed to be aware that the invisible acting is performed by someone behind the stage, thus encounters a moment of liminal experience because the offstage area is offered as another reality—one that only partially fits into the commonly acknowledged schema of the normal cognitive world. While the play room is still the actor's space, just as the stage is, its spatial nature is thus fluid and its boundary ambiguous.

THE THEATRICAL CONCEPTS OF INSIDE (*NEI*) AND OUTSIDE (*WAI*) SPACES

A similar ambiguity is created by certain stage directions in the texts of Yuan period plays, revealing subtly complex ways in which onstage and offstage spaces were conceived by play producers and theatergoers of that period. A particular conflation of the ways in which the plays' authors referred to the area behind the stage draws our attention.[56] Take, for example, a scene from a play by the early Yuan playwright Fei Tangchen (fl. 1273) about the celebrated Song literatus Su Shi:

> EMPEROR: My heart desires this. Officials nearby, quickly summon
>   Su Shi.
> *([Someone] from inside responds.)*
> MALE LEAD: *(Enters and speaks.)* My name is Su Shi.[57]

Here the word "inside" (*nei*), in the stage direction "[Someone] from inside responds" (*nei ying*), refers to the play room or the backstage area. To quote Marvin Carlson, it is the "hidden 'other' world of the actor, the place of appearance and disappearance, the realm of events not seen but whose effects conditioned the visible world of the stage."[58]

What, then, would its dichotomous counterpart, "outside" (*wai*), signify? To an audience, the stage area would be outside because of its visibility—that is, what is shown onstage would be considered exterior, whereas what is hidden behind the stage, only suggested by unseen actors speaking and performing audible but unseen actions, would be considered interior. But another type of stage direction, recurring in a number of Yuan play texts, mostly in the Maiwang guan edition (which is thought to preserve more archaic elements, with fewer emendations by later literati),[59] disrupts such a commonsensical expectation: the person performing in the play room is sometimes referred to as "outsider" (*wai*):

> COURT OFFICIAL: You, maid back there, ask the lady to come out and
>   discuss the matter.
> [SOMEONE] FROM OUTSIDE: Yes, sir.[60]

In this scene, someone in the back (*houmian*) is referred to as *wai,* and the room behind the stage is thus indicated as outside. Note especially that the stage direction takes a form like that of the previous example of the insider (*nei ying*)—in this case, the outsider (*wai ying*).

It becomes clear that the relationship between *nei* and *wai* is more complicated than what the terms literally signify. Yan Dunyi suggested in 1960 that the term *nei* used in certain Yuan drama texts could have been a replacement of the term *wai,* which seems to have been in use earlier.[61] This suggestion was based on a comparison between two different versions of the same comic play written by the early Yuan playwright Zheng Tingyu (fl. 1251). The comparison concerns a stage direction in the prologue (*xiezi*), after a monologue by the male lead as he is about to break into and rob a house. While the Maiwang guan version of the play text uses *wai* to refer to the invisible performer in the play room, the *Yuanqu xuan* edition refers to the person as *nei.*[62] Yan points out that these different stage directions were meant to be enacted by the same performer, and further suggests that the *wai* in the earlier (Maiwang guan) version would have been the original form of the stage direction—which, in the course of editing by various literati in later times, was changed to *nei.*[63] This argument is part of Yan's larger thesis that *wai* in *wai ying* (or in another common form, *wai chengda*[64]) is categorically homogeneous with the use of *wai* to mean a role type—that is, a supporting role for the female or male lead, which is fully developed in later dramatic texts and actual performances.[65] Given the relative fidelity of the Maiwang guan edition to early forms of Yuan texts, this suggestion is plausible.

Yet Yan's "developmental" model does not actually prove whether one term replaced the other or whether they had at first coexisted but later one of the two became more dominant. As is often the case with the scant early dramatic texts, it is impossible to determine with any certainty a chronology of such terms based on a few extant cases. For example, even among the Yuan plays included in the Maiwang guan collection both terms, *nei* and *wai,* coexist.[66] Furthermore, granted that the later role type *wai* derives from the early meaning of the word *nei* as an extra actor or another member of the troupe who would perform in the offstage area,[67] it is likely that the meaning of *wai* as an actor who "less visibly" performed to support the main characters persisted in later times, and that this term exists in the stage directions of Ming and Qing texts. Thus, there is not enough evidence to confirm that one term replaced the other term or that one term is the origin of the other.

I take seriously such inconclusive results, which indicate that play texts may have taken shape in a variety of forms/versions, and believe that these kinds of disjunctures in theater terminology and practices must be acknowledged and accepted as the mingling of two literally antonymic terms indicating the same thing. In addition, each of the terms was understood by play producers and theatergoers as indicating multiple things: a role type, an actor's space, or both. The conflation of the concepts *wai* and *nei* reflects a slippage between person and space as well as between two points of view, *in* and *out*. Regarding this, Yan Dunyi has succinctly yet rather simplistically characterized the relationship between the role type and space in no uncertain terms: *wai* signifies the outsider of *dramatis personae,* and *nei* signifies the inside of the play room.[68] As a brief explanation of the development of role types and the stage, this statement positions the two terms in epistemologically separated realms, as if the term *wai* was invented only to refer to a newly emerging role type, whereas the term *nei* was exclusively used to emphasize the spatial nature of the play room. Taking a strongly evolutionary perspective, such an approach glosses over the process in which the two already existing terms came to signify the same thing.

It is a commonplace that a single word can be used and circulated in multiple epistemological spheres, signifying different concepts. What makes this case extraordinary, however, is the intensity of such convertibility: a pair of *antonymic* words was used in the shared theatrical field to indicate the same space. This unusual conflation between the antonyms themselves may have been the result of the powerful visual and theatrical experiences of the people of that time. As I pointed out in the earlier discussion of the role of the play room, the scenes acted onstage were supplemented by unseen occurrences in the unseen area behind the stage, thus breaking out of the expected dichotomous frame of the theater versus the real world. The intense theatricality created through such dismantling of the normal world order resonates deeply with the effect of conflation between the two heterogeneous terms: the interchangeability of the antonyms would have been shaped by the fluid characteristic of the play room and, by extension, the theater itself.[69]

ANCIENT DOORWAYS AND GHOST DOORWAYS

The origins of the interchangeable use of the terms *nei* and *wai* also lie in the spatial construction of the stage—in particular, the marginal space between onstage and off-stage. References to a pathway between the two areas appear in some Yuan play texts, distinct from the terms for play room—for example, "room" (*fang*) or "(inner) stage" (*chang*); the term "doorways" (*mendao*) appears frequently in many stage directions in Yuan play texts. As a compound of a straightforward combination of two words, "door" or "gate" (*men*) and "road" or "way" (*dao*), *mendao* was a word used in everyday life to indicate the passageway that leads to a door. It was not a special theater term per se; the term appears in *Yingzao fashi* (Treatise on architectural methods) where it is referred to as an independent component of an architectural structure.[70] When used in stage directions of Yuan play texts, however, this common word seems to carry richer connotations than its original meaning in everyday life. Referring to the connecting area between the stage and play room as a passageway, it provides an important insight into the meaning of the potential movement of the actors that is implied in the image of the performance area on the Pan sarcophagus.

Accompanied with a prefix, *mendao* in play texts appears in stage directions to indicate unseen offstage space that leads to a play room. As yet, there has been no consensus among scholars of Chinese drama about the etymological relationship among terms referring to the play room that are phonetically close but use different prefixes. In surviving play texts of the Yuan, however, one comes across two principal terms that seem to have circulated among play producers and theatergoers: "ancient doorways" (*gu mendao*)—sometimes in an abbreviated form as "ancient doors" (*gu men*)[71]—and "ghost doorways" (*gui mendao*). Here are two excerpts of dialogue that include these terms, the first from a scene in a late thirteenth-century Yuan *zaju* written by Yue Bochuan (fl. 1279), and the second from one of the various editions of *Xixiang ji* (The romance of west chamber), both of which clearly show the kind of circumstance in which the two terms were used:

I.
MALE LEAD: *(Enters and speaks.)* My name is Yue Shou. I've come here hoping to find my sister-in-law and her kid. But I forgot where they live. I'd better ask someone. *(Turns toward the gu mendao and calls.)* Hey, you brother there! Where is the home of Yue the Kongmu?
[OFFSTAGE] VOICE FROM INSIDE: It's the house with the new gate tower.[72]

II.
MONK: *(Turns to the gui mendao and calls.)* General, speak please.
FEIHU: *(Abruptly enters the stage and speaks.)* Send Oriole out here quickly!
MONK: Calm down, general.[73]

In the first scene, where the hero looks for his old family house and asks someone on the street for directions, he turns toward a doorway,[74] as if there were an extension of the onstage space behind it. An invisible actor (or another member of the troupe) responds from within the hidden space behind the doorway—that is, the play room. This action suggests that in this fictive reality, he shares the same space as the actor on the real stage but stays somewhere beyond the audience's sight. The second example shows another major role of the doorway as a site through which an actor emerges on the stage. It is noteworthy that in both the stage directions quoted above, the function of doorways can be almost equated to that of the play room, which suggests that there would be no different consequence even if both terms were replaced with "play room" (*xifang*). It is precisely this conscious signification of the space as "doorways," as opposed to "play rooms," that deserves special attention: the term "doorways" seems to have been chosen over "play room," even though there would have been no difference between the two in the actual scenes being performed. Choosing a term referring to a spatially transient site, as opposed to dichotomizing the entire performance space into onstage and offstage areas, alludes to the contemporary recognition of the extended arena of fictive reality.

In addition, this selection further highlights the doorway's symbolic quality as a passageway. In both examples, the actors are expected and imagined by the audience to pass through a doorway and metamorphose from a natural being into a theatrical being, or vice versa. The doorway is thus transformative by nature. As a threshold to both the play room and the stage, it is also liminal, located midway between onstage and offstage spaces, and hence between the fictive world and the real world. Therefore, while the play room signifies a "fictive 'elsewhere,'"[75] the doorways to the play room demarcate the boundary between the fictive and the nonfictive.

It was probably thanks to such transformative and liminal characteristics of doorways as they were conceived of by people of that period that two seemingly unrelated prefixes, "ancient" and "ghost," were attached to the term "doorways," intensifying a sense of transience. The etymologies of these intriguing terms have been the subject of many studies of Chinese drama, and it is not my intention here to provide a new understanding of them. The oft-cited passage by the Ming dynasty prince and playwright Zhu Quan (1378–1448) has singlehandedly nurtured modern scholars' curiosity about the possible etymologies of these terms:

> Ghost doorways [*gui mendao*] are the places in a theater from which someone exits and enters the play room [*xifang*]. The reason the word "ghost" is used is because those whom the actors dress up as are all people from the past. Because a drum is placed by the doors, ignorant and vulgar folks call them "drum doorways" [*gu mendao*], but this contravenes the principle involved. They are also called "ancient doorways" [*gu mendao*], but this, too, is incorrect. Su Shi's poem, which reads "Performing events of then and now / Through ghost doorways, actors come and go," refers precisely to this.[76]

Although this passage provides us with a useful perception of how theater and performance were understood in the late fourteenth and early fifteenth centuries, it should be dealt with cautiously. It is not easy to locate the term "ghost doorways" in a satisfyingly historical context due to two contrasting situations. On the one hand, the Yuan play texts in which the term makes its appearance are thought to be heavily modified versions by Ming literati who edited and printed them. On the other hand, according to Zhu, the term appears in one of Su Shi's poems, described as functioning exactly in the same way as in the Ming, but the poem is not found in any of Su's surviving anthologies.[77]

As a passage written by one Ming period observer, however, it concerns us less as a source of accurate etymologies of related terms than as a reflection of various receptions of the characteristics of doorways during that time. Regarding the use of these terms during the Ming and Qing periods, Judith Zeitlin has shown that both "ancient doorways" and "ghost doorways" appear in the texts of Ming and Qing southern dramas, but "drum doorways" seldom, if ever, appears.[78] In terms of the historical development of these terms, J. I. Crump has suggested that the *guimen dao* ("Gate of Ghosts," in his translation) is the oldest of the three terms, and he emphasizes that the authors of Chinese drama in traditional times were always deeply conscious of the power of the stage to resurrect the past and its ghost, exemplified by Zhong Sicheng (fl. 1321), who compiled a record of dramas and playwrights that he titled *Lugui bu* (Register of ghosts).[79] When considered together with the "lost" poem by Su Shi, this is a reasonable suggestion. Yet my concern lies in how to understand the interrelationship of the three terms—and especially between "ancient doorways" and "ghost doorways"—and a particular discourse in which such different terms became commingled rather than giving historical authority to a single term. In fact, it is noteworthy that Zhu, a highly learned literary playwright, felt the need to sort out terms that were in circulation and to authorize one over the others. The passage thus ironically proves the popularity of the other terms among regular theatergoers and further reflects the degree to which they were engaged with the performance and theater of the time.

In fact, regardless of which term was coined first and therefore may be more "authentic," there is an overlapping meaning conveyed by both "ancient doorways" and "ghost doorways," which is why Zhu did not bother providing any further explanation about the etymology of the former term. Although he identified the term "ghost doorways" as the authentic one, it is obvious that he felt no need to explain why the term "ancient doorways" was "mistakenly" used by his contemporaries, since he had already given the definition of "ghost doorways"; it is so named because "those whom the actors dress up as are all people from the past." This reasoning may seem odd, since during the middle period (as in the modern period) people who lived in the past were not necessarily equated with ghosts; they were usually considered as categorically different beings. Yet what made these otherwise heterogeneous concepts interchangeable to people at that time is their fascination with the transformative nature of the doorways. Both terms highlight the quintessential function of doorways as transmitting people and narrative from the past that come to life only by going through them. Doorways were thus the boundary where the present cuts across the past and, by extension, where the worlds of the living and the dead intersected.

THE ACTORS, THE DEAD, AND THE PERFORMANCE

We can now understand the reasons for the seemingly unnecessary rendering of certain details on the Pan sarcophagus—that is, the meticulous depiction of the doorways and the partially exposed interior space behind the partly open louvered doors. As I have noted above, the stage depicted there constitutes an organic part of the actors' performance by implying the actors' potential movement through the doors for their entrances and exits, but what lies through those doors is unseen and remains unknown to the audience. Remember also that the balcony on which the actors stand, which projects out from the second floor of the central bay, is directly above the square opening in that central bay, which in fact is an actual opening in the stone panel. Thus the implied interior space on the second floor, behind what is represented on the coffin panel, is part of the dark, unknown space—the actual space—behind the sarcophagus surface.

As the popular medieval fantasy of a man walking into a hole in a ceramic pillow—prominently featured in the eighth-century tale "Record of the World in a Pillow" (Zhen zhong ji) by Shen Jiji—would suggest, the spatial transition between ontologically heterogeneous spaces was something readily conjurable. In the story, the protagonist scholar Lu finds a hole in the pillow, and as he gazes at it, "the hole gradually widens and brightens; Lu stands up and walks into the pillow."[80] In this sense, the distinctive interface between the inner space of the coffin and the margin of the image world that is implied as existing behind the doors resonates with the sensibility revealed in the characterization of the doorways during the early Ming dynasty: the doorways through which the "people from the past" and "ghosts" became interchangeable.

Recalling the function of this image-bearing object—the sarcophagus—we should not forget what lies behind such unusual spatial linkage: the deceased. A way to emphasize the existence of the body while maintaining the physicality of its container and transform it into a symbolic realm was to make an opening on the head panel. In this way, the dark space framed in the square opening alluded not only to the body's transcendent realm but to the body itself, which would ideally exist in a timeless manner. The spatial overlap between the "backstage" behind the depicted doorways and the physical space of the body inside the coffin gave the actors access to the symbolic realm of the deceased. By exiting and entering the stage through the doorways, the actors were to oscillate between two distinct worlds: the idealized, timeless microcosm of the deceased and the arrested momentum of the fictive world of theater.

The actors' pseudo–tableau vivant then finally finds its fullest meaning in this context. On the one hand, as in the case of the actor figurines and their stage in the Dong couple's Houma Tomb No. 1, the actors depicted here serve as a visual deictic that theatricalizes the surface of the head panel of the coffin. It is the vertical juxtaposition of the actors' stage and the actual opening in the stone that intensifies the performativity of the entire image. Posing for an imaginary spectator on the stage of a fictive world,[81] the actors—with their distinctive theatrical regalia and gestures—overtly signal their space to be a theater. Yet their formulaic postures and

their simultaneous presence on stage constitute a hollow performance, only signifying that the actual performance would be in another space—that is, while sending
the imaginary viewer a visual reminder that would say, "We are the actors on stage,
and you are supposed to be watching a performance," the actors introduce a virtual
performance by showing the framed stage—that is, the actual opening below their
own stage.

On the other hand, the image's larger spatial and conceptual contexts differenti-
ate the meaning of the actors' virtual performance from that of Houma Tomb No. 1.
The virtual stage shown here is located closest to the body—the focal point of the
entire burial space. The performance of *presenting* the virtual theater introduced
an ideal microcosm of the body whose life was intended to continue in the physically confined yet conceptually infinite world. The actors' implied movement within
and beyond the pictorial space altered the fixed spatiotemporal order in the interior
space behind the image and converted it into a living microcosm rather than a life-
less, limited space of the dead.

IN AND OUT OF THE THEATER

After analyzing the connections between the worlds of the theater and the dead
inscribed in this complex performance image, we are still left with some questions.
How was this innovative design accepted and appreciated by the patrons of the
sarcophagus? Did Pan Dechong's life have anything to do with the motif? The lack
of extant records concerning local artisans or Pan's social life might seem to make it
impossible to address these questions. But expanding our scope from the coffin itself to the larger built environment where Pan lived and died, we find a meaningful
context in which the local society and the realm of the sacred were mediated
through the theatrical vision.

The unprecedentedly intense theatricality manifested in the coffin design itself
is evidence of the popularity of theatrical performance in the Pingyang area. The
image was most likely born out of local people's experience of performances held
at temples in the community, including the Palace of Eternal Joy itself. As described in the commemorative stele erected in Guangsheng Monastery—the principal monastery in the Pingyang area, with a mural depicting a theatrical performance (see fig. 4.5)—folks from near and far, young and old, nobles in sedan chairs,
and commoners with their canes would all flock to the nearest monastery to watch
performances for days and days until they got tired.[82] In fact, one of the main halls
at the Palace of Eternal Joy gives us some insight into how local templegoers would
have perceived such performances. Like other Daoist temples, the Palace of Eternal
Joy comprises several buildings within a landscaped compound. When the townspeople came to visit the temple, the first building they encountered was the Hall of
Dragon and Tiger (Longhu dian), also called the Gate of Ultimate Limitlessness
(Wuji men; see fig. 4.15a), which they had to pass through to reach the temple—that
is, the central hall dedicated to the Three Purities (Sanqing dian). The Hall of
Dragon and Tiger features a courtyard between two lateral wings, and on one wall
facing the courtyard was a U-shaped platform that used to be encircled by wooden

railings and was most likely used as a stage (fig. 4.15b).[83] Rarely has notice been taken of the fact that the hall also functioned as the main gate of the monastery until the Qing period, when the current temple gate was built. It thus had a double function as gate and stage during the late thirteenth century, a particular form often termed "gate-stage" (*menting*) or "pass-through stage" (*guoting*).[84]

The construction of the Hall of Dragon and Tiger was completed about three decades after Pan's death, and therefore it is not considered here as the model for the stage depicted on the coffin. However, as has been discussed in this chapter, as well

Above, **FIGURE 4.15A.**
Facade of the Hall of
Dragon and Tiger,
Palace of Eternal
Joy. Yuan, ca. 1279.
Left, **FIGURE 4.15B.**
Platform of the Hall
of Dragon and Tiger,
seen from the south.

FIGURE 4.16. Theatrical performance on the *shanmen* stage of Bixia Palace, Lucheng, Shanxi Province. Photographed in 2005.

as in chapter 3, what concerns us here is a shared spatial logic between the actual building and the image of the building, rather than any particular formal resemblance between them.[85] Embedded in the logic of the Hall of Dragon and Tiger during that period was the experience of visitors passing through a temple gate that also served as a stage. Whoever came to such a monastery for a service or festival would enter through the gate, watch a performance or two inside, and pass through the gate again at the end of the event. This was a common ritual practice in temples and in the shrines of local deities, and it continues to be reenacted in the small towns of Shanxi and other provinces today (fig. 4.16). The entire process of such a chain of events would have shaped particular memories in the templegoers' minds.[86]

For those people, the site of performance in the temple's gate-stage thus served as the path between the worlds of everyday life and the sacred. Mediated through the connected experiences of the transitional space and theatrical spectacles, the boundary between these realms would seem to have been quite flexible in their minds. It was probably such psychological flexibility that nurtured the creative vision of the actors depicted on the Pan sarcophagus, who might also freely move between the two realms.

The virtual performance alluded to in the performance image doubly intersected the realms of life and death, the everyday and the ritual. In so doing, the power of such reversibility nascent in this performance image reveals a tangible sense of theatricality deeply inscribed in the lives of ordinary people during this time period.

POSTLUDE

A SOCIAL TURN IN CHINESE FUNERARY ART

By the early fourteenth century, the wave of theatrical spectacle infiltrating the tomb space reached its peak—so much so that it became embodied in the lyrics of dramatic songs, unaccompanied by a single image of actors or a stage. One such song is written on a painted screen in the tomb of a man named Wu Qing and his wife Jing, who were buried around 1309 in Hongyu Village in Xing County, Shanxi Province:

> Withered vines, an old tree, crows at dusk;
> A humble bridge, flowing stream, a few houses;
> Ancient road, the west wind, a haggard horse;
> Evening sun sets in the west, [yet]
> It is only me who is not on that horizon.
> [To the tune of] West River Moon [*Xi jiang yue*][1]

At first reading, these seem like they might be lyrics from one of those melancholic old songs about a lone traveler. But as the location of the image implies, the choice

FIGURE PO.1. Mural of tomb occupants seated in front of a screen, north wall of a tomb discovered in Hongyu Village, Shanxi Province. Yuan, ca. 1309.

of the subject was undoubtedly shaped by the funerary context: the burial of a couple who are depicted on the same tomb wall (fig. Po.1). In fact, the lyrics are almost identical to the well-known song "Autumn Thoughts" (Qiu si) attributed to one of the most prominent playwrights of the Yuan dynasty, Ma Zhiyuan (ca. 1260–1325).[2] Whether the lyrics were based on Ma's work or on the popular lyrics that had been widely circulated and later collected in Ma's anthology is an open question.[3] Nonetheless, a discrepancy between the textually transmitted versions and this tomb inscription indicates that the song was adapted specifically for this funerary occasion. The last line in all transmitted versions of the song is "a heartbroken man [*duanchang ren*] is on the horizon," but the line as written on the tomb wall replaced "heartbroken man" with "I" (*ji*)—referring to Wu Qing himself—and added the word "not," thus changing the rest of the line to "who is not on that horizon" (*bu zai tianya*), clearly alluding to his nonexistence in this world. These changes in the poem's wording could have been made by the sponsors of the tomb, or anonymously (prior to the burial) and circulated in the local community. Even without the changes, the poem's overall tone of loneliness, together with the images of old age, approaching darkness, and autumn (traditionally associated with death) would have been considered appropriate for the funerary occasion. Yet with such alterations, "Autumn Thoughts" was effectively transformed into an elegy for Wu Qing.

While it was certainly not unprecedented by the fourteenth century to have elegies such as this inscribed in burial chambers,[4] the format of this particular song points to its direct connection to a recent development in funerary art: the theatricalization of the tomb space. It was written as a song suite (*sanqu*)—a literary genre based on the language of the streets, which was closely linked to theatrical performances during the Jin and Yuan periods.[5] With lyrics written to fixed metrical patterns, *sanqu* often contained several arias or song segments in a single suite. The implication of this choice of literary form over a poem (*shi*) or a prose poem (*ci*) is significant; it confirms the broad popularity of this particular genre and its accessibility to the common folk, not just exclusively to the literati. Moreover, for people like Wu and his wife, identified as members of the nonliterati local elite,[6] *sanqu* lyrics were most likely enjoyed as performances enacted onstage rather than as written texts. The elegiac lyrics written on the tomb wall thus carry a strong sense of performance: they were meant to be sung and heard in dramatic contexts. Such performativity embedded in inscriptions of song lyrics is further revealed in the burial chamber (ca. 1200) of one Madame Zhang that was unearthed in Ershui, Houma, Shanxi Province. The walls adjacent to the body (the east, north, and west walls) were covered with songs written in ink in the format of another popular song suite for dramatic performances, the *zhugongdiao* (all keys and modes; see fig. Po.2). Surrounded by the lyrics, which are framed in what appears to be the representation of freestanding screens, the deceased would have been envisioned as enjoying the sound of the songs. As in the case of the *sanqu* in Wu Qing's tomb, it is the format of the text that transforms the tomb space into a place of imaginary performance, a realm filled with the sound of music from the worldly theater—in this case, the lyrics' *zhugongdiao* melodies.[7]

The dramatic song's accessibility to both literate and illiterate audiences and its performativity mark the mature phase of transforming the burial chamber into a theatrical space, the many aspects of which have been the focus of the present volume. Especially noteworthy is the performativity shared by both the words and images of theater. With their sources deeply rooted in the language of the streets and in theater, such lyrics inevitably brought those social worlds into the burial chamber, just as the vivid representations of actors and miniature theaters did so by transferring the spectacle of theatrical performances from the realm of the living into that of the dead.

The quintessentially social character of this theatricality is doubly articulated in its content and structure: its everydayness in living society was emulated in the

FIGURE PO.2. Arias written on the wall of Madame Zhang's tomb. West wall of Ershui Tomb No. 4, Houma, Shanxi Province. Jin, ca. 1200.

tomb space, and the boundaries of the afterworld were framed within the conceivable domain of the living—that is, society. The two aspects were interconnected, and this constituted an important development in the funerary culture of the middle period that is best illustrated in visual form, as it has been in this volume. The representation of the theatrical performance in the funerary blessing (*zi mingfu*) ceremony featured in Zhu Sanweng's coffin (see chapter 1) demonstrated how the classical motif of entertainment in a funeral became deliberately descriptive, emphasizing the mundane and vernacular details of the event. While such images from daily life rejuvenated the content of the traditional entertainment motif, the mode of representation itself began to evolve in another direction. This burgeoning new mode is encapsulated by the bas-relief of the five actors from the Yanshi tomb and its particular position therein (see chapter 2). Unlike the entertainment scenes in earlier tombs, this set of actor images was prepared to be "activated" for performing through the figures' distinctive illusionism as the sole focus of the gaze of the deceased. In such a way, the spectacles experienced in the world of the living were envisioned to be vividly reenacted in the space designed for the dead.

As various types of theatrical performance evolved aboveground, the new kind of performance images proliferating in underground chambers became loaded with complex conceptions of theatricality, fully utilizing such dualisms as world versus theater or self versus persona. Like the examples prominently featured in the Houma

Tomb No. 1 (see chapter 3) and in Pan Dechong's sarcophagus (see chapter 4), they did more than just bring the spectacle of the social world into burial chambers. These images of actors on the stages of miniature theaters, refashioned as deictic icons signifying the *idea* of the theater (and therefore self-reflexively doubling the theatricality inherent in them), yielded their role as performers to the deceased who are "virtual actors" within the stage set of the theatricalized burial space. In other words, such images served at once as a deictic sign of the society of the living from which their prototypes originated and of the afterworld to which these virtual actors were destined.

By fashioning the space of the dead through the theatrical lens, which was itself densely imbued with social experiences of the sponsors and makers, the performance images in this new mode subsumed the idea of the afterworld within the frame of living society. This phenomenon, which I refer to as a "social turn," reveals a major development not only in funerary art but also in society at large in middle period China. It is closely linked to the interest of particular members of the local elite in the world of the dead and to their tendency to conceive of their own view of society as an all-inclusive cognitive world. Since the term "social" has a multifaceted meaning, some explanation is necessary. Rather than the narrow usage of the word—that is, "the social" as a characteristic or aspect that constitutes society (comparable to the "cultural," "legal," or "religious," for example, as other constituents of society)—I use it in the most inclusive sense of the term. Here the social should not be regarded as an individual part that, together with other individual parts, comprises a whole; rather, the social *is* a whole that consists of associations among things and the actions of human agents. The social, rather than existing as a separate element or domain, is therefore composite by nature.[8] This definition, which provides a baseline against the compartmentalized notion of the social that is predominant in the modern usage of the term, approximates the workings of the theatrical images explored in this volume.[9] Their theatrical content and modality do not merely describe social aspects of the funerary art but present a paradigm in which the idea of the afterworld is filtered and projected through the frame of the society of the living as a larger whole. As has been shown throughout this book, especially in chapters 3 and 4, the idea of the world of the dead was often juxtaposed to that of the living as a pair of objectified—and objectifiable—realms. As "abstractions," these two realms were brought together into the single sphere essentially belonging to the "here and now" of living society—a new dimension unprecedented in earlier tomb spaces.[10] Thus, the afterworld was socialized not in the sense that it was visualized as mimetically reflecting the social world of the living (the "content" of society) but in the way that the afterworld was conceived of as an abstraction operating within the cognitive world of contemporary society.

In this schema, the lived social space that was implied by means of theatrical images thus mediated the worlds of the living and the dead and did not follow the classical dualism that was part and parcel to envisioning the afterworld and the posthumous soul. The classical paradigm of the dualistic soul (i.e., *hun* and *po*) that has been accepted by scholars of religion and history specializing in early and medieval time periods remains a useful framework for understanding the basic philosophical ground for traditional Chinese thought in a broad cultural sense.[11] But the visual and material evidence from the burial sites presented in this volume fails to support the idea that any clear pattern existed during the middle period; that is, there is no evidence of an overarching belief in abstract dualism for understanding the notion and whereabouts of the soul, especially among the local elite. In fact, this absence of a single dominant pattern is an important characteristic of the conceptions on the posthumous soul in middle period China, which is best explained through the new mode of framing these ideas—the socialization of the mortuary sphere.

The social turn visually and conceptually manifested in the tomb space was linked to ongoing changes in middle period Chinese society. Conveying the perspective of members of the nonliterati local elite, the series of theatrical images reveals the rare voice of those who had never owned a cultural means to express their views on life and death. As was emphasized in the prelude to this volume, the sponsors of the funerary images examined herein were members of a type of local elite—undereducated, yet relatively affluent—who were not categorized by a single ritual, legal, or administrative term during that time period. Beyond their similar educational and economic backgrounds, what connected their otherwise disparate ways of life and social practices was their shared cultural taste as it pertained to tomb making. The kinds of spaces created in burial chambers were not made by the nonelite, such as landless farmers who could not afford any decent burial; nor were they the products of those who despised luxurious burial as a token of their devotion to Confucian tenets—the educated yet otherwise underprivileged individuals aspiring to be officials someday (and who therefore might well have identified themselves as *shi* (litertati). The reality that their own social standing was not officially recognized on its own terms may have contributed to the construction of such exuberant funerary monuments, since wealth was their greatest asset and they were comparatively free from the constraint of the orthodox principle of frugal burial.

The display in burial chambers of images created using the newest artistic techniques and motifs was not merely a material statement of opulence, however, as is apparent from their unusual rendering of the funerary realm, framed as if it were a staged environment from their social world (i.e., the theater); rather, it reveals a distinctive set of attitudes that these individuals held about their society. Furthermore, such interest in their own social space resonated with the ongoing formation of new social strata during the middle period. The boundaries among social groups were shifting, and new social spaces beyond those aligned with the established categories of family and state were being created accordingly (a phenomenon that has been uncovered by earlier studies concentrating on the emergence and development of the literati elite). Here, I am referring to the emergence in the eleventh century of new members of the literati whose successes were achieved through cultural performances rather than aristocratic pedigree, and to the extensive increase after the eleventh century in social interactions between these new members of the literati and other members of the community in local societies, especially in the south.[12] One indication of the expansion of the social landscape that was in progress is

FIGURE PO.3. *Parinirvāṇa* scene painted on east wall of Hancheng tomb, Shanxi Province. Northern Song. App. W 7.4 m.

the scope of "society" inscribed in the funerary monuments of members of local nonliterati elites discussed in the present volume. These individuals, even though they did not have the textual means for delivering their ideas and thoughts, were able to express their existence in society, distinguishing themselves from both the literati elite and underprivileged commoners.

An equally important implication of the social turn in this broad phenomenon of boundary shifting in middle period society is in the religious sphere. In retrospect, the "socialization of the sacred realm" discussed in chapter 2 as a new development in middle period religiosity in China is most fully understood when reckoned through the extended context of the social turn. While this easier, more open access to the sacred realm for the common folk can be seen as a medieval phenomenon, the role of theatrical images in the funerary context has revealed that the sacred realm itself was becoming socialized during the middle period.[13] While the conceptual boundary between the mundane and the sacred—the world of the dead, in this case—was always to be maintained, those images configured the afterworld within the cognitive frame of society.

OPPOSITE PAGE
FIGURE PO.4. Funerary urn adorned with multiple Buddha images, earthenware with green glaze. From Zhejiang or Jiangsu Province, ca. 3rd century. H 45.4 × W 30.3 cm. Image © Metropolitan Museum of Art. Source: Art Resource, New York.

The prevalence of this tendency provides a reasonable explanation for the unprecedentedly flexible attitude of the Chinese during and after the middle period in embracing conflicting ritual systems or multiple religious beliefs within the funerary field, even when the major belief systems (i.e., Buddhism and Daoism) had been firmly institutionalized as completely independent religions. For example, several tombs containing the bodies of the deceased from this time period overtly displayed icons of the Buddha or other Buddhist deities painted on the walls (fig. Po.3).[14] Some of the early images of the Buddha in a tomb space, such as the well-known seated Buddha in a bas-relief in Mahao Cave, Sichuan Province, or multiple Buddha icons on funerary urns (fig. Po. 4), might seem to show similar efforts. Yet these images are distinguished from those of the middle period because they mark the transitional status of Buddhism, which often had to adopt indigenous deities— such as the Queen Mother of the West (Xiwangmu)—as equivalent to the Buddha when they appeared in the tomb space as appropriate pictorial motifs. In contrast, Buddhist images in middle period tombs often followed iconographic details faithful to sutras and represented in a far more prominent manner, which clearly indicate the sponsors' willingness to render Buddhist icons as completely independent from any indigenous deities. Such practices not only indicate that cremation— the orthodox Buddhist burial method—was merely an option but also show that, for some lay believers, tomb making was still the core funerary practice and their Buddhist faiths were expressed only as a part of the tomb imagery in which the worshiping of the deceased ancestor was central. Sometimes the expression of multiple religious beliefs commingled in a single tomb space, as in the well-known cemetery of the Zhang family in Xuanhua, Hebei Province (1093–1117), which exemplifies the intricate intersection of Buddhist, Daoist, and even exorcistic images and objects

FIGURE PO.5. Mural of five exorcists in Xuanhua Tomb No. 7, Hebei Province. Liao, ca. 1093. H 47.8 × W 105.7 cm.

within a single tomb chamber to compose a hybrid burial space (fig. Po.5).[15] I suggest that an underlying condition for such an extreme assimilation of heterogeneous elements within the funerary realm during this period was the growing tendency to socialize the funerary realm. The fluid characteristics of Chinese religions in general have been addressed in an impressive number of studies in the past several decades. Roughly put, in contrast to earlier scholarship, which maintained rather rigid divisions between orthodox religious practices and less orthodox ("diffused" or "popular") ones, later studies tend to emphasize the local and vernacular practices—which are not necessarily separate from core or orthodox practices—by embracing both the historical and the anthropological analyses.[16] While corresponding to the general direction of the recent scholarship, the socialization of the funerary realm detected in the new practice of funerary art in the middle period helps us further recognize more nuanced textures of this remarkable and flourishing cultural phenomenon. Seen from a perspective deeply rooted in the social world, where all types of conflicts coexisted, the ritual or doctrinal conflicts would not have been regarded as incompatible by the people of the middle period. In this sense, theological or doctrinal consistency was probably sought only within the narrow field of each belief system, whereas the kind of consistency that governed the funerary realm was, ironically, the commingling of variegated elements and the composite nature of society.

The social turn in Chinese funerary art thus manifests a significant aspect of the larger wave of boundary shifting during the middle period: it reveals a rare view of members of the nonliterati elite in the changing boundaries among social groups and also resonates with the increasingly flexible boundaries among disparate rituals and religious practices. As a response to the changing social landscape, the local elite's cultural taste and its view of life and death were manifested in opulent funerary monuments. Although it was obscured in the official narrative of history, this elite's voice can still be heard—and its socialized notion of death seen—in these burial chambers connecting the worlds of the living and the dead as expressed through theatrical spectacles.

APPENDIX

Images of Theatrical Performance Unearthed and Reported in Northern China, Eleventh to Fourteenth Centuries

ABBREVIATIONS

HXKG	*Huaxia kaogu*	华夏考古
KG	*Kaogu*	考古
KGYWW	*Kaogu yu wenwu*	考古与文物
WW	*Wenwu*	文物
WWJK	*Wenwu jikan*	文物季刊
WWSJ	*Wenwu shijie*	文物世界
ZYWW	*Zhongyuan wenwu*	中原文物

TOMB/OBJECT NAME	TIME PERIOD	LOCATION	MEDIUM	REFERENCE
Xingyang Zhu Sanweng Sarcophagus	Northern Song (1096)	Xingyang, Henan	Engraving on sarcophagus	ZYWW 4, 1983
Luoning Yueshi Sarcophagus	Northern Song (1117)	Dasongcun, Luoning, Henan	Engraving on sarcophagus	WW 5, 1993
Baisha Song Tomb No. 1	Northern Song	Baisha, Yuxian, Henan	Brick relief	Su Bai, *Baisha Song mu*, 1957
Yanshi Jiuliugou Song Tomb	Northern Song	Jiuliugou, Yanshi, Henan	Brick relief	WW 9, 1959
Luolong Guanlinmiao Song Tomb	Northern Song	Guanlinmiao, Luolong, Henan	Brick relief	WW 8, 2011
Ding Dusai Brick	Northern Song	Reportedly found in Yanshi, Henan	Brick relief	WW 2, 1980
Wenxian Wangcun Song Tomb	Northern Song	Wangcun, Wenxian, Henan	Brick relief	ZYWW 1, 1983
Wenxian Museum Actor Bricks 1	Northern Song	Wenxian, Henan	Brick relief	Zhou Dao, *Xiqu yishu* 2, 1984
Wenxian Museum Actor Bricks 2	Northern Song	Wenxian, Henan	Brick relief	KGYWW 3, 1988
Luoyang Jianxi Tomb No. 15	Northern Song	Jianxi, Luoyang, Henan	Brick relief	WW 8, 1983
Wenxian Xiguan Song Tomb	Northern Song	Xiguan, Wenxian, Henan	Brick relief	HXKG 1, 1996
Luoning Shangcun Song–Jin Tomb	Late Northern Song–Early Jin	Shangcun, Luoning, Henan	Brick relief	ZYWW 4, 1988
Mianxian Yangzhai Tomb	Northern Song	Yangzhai, Mianxian, Shaanxi	Brick relief	*Zhongguo xiqu zhi* (Shaanxi juan), 1990
Hancheng Panle Song Tomb	Northern Song	Panle, Hancheng, Shanxi	Wall painting	Xu Guangju, ed., *Zhongguo chutu bihua quanji* 7
Houma Niucun Jin Tomb	Jin (1151)	Niucun, Houma, Shanxi	Brick relief	WWJK 3, 1996
Tunliu Jin Tomb	Jin (1153)	Tunliu, Changzhi, Shanxi	Wall painting	WW 3, 2003
Yuanqu Podi Jin Tomb	Jin (1163)	Podi, Yuanqu, Shanxi	Brick relief	Liao Ben, *Song Yuan xiqu yu wenwu yu minsu*
Houma Dali Jin Tomb	Jin (1180)	Dali, Houma, Shanxi	Brick relief	WWJK 3, 1999

TOMB/OBJECT NAME	TIME PERIOD	LOCATION	MEDIUM	REFERENCE
Anyang Jiangcun Jin Tomb	Jin (1186)	Anyang, Henan	Clay figurine	Yang Jianmin, *Zhongzhou xiqu lishi wenwu kao*
Houma Zhiyaochang Jin Tomb	Jin	Houma, Shanxi	Brick relief	WWSJ 3, 1996
Houma Tomb No. 1	Jin (1210)	Houma, Shanxi	Clay figurine	WW 6, 1959
Houma Tomb No. 2	Jin (1210)	Houma, Shanxi	Clay figurine	WW 6, 1959
Houma Tomb No. 104	Jin	Houma, Shanxi	Clay figurine	WW 6, 1983
Huafeichang Jin Tomb	Jin	Jishan, Shanxi	Brick relief	WWSJ 4, 2011
Macun Tomb No. 1	Jin	Macun, Jishan, Shanxi	Clay figurine	WW 1, 1983
Macun Tomb No. 2	Jin	Macun, Jishan, Shanxi	Brick relief	WW 1, 1983
Macun Tomb No. 3	Jin	Macun, Jishan, Shanxi	Brick relief	WW 1, 1983
Macun Tomb No. 4	Jin	Macun, Jishan, Shanxi	Brick relief	WW 1, 1983
Macun Tomb No. 5	Jin	Macun, Jishan, Shanxi	Brick relief	WW 1, 1983
Macun Tomb No. 8	Jin	Macun, Jishan, Shanxi	Brick relief	WW 1, 1983
Wucheng Jin Tomb	Jin (1199)	Wucheng, Jishan, Shanxi	Brick relief	Liao Ben, *Song Yuan xiqu wenwu yu minsu*
Huayu Tomb No. 2	Jin	Huayu, Jishan, Shanxi	Brick relief	WW 1, 1983
Huayu Tomb No. 3	Jin	Huayu, Jishan, Shanxi	Brick relief	WW 1, 1983
Miaopu Tomb No. 1	Jin	Miaopu, Jishan, Shanxi	Brick relief	WW 1, 1983
Houma 65H4 Tomb No. 102	Jin	Houma, Shanxi	Brick relief	WWJK 4, 1997
Houma Jin'guang Tomb No. 1	Jin (1210)	Jin'guang, Houma, Shanxi	Brick relief	WWJK 3, 1996

TOMB/OBJECT NAME	TIME PERIOD	LOCATION	MEDIUM	REFERENCE
Xinyang Jin Tomb	Jin (1202)	Songzhaicun, Xinyangxian, Henan	Brick relief	Liao Ben, *Song Yuan xiqu wenwu yu minsu*
Yima Jin Tomb	Jin (1216)	Yima, Henan	Brick relief	HXKG 4, 1993
Jiaozuo Xifengfengcun Jin Tomb	Jin	Xifengfengcun, Jiaozuo, Henan	Brick relief	ZZYW 1, 1983
Yuanqu Gucheng Jin Tomb	Jin	Guchengcun, Yuanqu, Shanxi	Brick relief	Shanxi shifan daxue xiqu wenwu yanjiusuo, *Song Jin Yuan xiqu wenwu tulun*
Xiuwu Dawei Jin Tomb	Jin	Daweicun, Xiuwuxian, Henan	Brick relief	WW 2, 1995
Ruicheng Pan Dechong Sarcophagus	Yuan	Yonglezhen, Ruicheng, Shanxi	Engraving on sarcophagus	KG 8, 1960
Xilizhuang Yuan Tomb	Yuan	Xilizhuang, Yuncheng, Shanxi	Wall painting	WW 4, 1988
Wulingzhuang Yuan Tomb	Yuan (1279)	Wulingzhuang, Xinjiangxian, Shanxi	Brick relief	WW 1, 1983
Diantou Yuan tomb	Yuan (1289)	Diantoucun, Jishan, Shanxi	Brick relief	Liao Ben, *Song Yuan xiqu yu wenwu yu minsu*
Xinjiang Zhaili Yuan Tomb	Yuan (1311)	Zhaili, Xinjiang, Shanxi	Brick relief	KG 1, 1966

NOTES

Unless otherwise noted, all translations are my own.

ABBREVIATION

SKQS   *Wenyuan ge siku quanshu.* 1,500 vols. Taipei: Taiwan shangwu yin
         shuguan, 1983–1986.

PRELUDE

1. Cheng Dachang, *Yanfanlu,* juan 6, in *Congshu jicheng chubian* edition
    (Beijing: Zhonghua shuju, 1991), 293:65; Meng Yuanlao, *Dongjing
    menghua lu,* juan 7, "Jiadeng Baojin lou zhujun ting baixi," in *Dongjing
    menghua lu jianzhu,* annotated by Yi Yongwen (Beijing: Zhonghua shuju,
    2006), 2:688.
2. Liu Nianzi, "Song zaju Ding Dusai diaozhuan kao," *Wenwu* 1980, no. 2
    (1980): 58. Here the term "actors" specifically refers to players of dramatic

performances. As will be discussed in a later section of this chapter, representations of other entertainers such as acrobats or musicians had appeared earlier.

3. For classical studies of economic development and urbanization in the course of the Tang and Song dynasties, see Miyazaki Ichisada, *Tōyō teki kinsei* (1950), reprinted in *Miyazaki Ichisada zenshū* (Tokyo: Iwanami shoten, 1991), 2:131–241; and Shiba Yoshinobu, *Sōdai shōgyōshi kenkyū* (Tokyo: Kazama shobo, 1968). For the early development of theater, see Wang Guowei, *Song Yuan xiqu shi* (Shanghai: Shanghai guji chubanshe, 1998); Stephen H. West, *Vaudeville and Narrative: Aspects of Chin Theater* (Wiesbaden, Germany: Steiner Verlag, 1977); and Xue Ruizhao, *Song Jin xiju shi gao* (Beijing: Sanlian shudian, 2005).

4. For the records of such occasions, see Zhou Nan, "Liu xiansheng zhuan," *Shanfang ji,* in *Siku quanshu zhenben san ji,* ed. Wang Yunwu (Taipei: Taiwan Shangwu yin shu guan, 1972), vol. 242, juan 4, 12b; Guo Tuan, *Kui che zhi,* juan 5, in *Tang Song biji xiaoshuo san zhong,* ed. Xu Lingyun and Xu Shanshu (Hefei: Huangshan shushe, 1991), 139; Tao Zongyi, "Goulan ya," *Nancun Chuogeng lu,* juan 24 (Beijing: Zhonghua shuju, 2004), 289–290.

5. The vibrancy of performance culture in these regions can be still observed in small towns in China today. On dynamic performances in village rituals in Shanxi, see David Johnson, *Spectacle and Sacrifice: The Ritual Foundations of Village Life in North China* (Cambridge, MA: Harvard University Asia Center, 2009). So far, no representation of theatrical performances has been found in southern tombs constructed during the Northern Song period. A few tombs of the Southern Song period decorated with representations of theatrical performances—modeled after southern-style performances (e.g., *xiwen*)—were excavated in Sichuan and Jiangxi provinces. These cases are not included in this book, as they belong to different traditions of visual practices, cultural prototypes, and tomb making from those of northern China and deserve a separate study. See, for example, Liao Ben, "Guangyuan Nan Song mu zaju, daqu shike kao," *Wenwu* 1986, no. 12 (1986): 25–35; and Tang Shan, "Jiangxi Poyang faxian Song dai xiju yong," *Wenwu* 1979, no. 4 (1979): 6–7.

6. Liao Ben, *Zhongguo xiju tushi* (Zhengzhou: Henan jiaoyu chubanshe, 1996).

7. One exception is Robert Maeda's article on some of the published images; see Maeda, "Some Sung, Chin, and Yüan Representations of Actors," *Artibus Asiae* 41, nos. 2–3 (1979): 132–156.

8. Liu, "Song zaju Ding Dusai diaozhuan kao," 58–62.

9. As I will discuss further in this introduction, exactly how the artisans' workshops were run, as well as what their lives were like, remain somewhat of a mystery. Occasionally the costs of funerary objects such as sarcophagi were carved on the stone (see the Yongji sarcophagus, discussed in chapter 4), names of stonemasons/carvers were engraved on stone panels, or painters'

names were written on murals. See, for example, Yan Xiaohui, "Shanxi Changzi xian Shizhe Jin dai bihua mu," *Wenwu* 1985, no. 6 (1985): 45–54; Wang Jinxian and Zhu Xiaofang, "Shanxi Changzhi Anchang Jin mu," *Wenwu* 1990, no. 5 (1990): 76–85; and Yang Baoshun, "Jiaozuo Jin mu fajue jianbao," *Zhongyuan wenwu* 1979, no. 1 (1979): 14–24.

10. For details, see chapter 1. For records on the prohibition of such events see, among many published sources, Dou Yi, *Song xingtong,* juan 1, "Shi'e (Ten Evils)" (Beijing: Zhonghua shuju, 1984), 7; and Tuo tuo, *Song shi,* juan 125, "Shishuren sangli" (Beijing: Zhonghua shuju, 1977), 2918. In Northern Song law, the act of sponsoring performances for parents' funerals was described as unfilial, and was one of the ten major crimes. Since children of deceased parents were usually the major conductors of funerary rituals, this rule must have been applied to the majority of people who prepared funerals. For accounts of entertainments during funerary rituals, see Wang Dang, *Tang yulin jiaozheng,* annotated by Zhou Xunchu, vol. 1, juan 8 (Beijing: Zhonghua shuju, 1987), 705; and Sima Guang, "Zang lun," *Chuanjia ji,* juan 65, *SKQS* 1094:604.

11. Xue, *Song Jin xiju shi gao,* 144–52; Wilt Idema and Stephen H. West, *Chinese Theater, 1100–1450: A Source Book* (Wiesbaden, Germany: Steiner Verlag, 1982); and Liao Ben, *Zhongguo xiqu shi* (Shanghai renmin chubanshe, 2004), 138–142.

12. Zhou, "Liu xiansheng zhuan."

13. Du Renjie [Du Shanfu], "Zhuangjia bushi goulan," in *Lidai quhua huibian,* ed. Yu Weimin and Sun Rongrong (Hefei: Huangshan shushe, 2006), 212–213. Since this vividly written *sanqu* has been extensively studied by a number of experts in Chinese drama, I will not discuss its content here. See West, *Vaudeville and Narrative: Aspects of Chin Theater,* 1977; and Idema and West, *Chinese Theater,* 64–83. For a recent, refined translation in English, see Stephen H. West and Wilt L. Idema, *Monks, Bandits, Lovers and Immortals: Eleven Early Chinese Plays* (Indianapolis, IN: Hackett, 2010), xii–xv.

14. Liao Ben, "Song Yuan xitai yiji—Zhongguo gudai juchang wenwu yanjiu zhi yi," *Wenwu* 1989, no. 7 (1989): 82–95; Xue Linping and Wang Jiqing, *Shanxi chuantong xichang jianzhu* (Beijing: Zhongguo jianzhu gongye chubanshe, 2004).

15. See Feng Junjie, *Shanxi xiqu beike jikao* (Beijing: Zhonghua shuju, 2002); and Anning Jing, *The Water God's Temple of the Guangsheng Monastery: Cosmic Function of Art, Ritual and Theater* (Leiden, Netherlands: Brill, 2002).

16. For examples, see Xue, *Song Jin xiju shi gao,* 356–377.

17. "Spectacle" has manifold meanings, which can be largely divided into two categories—the ephemeral and the material. The primary definition of "spectacle," which belongs in the first category, is "a specially prepared or arranged display of a more or less public nature (especially one on a large scale), forming an impressive or interesting show or entertainment for those

viewing it." The other definition, which is one way the word was used during the fifteenth and sixteenth centuries, refers to "a means of seeing; something made of glass; a window or mirror." The definition I adopt here sits somewhere between the two, subtly recognizing its intermediary characteristic. This meaning is implied in yet another definition of the word (3.a): "A thing seen or capable of being seen; something presented to the view, esp. of a striking or unusual character; a sight." *Oxford English Dictionary* (online edition), s.v. "spectacle."

18. Guy Debord, *La société du spectacle* (Paris: Buchet/Chastel, 1967); reprinted in English as *The Society of the Spectacle,* trans. Donald Nicholson-Smith (New York: Zone Books, 1994), 12. Debord's characterization of spectacle is multifaceted, most aspects of which are applicable to modern capitalist societies. Yet the effect of transforming and/or contesting the regular order of everyday life is a fundamental characteristic of any spectacle, regardless of time and place, and therefore useful for my discussion. In particular, Debord's basic premise that it is "a social relationship between people mediated by images" is a recognition of spectacle's role as a medium, which opens up a useful theoretical approach to the ways in which it shapes the viewer's environment and interacts with it.

19. For discussions of *mingqi,* see chapter 3.

20. See Liu, "Song zaju Ding Dusai diaozhuan kao."

21. For a historical introduction to Chinese funerary epitaphs, see Zhao Chao, *Gudai muzhi tonglun* (Beijing: Zijincheng chubanshe, 2003). For the epitaphs of Song and Southern Song tombs, see Angela Schottenhammer, "Characteristics of Song Epitaphs," in *Burial in Song China,* ed. Dieter Kuhn (Heidelberg: Edition Forum, 1994), 253–306. For a discussion of the epitaphs made from the mid-ninth to the tenth centuries and their meanings in the formation of new elites, see Nicolas Tackett, *The Destruction of the Medieval Chinese Aristocracy* (Cambridge, MA: Harvard University Asia Center, 2014), 13–25.

22. Many tomb contracts follow the template published in the popular geomancy manual *Dili xinshu* (New book of earth patterns). See Wang Zhu, *Tujie jiaozheng dili xinshu,* 1192 ed. (Taipei: Jiwen shuju, 1985). For examples of middle period funerary land deeds, see Ina Asim, "Status Symbol and Insurance Policy: Song Land Deeds for the Afterlife," in Kuhn, ed., *Burial in Song China,* 307–370; and Valerie Hansen, *Negotiating Daily Life in Traditional China* (New Haven, CT: Yale University Press, 1995).

23. Dieter Kuhn, "Decoding Tombs of the Song Elite," in Kuhn, ed., *Burial in Song China,* 12. Kuhn's definition of local elite is based on Robert Hymes's classical study of the local elite. See Robert P. Hymes, *Statesmen and Gentlemen: The Elite of Fu-chou, Chiang-hsi, in Northern and Southern Sung* (Cambridge: Cambridge University Press, 1986), 7. For a seminal discussion of the change of elite society from the Tang through the Song to the Ming, see Robert M. Hartwell, "Demographic, Political, and Social Transformations of China, 705–1550," *Harvard Journal of Asiatic Studies* 42, no. 2 (1982):

365–442. For the intellectual transformation of the elite during the course of the Tang and the Song from a social perspective, see Peter K. Bol, *"This Culture of Ours": Intellectual Transitions in T'ang and Sung China* (Stanford, CA: Stanford University Press, 1992).

24. The official aspect of such preference is best exemplified by the categorization of the two types of burial in the government-issued encyclopedia of statecraft, *Cefu yuan gui* (1013), in which an entire chapter (juan 907) is dedicated to humble burial (*bozang*), whereas lavish burial (*houzang*) appears along with two other morally problematic practices such as inappropriate ritual decorum (*shili*) and extravagance (*shechi*). See Wang Qinruo, *Cefu yuan gui*, juan 946 (Beijing: Zhonghua shuju, 1989), 4:3775–3779.

25. See Chao Ruyu, *Song mingchen zouyi*, juan 93, *SKQS*, 432:153–156.

26. The plain burial was encouraged because it corresponded to the teachings of Confucius and other orthodox Confucian scholars, and also because it was considered a preemptive effort to avoid tomb robberies. For a brief discussion of *bozang* and *houzang* during the Song, see Kuhn, "Decoding Tombs of the Song Elite," 18–20.

27. Sima Guang, *Sima shi shuyi*, in *Congshu jicheng chubian* edition, vol. 1040, juan 7 (Beijing: Zhonghua shuju, 1985), 78.

28. Kuhn, "Decoding Tombs of the Song Elite," 20. Scholar-officials being entitled to include epitaphs in their tombs was not only sanctioned by the government but also actually practiced. For a succinct statement of the distinction between those who could make their epitaphs and those who could not, see Huang Minzhi, "Jining Li shi zuyingbei" (1195), in *Quan Liao Jin wen* (Taiyuan: Shanxi guji chubanshe, 2002), 2:1994.

29. Qin Dashu, *Song Yuan Ming kaogu* (Beijing: Wenwu chubanshe, 2004), 137–145.

30. For a detailed introduction to Tang mural tombs, see Li Xingming, *Tang dai mushi bihua yanjiu* (Xi'an: Shanxi renmin chubanshe, 2005).

31. Between the two kinds of brick tombs in the early middle period (tenth and eleventh centuries), the simple brick tombs with no interior decoration were made and occupied mostly by scholar-officials. The other and comparatively new type, the brick tombs that imitate wooden architecture, emerged in the late Tang period and were adopted by some members of the royal family in the Song. Around the mid-eleventh century, the patrons of the latter type shifted to local elites. See Qin, *Song Yuan Ming kaogu*, 137–145. For my own discussion of wood-imitation brick architecture, see chapters 2 and 3.

32. The size is recognized as unusually large, since most excavated epitaphs (from both medieval and postmedieval periods) are much smaller, measuring between approximately forty and one hundred centimeters on each side.

33. For a full report, see Henan sheng wenwuju, ed., *Anyang Han Qi jiazu mudi* (Beijing: Kexue chubanshe, 2012).

34. Shanxisheng kaogu yanjiusuo Houma gongzuozhan, "Houma 65H4M102 Jin mu," *Wenwu jikan* 1997, no. 4 (1997): 28–40. This calculation is based on

one of the inscriptions in the front chamber, and on the discussion of it in Yang Fudou and Yang Jigeng, "Jin mu zhuandiao congtan," *Wenwu jikan* 1997, no. 4 (1997): 66–77, esp. 75–77.

35. Of course, these scenes cannot be exclusively interpreted as visual documents of their daily lives. And yet, both the increased number of such scenes in tombs during the middle period, and, more important, the specificity of such images—which suggests sophisticated knowledge of such activities based on firsthand experiences—point to the possibility that these representations were derived from the occupations of the tomb sponsors.

36. For a detailed discussion of the burial practices by the group defined here as the "nonliterati," see Jeehee Hong, "Changing Roles of the Tomb Portrait: Burial Practices and Ancestral Worship of Non-literati Elite in North China (1000–1400)," *Journal of Song-Yuan Studies* 44 (forthcoming).

37. For a discussion of the social status of artisans in early China, see Anthony J. Barbieri-Low, *Artisans in Early Imperial China* (Seattle: University of Washington Press, 2007), esp. chapter 2, 31–66. For a case study on workshops and the roles of artisans in early China, see Lillian Lan-ying Tseng, "Zuofang, getao yu diyuzhe chuantong: Cong Shandong Anqu Dongjiazhuang Han mu de zhizuo henji tanqi," *Taida meishushi yanjiujikan* 8 (2000): 33–86.

38. Martin Powers, *Art and Political Expression in Early China* (New Haven, CT: Yale University Press, 1991), 1–30; Wu Hung, *Monumentality in Early Chinese Art and Architecture* (Stanford, CA: Stanford University Press, 1995), 189–250. Although these works take different perspectives on the relationship between the patron and the artisan, both recognize the clear gap in the social status of the two parties.

39. They were variously referred to as *gong, gongjiang,* or *jiang,* with affixes indicating their specialties such as *huajiang* (painter), *qiejiang* (brick- or stoneworker), *shijiang* (stoneworker) or, more rarely, *shaozhuanjiang* (brick baker).

40. Even though there existed a special register for civil artisans (*jiangji*), it was merely a list of names of individuals who were active as artisans (regardless of their principal occupation) rather than a designation of special status separate from what was listed in the register for all private households (*huji*). See Bao Weimin, "Song dai minjiang chagu zhidu shulue," in *Chuantong guojia yu shehui* (Beijing: Shangwu yin shu guan, 2009), 166–209.

41. Zhen Dexiu, "Shen Shumiyuan qizhuzhu chizhou chengbi," juan 6, *Xishan ji,* SKQS 1174:102–103.

42. Wu, *Monumentality,* 192.

43. In this respect theatrical culture as "popular" culture was not confined to the lower class but cut across multiple social strata. On such an open notion of popular culture in historical studies, see Roger Chartier, *The Cultural Uses of Print in Early Modern France,* trans. Lydia G. Cochrane (Princeton, NJ: Princeton University Press, 1987); and Peter Burke, "Learned Culture and Popular Culture in Renaissance Italy," in *Varieties of Cultural History* (Ithaca, NY: Cornell University Press, 1997), 124–135.

44. I use the term "agency" in the sense that Alfred Gell proposed in his influential work *Art and Agency: An Anthropological Theory* (Oxford: Clarendon Press, 1998). Among several conceptual suggestions made by Gell, I particularly subscribe to the view that considers art as the nexus of social relationships and interactions rather than simply a medium for communicating meaning.

45. A central mode in the theatrical images to be examined in the following chapters, the notion of visual theatricality, belongs to the larger category of visuality. Distinguishable from "vision," which belongs to the natural realm of the visual, the notion of visuality assumes a particular time and space that shapes natural vision in social and historical contexts. For discussions of visuality, see Hal Foster, ed., *Vision and Visuality* (Seattle: Bay Press, 1988); and Robert Nelson, ed., *Visuality Before and Beyond the Renaissance* (Cambridge: Cambridge University Press, 2000). Although the concept still suffers from the fundamental dilemma of how to distinguish what is natural from what is constructed, its basic premise of contextualizing the practice of "seeing" offers a productive methodological insight.

46. While this is my own definition of "theatricality," synthesized through close analyses of the selected examples in this book, the idea has acquired various meanings in diverse academic fields. For a useful discussion of the usage of the term and relevant scholarship, see Thomas Postlewait and Tracy C. Davis, "Theatricality: An Introduction," in *Theatricality*, ed. Thomas Postlewait and Tracy C. Davis (New York: Cambridge University Press, 2003), 1–39.

CHAPTER 1: THEATER AND FUNERAL

1. See Liu Yiqing, *Shishuo xinyu*, juan 23, "Rendan," in *Shishuo xinyu jiaojian*, annotated by Xu Zhen'e (Beijing: Zhonghua shuju, 1984), 2:407. On performances at funerary occasions in the north before the Tang dynasty, see Xie Baofu, *Beichao hunsang lisu yanjiu* (Beijing: Shoudu shifan daxue chubanshe, 1998), 127–134.

2. For records on the prohibition of such events see Dou Yi, *Song xingtong*, juan 1, "Shi'e" (Beijing: Zhonghua shuju, 1984), 7; and Tuo tuo, *Song shi*, juan 125, "Shishuren sangli" (Beijing: Zhonghua shuju, 1977), 2918.

3. Sima Guang, "Zang lun," *Chuanjia ji*, juan 65, *SKQS*, 1094: 604.

4. Lu You, "You jin shu," in *Fangweng jiaxun*, in *Zhibuzuzhai congshu*, Baibu congshu jicheng no. 29, box 22 (Taipei: Yiwen, 1966), 3b.

5. Feng Yan, "Dao ji," annotated by Zhao Zhenxin, *Feng shi wenjian ji jiaozhu*, juan 6 (Beijing: Zhonghua shuju, 2005), 61. The event is also recorded in Wang Dang, *Tang yulin jiaozheng*, annotated by Zhou Xunchu, vol. 1, juan 8 (Beijing: Zhonghua shuju, 1987), 705.

6. The Three Kingdoms saga is a famous story set at the time just after Liu Bang (d. 195 BCE) conquered the heartland of the Qin (221–206 BCE), an achievement that Liu's rival Xiang Yu (232–202 BCE) had believed was reserved for his

own accomplishment. In revenge, Xiang offers a feast at the Goose Gate, where his army is camping, thus giving him an opportunity to assassinate Liu. During the banquet Xiang has one of his generals perform a sword dance in an attempt to stab Liu. Seeing through the ruse, Liu's military adviser also begins a sword dance in defense. This was one of several historical episodes frequently represented in Later Han tombs and widely circulated by the time of the Late Tang dynasty. For a complete account of this episode, see Sima Qian, "Xiang Yu benji," in *Shi ji* (Beijing: Zhonghua shuju, 1959), 312–313. For a discussion of this motif in Later Han tombs, see Zhou Dao and Wang Xiao, *Han hua: Henan Handai huaxiang yanjiu* (Zhengzhou: Zhongzhou guji chubanshe, 1996), 58, 75–76. The combat scene is that of the Uigur-origin general Weichi Jingde of the Tang dynasty versus a military officer from Tujue, an episode from the more recent past. See Feng, "Dao ji."

7. One of the earliest usages of this term appears in the criticism by Qiao Zhou (cited in Liu Yiqing, *Shishuo xinyu jiaojian,* annotated by Xu Zhen'e, vol. 2 [Zhonghua shuju, 1984], 407), and it continued to be in use during the Tang dynasty (618–907). See Duan Chengshi, "Shixi," *Youyang zazu,* juan 13, *SKQS,* 1047:717. Qin Dashu further equates the notion of *yuesang* with *yushi* (pleasing the corpse), an expression that appears in a late nineteenth-century gazetteer of Jishan County, Shanxi Province; Qin Dashu, *Song Yuan Ming kaogu* (Beijing: Wenwu chubanshe, 2004), 146–148. Aside from the problem of definitively identifying the notion of *yuesang* as the function of entertaining performances at funerals, Qin's equating of *yuesang* with *yushi* needs to be rethought. The ritual function of "accompanying music to the funeral" should be understood differently from that of "pleasing the corpse," since the former does not indicate specific audiences and involves a much larger context.

8. On the *yuji,* a worship ceremony conducted when the mourners returned home from the burial site, see *Yili,* juan 40, "Jixi li," in *Yili zhushu,* with commentary by Zheng Xuan and compiled by Jia Gongyan (Shanghai: Shanghai guji chubanshe, 2008), 3:1216; and Sima Guang, *Sima shi shuyi,* juan 8 (Beijing: Zhonghua shuju, 1985), 93–95.

9. For a general discussion of the traditional Chinese funerary program, see James L. Watson and Evelyn S. Rawski, eds., *Death Ritual in Late Imperial and Modern China* (Berkeley: University of California Press, 1988), esp. pt. 1. For influential middle period texts written by scholar-officials about rituals, including the funeral, see Sima Guang, *Sima shi shuyi;* and Zhu Xi, *Jiali, SKQS* 142. For a translation with annotation and an introduction to Zhu Xi's text, see Zhu Xi, *Chu Hsi's Family Rituals: A Twelfth-Century Chinese Manual for the Performance of Cappings, Weddings, Funerals, and Ancestral Rites,* translated and annotated by Patricia Buckley Ebrey (Princeton, NJ: Princeton University Press, 1991); see also Patricia Buckley Ebrey, *Confucianism and Family Rituals in Imperial China: Social History of Writing about Rites* (Princeton, NJ: Princeton University Press, 1991). For a recent examination of

the ritual texts from the Tang to the Song dynasties, see Chang Wen-chang, *Zhili yi jiao tianxia—Tang Song lishu yu guojia shehui* (Taipei: Guoli Taiwan daxue chubanshe, 2012).

10. For multifaceted ritual meanings constructed around the body of the deceased in early funerary contexts, see Joy E. Beckman, "Layers of Being: Bodies, Objects, and Spaces in Warring States Burials," PhD diss., University of Chicago, 2006.

11. For brief discussions of Zhu Sanweng's sarcophagus, see Lü Pin, "Henan Xingyang Bei Song shiguan xianhua kao," *Zhongyuan wenwu* 1983, no. 4 (1983): 91–96; Zhou Dao, "Xingyang Songdai shiguan zaju tu kao," *Xiqu wenwu* 4 (1983): 104–105; and Xu Pingfang, "Song Yuan mu zhong de zaju diaoke," in *Zhongguo lishi kaoguxue luncong* (Taipei: Yunchen wenhua shiye gufen youxian gongsi, 1995), 496–510.

12. Lü, "Henan Xingyang Beisong shiguan," 91.

13. Shanxisheng kaogu yanjiusuo, ed., *Zoujin kaogu buru Sing Jin—Yi ci gongzhong kaogu huodong de tansuo yu shiqian* (Beijing: Kexue chubanshe, 2009), 23.

14. The iconicity of this motif would have been derived from actual funerary practice. According to *Yili,* horses were to be prepared in the courtyard during the first stage of the mourning ritual. See *Yili,* juan 39, in *Yili zhushu,* 3:1184.

15. Although some of them carried specific symbolic meanings (such as images of a cat capturing a sparrow depicted in some Song and Jin tombs, which could be seen as visual puns on terms signifying longevity), others were simply playful elements intended as details of everyday life. On the visual pun in the images of cats and sparrows in some Song and Jin tombs, see Yuan Quan, "Song Jin muzang maoque ticai kao," *Kaogu yu wenwu* 2008, no. 4 (2008): 105–112.

16. See Su Bai, *Baisha Song mu,* 2nd ed. (Beijing: Wenwu chubanshe, 2002), 48–49. A line of new scholarship suggests that the image of the deceased and the ceremonial wares on the table in the tomb design together evoke a ritual setting at ancestral shrines or image halls (*yingtang*). See Yi Qing, "Song Jin zhongyuan diqu bihua mu 'muzhuren dui (bing) zuo' tuxiang tanxi," *Zhongyuan wenwu* 2011, no. 2 (2011): 73–80; Li Qingquan, "'Yitang jiaqing' de xin yixiang—Song Jin shiqi de muzhu fufu xiang yu Tang Song muzang fengqi de bian," in *Gudai muzang meishu yanjiu,* ed. Wu Hung and Zheng Yan (Changsha: Hunan meishu chubanshe, 2013), 2:318–35; Jeehee Hong, "Changing Roles of the Tomb Portrait: Burial Practices and Ancestral Worship of Non-literati Elite in North China (1000–1400)," *Journal of Song-Yuan Studies* 44 (forthcoming).

17. Images of chairs appear in sixth-century Buddhist murals and stele, and it is generally accepted that chairs were commonplace in Chinese houses and temples by the eleventh century. On this issue, see John Kieschnick, *The Impact of Buddhism on Chinese Material Culture* (Princeton, NJ: Princeton University Press, 2003), 222–240.

18. For one of earliest descriptions of the basic role types of the Song period *zaju,* see Wu Zimu, *Mengliang lu,* in *Dongjing menghua lu wai si zhong* (Beijing: Zhonghua shuju, 1962), 308–309.

19. Among several studies that provide an overall picture of the Song period *zaju,* see Zhou Yibai, *Zhongguo xiju shi* (Shanghai: Zhonghua shuju, 1953), 99–124; Wilt Idema and Stephen H. West, *Chinese Theater, 1100–1450: A Source Book* (Wiesbaden, Germany: Steiner Verlag, 1982); Xue Ruizhao, *Song Jin xiju shi gao* (Beijing: Sanlian shudian, 2005), 144–152. Some of the important details about each role type are discussed further in chapter 2.

20. Among numerous writings addressing the importance of the excavated material, see Liu Nianzi, *Xiqu wenwu congkao* (Beijing: Zhongguo xiju chubanshe, 1986); Liao Ben, *Song Yuan xiqu wenwu yu minsu* (Beijing: Wenhua yishu chubanshe, 1989); and Che Wenming, *Ershi shiji xiqu wenwu de fazhan yu quxue yanjiu* (Beijing: Wenhua yishu chubanshe, 2001).

21. At this point in the early development of *zaju,* the visual codification of each role type was still in flux, and it is difficult to decisively determine which visual traits were exclusively associated with certain role types. I therefore use the expression "which became" as regards the later Jin theater, when such codification became firm and consistent. The thirteenth-century texts *Mengliang lu* and *Ducheng jisheng* (1235) briefly mention the *fumo*'s role as that of "telling jokes." See Wu, *Mengliang lu,* 309; and Nai Deweng, *Ducheng jisheng,* in *Dongjing menghua lu wai si zhong* (Beijing: Zhonghua shuju, 1962), 96.

22. Initially a symbol of high literary talent, this type of hat gained popularity among literati of the mid-Song period. See Li Zhi, "Dongpo mao," in *Shiyou tanji* (Beijing: Zhonghua shuju, 2002), 11–12. On the origins of the *zhugan zi* as a prop often used in short comic skits during the Tang period, see Meng Yuanlao, *Dongjing menghua lu,* juan 9, in *Dongjing menghua lu jianzhu,* annotated by Yi Yongwen (Beijing: Zhonghua shuju, 2007), 2:833, esp. note 30.

23. For a brief description of the comic role types in the early theater, see Nai, *Ducheng jisheng,* 97.

24. Tao Zongyi, "Yuanben mingmu," *Nancun Chuogeng lu,* juan 25 (Beijing: Zhonghua shuju, 2004), 306.

25. I am referring to *Mengliang lu, Ducheng jisheng,* and *Chuogeng lu.* Some of the details that are more relevant to later representations of actors are discussed in chapters 2 and 3.

26. Lü, "Henan Xingyang Beisong shiguan," 92.

27. For general discussions on *zhancui,* see *Yili,* juan 28, 2:862–882.

28. *Yili,* juan 34, in *Yili zhushu,* 2:1030.

29. Ibid.

30. Nie Chongyi, "Sangfu tu 15," in *Xin ding Sanli tu* (Beijing: Zhonghua shuju, 1963), 2:1b (reprint of Zhenjiang fu xue ed., 1175); Chen Yuanjing, *Shilin guangji* (Beijing: Zhonghua shuju, 1999), 48 (reprint of Jianan Chunzhuang shuyuan keben, 1330–1333, in Palace Museum, Beijing).

31. *Yili,* juan 28, 2:862, and juan 34, in *Yili zhushu,* 2:1027–1028. Notice that the *chang* was not exactly the same thing as a modern-day skirt, as it was also worn by men, usually underneath a robe.

32. Nie, "Sangfu tu shang 15," 2:1b; Chen, *Shilin guangji,* 48. The overall form of the pleats corresponds to the prescriptive measurements for the mourning skirts given in *Yili,* juan 34, in *Yili zhushu,* 2:1027–1028. By the time Nie wrote *Sanli tu,* variations of pleated skirts—such as the *Daogongbu chang* or *Sicui chang,* both of which had multiple pleats—were used as mourning attire. See Nie, "Sangfu tu shang 15," 2:4a; and "Sangfu tu xia 16," 2:4b.

33. Roland Barthes emphasizes this "nesting" nature of a narrative by characterizing it as "international, transhistorical, transcultural"; see Barthes, *Image, Music, Text,* translated by Stephen Heath (New York: Hill and Wang, 1977), 79.

34. For a discussion of the relationship between the viewing experience and the format of this painting, see Wu Hung, *The Double Screen: Medium and Representation in Chinese Painting* (Chicago: University of Chicago Press, 1996), 29–71; and De-nin D. Lee, *The Night Banquet: A Chinese Scroll through Time* (Seattle: University of Washington Press, 2010).

35. For a southern example, see Jiangyinshi bowuguan, "Jiangsu Jiangyinshi Qingyangzhenli Jingba Song mu," *Kaogu* 2008, no. 3 (2008): 92–96.

36. The use of the *mingjing* banner in a funeral has been traced back to antiquity. It was used throughout the funerary ritual, from the initial stage, along with a spirit seat (*lingzuo*), until the coffin reached the tomb site. See *Yili,* "Shi sang li," juan 35, in *Yili zhushu,* 3:1055; and Nie, "Xilian tu 17," 2:6b.

37. While Cheng Yi's main criticism against using cymbals and gongs focused on their origin in India, where they were used by monks for begging, Yu Wenbao complained about their inappropriateness as a means of expressing grief. For detailed discussions of such criticisms, see Ebrey, *Confucianism and Family Rituals in Imperial China,* esp. chap. 4. See also Patricia Buckley Ebrey, "The Response of the Sung State to Popular Funeral Practices," in *Religion and Society in T'ang and Sung China,* ed. Patricia Buckley Ebrey and Peter N. Gregory (Honolulu: University of Hawai'i Press, 1993), 213–214.

38. Wang Yong, *Yanyi yimou lu,* juan 3 (Beijing: Zhongghua shuju, 1981), 24. The term *yanyue,* translated here as "vulgar music," has complex origins, but by the eleventh century it referred principally to vulgar music. For examples, see Ouyang Xiu, "Yue li zhi," juan 22, in *Xin Tang shu* (Beijing: Zhonghua shuju, 1975), 12:473–480; Shen Kuo, *Mengxi bitan,* juan 5, in *Mengxi bitan ji-aozheng,* annotated by Hu Daozheng (Shanghai: Shanghai guji chubanshe, 1987), 1:232. For *yanyue* as a court music during the Sui and Tang dynasties, see Yang Yinliu, *Zhongguo gudai yinyueshi kao* (Beijing: Renmin yinyue chubanshe, 1981), 1:213–232.

39. Xuanzang introduces the practice as indigenous to India; see Xuanzang, *Da Tang Xiyue ji,* juan 2 (Bingsi), in *Da Tang Xiyue ji,* annotated by Zhou Guolin (Changsha: Yuelu shushe, 1999), 103.

40. Among many examples, see Zhu Mu, *Gujin shiwen leiju,* qian ji, juan 54, *SKQS,* 925:864; and Guo Tuan, *Kui che zhi,* juan 4, in *Baibu congshu jicheng* 14, no. 576 (Taipei: Yiwenyin shuguan, 1965), 1b–2a.

41. Liu Xi, *Shi ming,* juan 8, in *Congshujicheng chubian,* vol. 1151, ed. Wang Yunwu (Changsha: Shangwu yin shu guan, 1939), 132. For the uses of the term *jiu* during the Han, see Wu Hung, *The Art of the Yellow Springs: Understanding Chinese Tombs* (Honolulu: University of Hawai'i Press, 2010), 128. This early definition persisted into the late imperial period. For early Song evidence, see Chen Pengnian and Li Shuchang, *Zhongxiu Guang yun,* juan 4, *SKQS,* 236:389.

42. "Chen Laizi," juan 257, in *Taiping guangji,* ed. Li Fang, *SKQS,* 1044:655.

43. Anna Seidel, "*Post-Mortem* Immortality or the Taoist Resurrection of the Body," in *Gilgul: Essays on Transformation, Revolution, and Permanence in the History of Religions,* ed. Shaul Shaked and Gedaliahu A. G. Stroumsa (Leiden, Netherlands: Brill, 1987), 223–237.

44. The commonality of certain programs such as entertainment or Buddhist services in both auspicious and inauspicious events was deeply rooted in the lives of ordinary people. For a comparable example from the Southern Song dynasty, see Ebrey, "The Response of the Sung State," 233n29.

45. Several murals in contemporaneous tombs in northern China also metonymically depict selected segments of funeral rites typically conducted among commoners. See Jeehee Hong, "'Hengzai' zhong de zangyi: Song Yuan shiqi zhongyuan muzang de yili shijian," in *Gudai muzang meishu yanjiu,* ed. Wu Hung, Zhu Qingsheng, and Zheng Yan, vol. 3 (Changsha: Hunan meishu chubanshe, 2015), 196–226.

46. The earliest known example of this particular motif appears on a stone coffin found in Mount Wohu Tomb No. 2, Zoucheng, Shandong Province, dating to the late Han period; see Zoucheng shi wenwu guanli ju, "Shandong Zoucheng shi Wohu shan Han huaxiangshi mu," *Kaogu* 199, no. 6 (1999): 43–51. During the Eastern Han, many tombs in Sichuan included images of this motif; for these early examples, see Sheng Lei, "Sichuan 'bankaimen zhong tan shen renwu' ticai chubu yanjiu," *Zhongguo Han hua yanjiu* 1 (2004): 70–88. Much scholarship has been dedicated to this topic, which is discussed further in the present chapter.

47. The inner coffin of Marquis Yi of the Zeng shows a window-shaped pattern on both side panels. Alain Thôte, comparing these patterns with rectangular openings made on some Western Zhou bronze vessels, convincingly argues that they represent openings; see Thôte, "The Double Coffin of Leigudun Tomb No.1: Iconographic Sources and Related Problems," in *New Perspectives on Chu Culture during the Eastern Zhou Period,* ed. Thomas Lawton (Princeton, NJ: Princeton University Press, 1991), 34–37.

48. See Wu Hung, "Myths and Legends in Han Funerary Art," in *Stories from China's Past: Han Dynasty Pictorial Tomb Reliefs and Archaeological Objects from Sichuan Province, People's Republic of China,* ed. Lucy Lim (San Francisco: Chinese Culture Foundation of San Francisco, 1987), 72–80. See also

Wu Hung, *Monumentality in Early Chinese Art and Architecture* (Stanford, CA: Stanford University Press, 1995), 257–259; and Lillian Lan-ying Tseng, *Picturing Heaven in Early China* (Cambridge, MA: Harvard University Press, 2011), 205–233. For examples with inscriptions referring to the image of *que* as *tianmen* (heavenly gate), see Zhao Dianzeng and Yuan Shuguang, "'Tianmen' kao—jian lun Sichuan Han huaxiangzhuan (shi) de zuhe yu zhuti," *Sichuan wenwu* 1990, no. 6 (1990): 3; and Wang Yu, "Sichuan Han mu chutu 'Xiwangmu yu zaji' yaoqianshu zhiye shitan," *Kaogu* 2013, no. 11 (2013): 72–83.

49. Wu, *Monumentality*, 75. There have been numerous studies on the motif of a figure peering out of a half-open door as represented on tomb walls and other funerary monuments. Since I consider the meaning of such images to be distinct from those appearing on the head panel of a sarcophagus, I will not introduce them here. For a thorough discussion of such scholarship that includes both tomb walls and coffin surfaces, see Zheng Yan, "Lun 'Ban ji men,'" in *Gugong bowuyuan yuankan* 3, no. 161 (2012): 16–36. For a study of this particular sarcophagus, see Lillian Lan-ying Tseng, "Funerary Spatiality: Wang Hui's Sarcophagus in Han China," *Res: Anthropology and Aesthetics* 61–62 (2012): 116–131.

50. A door image appearing on the surface of a reliquary potentially involves different philosophical and religious meanings, a topic that requires a separate study.

51. Nevertheless, this particular type of coffin should be distinguished from the much larger-scale burial structures that faithfully imitate the shape of a house as a whole; these began to appear in the northern dynasties during the sixth century; see Wu Hung, "A Case of Cultural Interaction: House-Shaped Sarcophagi of the Northern Dynasties," *Orientations* 137, no. 5 (2002): 34–41.

52. Jessica Rawson suggests that the door images would appear to indicate the liminal state of the tomb, with access both to the world of the living and the world of the dead; see Rawson, "Changes in the Representation of Life and the Afterlife as Illustrated by the Contents of Tombs of the T'ang and Sung Periods," in *Arts of the Sung and Yuan,* ed. Maxwell Hearn and Judith Smith (New York: Metropolitan Museum of Art, 1996), 35–36. Li Qingquan has suggested that the space beyond the doors symbolized a bedroom for the deceased (*qin*), as opposed to a hall, which was a more public part of a house (*tang*). See Li Qingquan, "Kongjian luoji yu shijue yiwei—Song Liao Jin mu 'furen jimen tu' xinlun," in *Gudai muzang meishu yanjiu,* ed. Wu Hung and Zheng Yan (Beijing: Wenwu chubanshe, 2011), 1:329–362. Zheng Yan, by recontextualizing the "icon" within a larger category of the representation of space dividers in tombs (including doors, screens, and windows), has explored the third spatial dimension that such images evoked; see Zheng, "Lun 'Ban ji men.'"

53. An eleventh-century architectural manual, *Yingzao fashi,* categorizes them as either single- or double-layer balustrades. See Li Jie, *Yingzao fashi,* juan 8 (Beijing: Zhongguo shudian, 2006), 170–174.

54. See Zhengzhou shi wenwu kaogu yanjiusuo. "Henan Xinmi shi Pingmo Song dai bihua mu," *Wenwu* 1998, no. 12 (1998): 26–32. This motif of the exemplars of filial piety already began to appear on tomb walls since the Han, but extended versions of it became extremely popular during the middle period. See Dong Xinlin, "Bei Song Song Jin muzang bishi suo jian 'Er shi si xiao' gu shi yu Gaoli *Xiaoxing lu,*" *Huaxia kaogu* 2 (2009): 141–152; and Deng Fei, "Guanyu Song Jin muzang zhong xiaoxing tu de sikao," *Zhongyuan wenwu* 2009, no. 4 (2009): 75–81.

55. Monks are known to have worn this type of hood by the eleventh century, but it became particularly associated with funerary occasions; see Daocheng, *Shishi yaolan* (ca. 1019), in *Taishō shinshū Daizōkyō,* ed. Takakusu Junjirō and Watanabe Kaigyoku, vol. 54, no. 2127 (Tokyo: Taishō Issaikyo Kankokai, 1914–1932): 308b.

56. The practice of chanting a sutra at a funeral began much earlier, and was already popular during the eighth century. Daniel Overmyer's introduction to some of the indigenous scripts found in Dunhuang, especially that of *Foshuo tiandi bayang shenzhu jing* (ca. 730) by a monk named Yijing provides a concrete picture of the popular practice among ordinary people; see Yijing, *Foshuo tiandi bayang shenzhou jing,* in *Taishō shinshū Daizōkyō,* ed. Takakusu Junjirō and Watanabe Kaigyoku, vol. 85, no. 2987 (Tokyo: Taishō Issaikyo Kankokai, 1914–1932); see Overmyer, "Buddhism in the Trenches: Attitudes toward Popular Religion in Chinese Scriptures Found at Tun-Huang," *Harvard Journal of Asiatic Studies* 50, no. 1 (1990): 197–222, esp. 216–218. For a brief account of Song period examples, see Ebrey, "Response of the Sung State," 212.

57. For historical records on Sengqie, see Zanning, *Song Gaoseng zhuan,* juan 18 (Beijing: Zhonghua shuju, 1987), 448–452; Zhipan, *Fozu tongji,* in *Taishō shinshū Daizōkyō,* ed. Takakusu Junjirō and Watanabe Kaigyoku, vol. 49, no. 2035 (Tokyo: Taishō Issaikyo Kankokai, 1914–1932), 372. On archaeological finds that reflect the popular worship of Sengqie during the Song, see Xu Pingfang, "Sengqie zaoxiang de faxian he Sengqie chongbai," *Wenwu* 1996, no. 5 (1996): 50–67; Chen Chang'an, "Luoyang chutu Sizhou dasheng shidi-aoxiang," *Zhongyuan wenwu* 1997, no. 2 (1997): 93–109; and Sonya S. Lee, *Surviving Nirvana: Death of the Buddha in Chinese Visual Culture* (Hong Kong: Hong Kong University Press, 2010), 252–255. Dieter Kuhn briefly discusses the image of Sengqie in this tomb; see Kuhn, "Religion in the Light of Archaeology and Burial Practices," in *Modern Chinese Religion,* ed. John Lagerway (Leiden, Netherlands: Brill, 2015), 1:534–538. For an introduction to extant sculptures portraying Sengqie, see Denise Patry Leidy, "A Portrait of the Monk Sengqie in the Metropolitan Museum of Art," *Oriental Art* 49, no. 1 (2003): 52–64; and Denise Patry Leidy and Donna Straham, *Wisdom Embodied: Chinese Buddhist and Daoist Sculpture in the Metropolitan Museum of Art* (New Haven, CT: Yale University Press, 2010), 126–129. The informal terms *weng* and *po* were commonly used during this time to refer to a couple either living or dead, as evident in the image of the deceased couple incised on

Zhang Jun's sarcophagus (dating to 1106); see Huang Minglan and Gong Dazhong, "Luoyang Bei Song Zhang Jun mu huaxiang shiguan," *Wenwu* 1984, no. 7 (1984): 79–81.

58. For another example of the *zi mingfu* ceremony, see Zhengzhou shi wenwu kaogu yanjiusuo, ed., *Zhengzhou Song Jin bihua mu* (Beijing: Kexue chuban-she, 2005), 38.

59. Raoul Birnbaum, "Light in the Wutai Mountains," in *The Presence of Light: Divine Radiance and Religious Experience,* ed. Matthew T. Kapstein (Chicago: University of Chicago Press, 2004).

60. Shih-shan Susan Huang labels this image as "a picture of *chaoyuan*" in the context of Daoist ritual imagery that features Daoist deities' procession; Shih-shan Susan Huang, *Picturing the True Form: Daoist Visual Culture in Traditional China* (Cambridge, MA: Harvard University Asia Center, 2012), 303–304. While the ubiquity of the pictorial motif in the ritual field (including Daoist, Buddhist, and funerary rituals) during the middle period is unquestionable, there is no evidence that these images depicted in the Pingmo tomb were something "appropriated" from a Daoist pictorial motif.

61. The idea and representation of "crossing a bridge" as the deceased's journey from this world to the afterworld became a common trope from the Han dynasty onward. See Wu Hung, "Beyond the 'Great Boundary': Funerary Narrative in Early Chinese Art," in *Boundaries in China,* ed. John Hay (London: Reaktion, 1994), 81–104.

62. For an in-depth discussion of the distinctive temporality emphasizing the presentness in the representations of funeral in middle period tombs, see Hong, "'Hengzai' zhong de zangyi."

63. I use the term "orthopraxy" in a broad sense, defined as "proper actions" rather than "proper beliefs." More specifically, I use it as a conceptual tool to help distinguish potential variations, conflicts, and interactions among those in the upper class of society. This conceptualization is distinguished from the much influential discussions on orthopraxy in death ritual initiated and expounded by James Watson, which focus on explaining the hierarchical dissemination of "the proper ritual form" from the elite (as a single entity) to the ordinary people in the late imperial period. See, among his many influential studies, James L. Watson, "The Structure of Chinese Funerary Rites: Elementary Forms, Ritual Sequence, and the Primacy of Performance," in *Death Ritual in Late Imperial and Modern China,* ed. James L. Watson and Evelyn S. Rawski (Berkeley: University of California Press, 1988); and James L. Watson, "Rites or Beliefs? The Construction of a Unified Culture in Late Imperial China," in *China's Quest for National Identity,* ed. Lowell Dittmer and Samuel S. Kim (Ithaca, NY: Cornell University Press, 1993), 80–103. For a reexamination of orthopraxy during the late imperial period and in modern China, see a series of articles in the special issue titled "Ritual, Cultural Standardization, and Orthopraxy in China: Reconsidering James L. Watson's Ideas," *Modern China* 33, no. 1 (2007).

64. For the excavation report on this sarcophagus, see Li Xianqi and Wang Liling, "Henan Luoning Bei Song Lezhongjin huaxiang shiguan," *Wenwu* 1993, no. 5 (1993): 30–39.

65. The narrative structure I am referring to here is borrowed from Paul Ricoeur's scheme of narrative time. Ricoeur defines the plot as an "intelligible whole that governs a succession of events in any story"; in both literary and visual narrative, this concept enables us to recognize the complex relationship between an event or events and the story: a story is made out of events to the extent that the plot makes events into a story. See Ricoeur, "Narrative Time," *Critical Inquiry* 7, no. 1 (1980): 171.

66. The Eastern Han tomb from Yinan, Shandong Province, is a good example. See Zeng Zhaoyu, Jiang Baogeng, and Li Zhongyi, *Yinan gu huaxiangshi mu fajue baogao* (Shandong: Wenwubu wenwu guanliju, 1956), 30; Lydia duPont Thomson, "The Yi'nan Tomb: Narrative and Ritual in Pictorial Art of the Eastern Han (25–220 CE)," PhD diss., New York University, 1998, esp. chap. 5; and Wu, *The Art of the Yellow Springs,* 194–204.

67. Wu Lan and Xue Yong, "Shanxi Mizhi xian Guanzhuang Dong Han huaxiang shi mu," *Kaogu* 1987, no. 2 (1987): 997–1001. For a discussion of the spatial configuration in the carved images in this tomb, see Tseng, *Picturing Heaven in Early China,* 228–233. A series of well-known stone slabs that covered the walls of a tomb at Cangshan County, Shandong Province (151 BCE), exemplifies the archetype of the performance image portrayed in symbolic ambiance as a component of the deceased's journey into the afterworld. For an in-depth discussion of the entire pictorial program, see Wu, "Beyond the 'Great Boundary,'" 81–104.

CHAPTER 2: THEATER FOR THE DEAD

1. As with any archaeological discoveries in China, this number should be assumed to be a minimum, as research on many discoveries has simply not seen publication. For example, during several research trips, I encountered dozens of such brick reliefs in northern Henan Province alone that have never been reported.

2. Dong Xiang, "Yanshi xian Jiuliu gou shuiku Song mu," *Wenwu* 1959, no. 9 (1959): 84–85. For detailed information about tomb furnishings, including utensils, published by the Song court mainly for commoners, see Zheng Juzhong, *Zhenghe wuli xinyi,* juan 239 (Taipei: Taiwan shangwu yin shuguan, 1983). For an overview of the materials of *shiqi* found in Song tombs, see Jessica Rawson, "Changes in the Representation of Life and the Afterlife as Illustrated by the Contents of Tombs of the T'ang and Sung Period," in *Arts of the Sung and Yuan,* ed. Maxwell Hearn and Judith Smith (New York: Metropolitan Museum of Art, 1996), 23–43.

3. Luoyangshi wenwu gongzuodui, "Luoyang Luolongqu guanlinmiao Song dai zhuandiaomu fajue jianbao," *Wenwu* 2011, no. 8 (2011): 31–46.

4. Two core aspects in the organization of images in the Luolong tomb are shared with the Yanshi case. First, the actor reliefs take the central position in the layout of all representations in terms of their prominent size (i.e., largest among all figures represented in the tomb); second, they are placed on the wall near the head of the deceased, without any representation of the deceased in the tomb as a potential spectator. The significance of this second aspect will be explained later in this chapter.

5. For the distribution of wood-imitation brick tombs in northern China, see Qin Dashu, *Song Yuan Ming kaogu* (Beijing: Wenwu chubanshe, 2004), 138–145. On the characteristics and symbolic meanings embedded in the tomb's structure, see Wei-cheng Lin, "Underground Wooden Architecture in Brick: A Changed Perspective from Life to Death in 10th- through 13th-Century Northern China," *Archives of Asian Art* 61 (2011): 3–36.

6. See Zhu Mu, "Louzeyuan zhi chuang," in *Gujin shiwen leiju*, qian ji, juan 56, *SKQS* 925:884. For excavated examples of *louzeyuan,* see Sanmenxia wenwu gongzuodui, *Bei Song Shanzhou louzeyuan* (Beijing: Wenwu chubanshe, 1999). For a general discussion of *louzeyuan,* see Silvia Freiin Ebner von Eschenbach, "Public Graveyards of the Song Dynasty," in *Burial in Song China,* ed. Dieter Kuhn (Heidelberg: Edition Forum, 1994).

7. Li Jifu, *Yuanhe junxian zhi,* juan 6, Henan dao yi, *SKQS* 468:197; Yue Shi, *Taiping huanyu ji,* juan 52, "Hebei dao 1" (Taipei: Wenhai chubanshe, 1963), 1:418; Ouyang Min, *Yudi guangji,* shang, juan 9, "Jingxi beilu" (Chengdu: Sichuan daxue chubanshe, 2003), 199.

8. Shao Bowen, "Sifang jiyi juji," *Shaoshi jianwen lu,* juan 17 (Beijing: Zhonghua shuju, 1983), 186.

9. The motif of women working in a kitchen was one of the popular themes adopted in tomb decoration during the Song period and later times. See Ellen Johnston Laing, "Patterns and Problems in Later Chinese Tomb Decoration," *Journal of Oriental Studies* 16, nos. 1–2 (1978): 15.

10. Among numerous examples, a short essay by Zhang Xian discusses sliced raw fish and wine as an ideal snack for an old man to enjoy during his leisure time. See Zhang, "Zuimian ting," in *Anlu ji,* in *Fugu bian* (Yangzhou: Huainan shuju, 1903), 1a. Paintings of this subject are recorded in *Xuanhe huapu* under the entries of Du Tingmu and Zhou Wenju. See *Xuanhe huapu,* juan 6 and 7, in *Zhongguo shuhua quanshu,* ed. Lu Fusheng (Shanghai: Shanghai shuhua chubanshe, 1993), 2:79–80. The imagery of a woman slicing fish also entered the world of theater, as can be seen in the play *Wangjiangting zhongqiu qiekuai dan* (Riverside pavilion at mid-autumn: A female slicing fish); see Hsien-yi Yang and Gladys Yang, trans., *Selected Plays of Kuan Han-ch'ing* (Shanghai: New Art and Literature Publishing House, 1958; repr. Beijing: Foreign Language Press, 1979), 225–271.

11. Xu Pingfang has suggested that these three women could represent the tomb occupant's servants, judging from the content of their activities as "domestic" labor, and that assertion has been seconded by Robert Maeda; Xu Pingfang,

NOTES TO PAGES 48-49

"Songdai de zaju diaozhuan," *Wenwu* 1960, no. 5 (1960): 40. See also Liu Nianzi, "Song zaju Ding Dusai diaozhuan kao," *Wenwu* 1980, no. 2 (1980): 58–62; and Shi Zhilian, "Bei Song funü huaxiangzhuan," *Wenwu* 1979, no. 3 (1979): 87.

12. Xu Pingfang was the first scholar who identified the three brick reliefs as representations of actors and suggested that they were designed as a group separate from the other three brick panels; see Xu, "Songdai de zaju diaozhuan," 40–42.

13. Although decorating clothes or hats with flowers for men was not uncommon for special occasions such as wedding ceremonies, the distinctive headgear here is clearly linked to later representations of actors in the Jin period, where the grouping and visual coding more explicitly identify them as actors. For an example, see Wu Zimu, "Jiyue," *Mengliang lu,* juan 20, in *Dongjing menghua lu wai si zhong* (Shanghai: Shanghai gudian wenxue chubanshe, 1956), 308–309.

14. See, for example, Zhou Nan, "Liu xiansheng zhuan," in *Shanfang ji,* ed. Wang Yunwu, in *Siku quanshu zhenben san ji* (Taipei: Taiwan Shangwu yin shu guan, 1972), vol. 242, juan 4, 12b.

15. Wu Zimu, *Mengliang lu,* 308–309.

16. See Chen Shan, "Shan'gu yanshi," *Menshi xinhua,* juan 7, in *Xuxiu Siku quanshu* (Shanghai: Shanghai guji chubanshe, 1995–2002), 1122:126.

17. The entire show was composed of at least five segments, including *qubo* (prelude dancing), *yanduan, zheng zaju, sanduan* (loose farce), and *duansong* (postlude); the main sections of the performance were *yanduan* and *zhengzaju.* For interpretations of the primary sources, see Zhou Yibai, *Zhongguo xiju shi* (Shanghai: Zhonghua shuju, 1953), 99–124; and Stephen H. West, "Some Remarks on the Development of Northern Music-Drama," *Chinoperl Papers* 6 (1976): 23–44.

18. For details of *jiangshi*'s role, see Victor Mair, *Painting and Performance: Chinese Picture Recitation and Its Indian Genesis* (Honolulu: University of Hawai'i Press, 1988).

19. The entire set of Yanshi reliefs now stored in Henan Provincial Museum was damaged and subsequently reassembled, and a photographic reproduction of the reliefs in their current condition fails to capture the subtlety of their pictorial quality. While I provide photographs taken by James Cahill in about 1977, reprinted in *Artibus Asiae* 12, nos. 2–3, (1979): 132–156, I encourage readers to compare them with the almost identical reliefs discovered in Luolong Song tomb, which are in mint condition (see fig. 2.3).

20. While the paintings themselves would have facilitated such visual codification, sketches or copybooks would also have contributed to this process. On the various types of sketches used for copying in the pictorial field of the middle period, see Sarah Fraser, *Performing the Visual: The Practice of Buddhist Wall Painting in China and Central Asia, 618–960* (Stanford, CA: Stanford University Press, 2004), chap. 3, 109–130.

21. According to the *Chuogeng lu*, in the past the *fujing* role was called *canjun* (as in *canjunxi*, or adjutant play), and the *fumo* was called *canghu*; see Tao Zongyi, *Nancun Chuogeng lu*, juan 25 (Beijing: Zhonghua shuju, 2004), 304. For a detailed discussion of the origins of these role types, see Wilt Idema and Stephen H. West, eds., *Chinese Theater, 1100–1450: A Source Book* (Wiesbaden, Germany: Steiner Verlag, 1982), 64–83.

22. Wu Zimu, *Mengliang lu*, 309.

23. Nai Deweng, *Ducheng jisheng* (1235), in *Dongjing menghua lu wai si zhong*, 97. This type of whistle could be identified as the so-called barbarian whistle, or *hushao*; see J. I. Crump, "Yuan-pen, Yuan's Rowdy Ancestor," *Literature East and West* 14, no. 4 (1970): 485.

24. Du Renjie [Du Shanfu], "Zhuangjia bushi goulan," in *Lidai quhua huibian*, eds. Yu Weimin and Sun Rongrong (Hefei: Huangshan shushe, 2006), 212–213.

25. Xu Pingfang proposes that this tableau-like image is a representation of a specific play and has suggested that the figures are enacting "Walking the Parrot" (*Zouying ge*), a Jin dynasty play listed in *Chuogeng lu*; see Xu, "Songdai de zaju diaozhuan." Zhao Jingshen also agrees with Xu's identification, but provides no evidence; see Zhao Jingshen, *Xiqu bitan* (Beijing: Zhonghua shuju, 1962), 230–236. This identification is not only problematic in terms of its anachronism but also unconvincing given our lack of knowledge on the content of this *yuanben* play, which has been lost. Robert Maeda also expresses similar caution on this issue; see Robert J. Maeda, "Some Sung, Chin and Yuan Representations of Actors," *Artibus Asiae* 41 (1979): 135.

26. As with the case of the *yanduan* figure, their gender is difficult to determine, and it is possible that these are images of women cross-dressing for a performance; see Xu, "Songdai de zaju diaozhuan."

27. See West, "Some Remarks on the Development of Northern Music-Drama."

28. Zhao Jingshen has proposed that this object wrapped inside could be an official's seal, and that assertion has been seconded by Robert Maeda; see Zhao, *Xiqu bitan*, 230–236; and Maeda, "Some Sung, Chin and Yuan Representations of Actors," 135–136.

29. Zhao Jingshen has gone so far as to suggest that this scene could represent a particular play from the Yuan period. It is unreasonable, however, to pair this image with one of these *yuanben* plays because the content of the play is unknown (lost) and only its title survived. See Zhao, *Xiqu bitan*, 231–232. For the surviving titles of Jin *yuanben*, including these two, see also Tao Zongyi, "Yuanben mingmu," *Nancun Chuogeng lu*, juan 25 (Beijing: Zhonghua shuju, 2004), 306–315.

30. On these two concepts, see Wu Hung, *The Wu Liang Shrine: The Ideology of Early Chinese Pictorial Art* (Stanford, CA: Stanford University Press, 1989), 132–140.

31. Laura Mulvey, *Visual and Other Pleasures* (Bloomington: Indiana University Press, 1989). The concept of "suture" helps identify this relief as a representation

of actors on stage, which involves the prototype (the actual theatrical performance), the representation (the brick relief), and the audience of the prototype
(the potential or imaginary viewer of this representation).

32. See Li Jie, *Yingzao fashi,* juan 25 (Beijing: Zhongguo shudian, 2006), 2:548–
549. For a detailed introduction to this text, see Else Glahn, "On the Transmission of the Ying-Tsao Fa-Shih," *T'oung Pao* 61, nos. 4–5 (1974): 232–265;
see also Jiren Feng, *Chinese Architecture and Metaphor: Song Culture in the
Yingzao Fashi Building Manual* (Honolulu: University of Hawai'i Press,
2012). For an introduction to tile making, see Tananka Tan, *Chūgoku kenchikushi no kenkyū* (Tokyo: Kōbundō, 1989), 355–424.

33. See the section "Hunzuo diao" (Mixed methods in carving) in *Diaozuo zhidu*
(Manual on carving) in Li, *Yingzao fashi,* juan 12, 1:250–255.

34. Robert Maeda and Liao Ben have suggested that the first stage of this process
must have been based on a painting or drawing, but it is difficult to prove this
point without solid evidence; see Maeda, "Some Sung, Chin and Yuan Representations of Actors," 136; and Liao Ben, *Zhongguo xiju tushi* (Zhengzhou:
Henan jiaoyu chubanshe, 1996), 153.

35. Xu Huadang, *Zhongguo chuantong nisu* (Beijing: Renmin meishu chubanshe,
2005).

36. Luoyangshi wenwu gongzuo dui, "Luoyang Luolongqu Guanlinmiao Song dai
zhuandiao mu"; Hebei sheng bowuguan, *Henan gudai taosu yishu* (Zhengzhou: Daxiang chubanshe, 2005), 143.

37. This set of reliefs was excavated in 2005. Official reports of these new finds
have not been published, but I was able to examine the reliefs that were on
view in the Jiaozuo Museum in September 2005. For the excavation report of
the Wenxian tomb found in 1982, see Zhang Siqing and Wu Yongzheng,
"Wenxian Song mu fajue jianbao," *Zhongyuan wenwu* 1983, no. 1 (1983): 19–20.

38. On the Baisha reliefs, see Su Bai, "Baisha Song mu zhong de zaju zhuandiao,"
Kaogu 1960, no. 9 (1960): 59–60.

39. Xu, *Zhongguo chuantong nisu,* 122–126.

40. The aforementioned brick reliefs excavated from Wenxian, Henan Province,
in 2005 display relatively vivid colors on all of the figures: black on hair,
eyebrows, headgear, and parts of clothes; red on lips, hats, and clothes; and
white on headgear, shoes, and clothes.

41. See Song Yingxing, "Zhuan," in *Tiangong kaiwu* (Guangzhou: Guangdong
renmin chubanshe, 1976), 184–190.

42. According to historical texts and the epitaph for Wang Chuzhi (d. 923), after
serving as a regional military governor at various places Wang finally became
king of Beiping; see Hebei sheng wenwu yanjiusuo and Baoding shi wenwu
guanlichu, *Wudai Wang Chuzhi mu* (Beijing: Wenwu chubanshe, 1998),
56–60.

43. A native of Gaotang County, Shandong Province, Feng Hui served in the
imperial courts and became king of Chenliu Prefecture; see Xianyang shi
wenwu kaogu yanjiusuo, *Wudai Fenghui mu* (Chongqing: Chongqing chubanshe, 2001): 57–61.

44. For an example of early models for this type of composition and medium, see the well-known Northern Wei relief of the imperial procession in Cave 1, Gongxian County, Henan Province, reproduced in Angela Falco Howard et al., *Chinese Sculpture* (New Haven, CT: Yale University Press and Beijing: Foreign Language Press, 2006), plate 3.47.

45. Going back to the Warring States period, the seat for the spirit of the deceased was commonly represented in a tomb, taking architectonic, pictorial, or mixed form; see Wu Hung, *The Art of the Yellow Springs: Understanding Chinese Tombs* (Honolulu: University of Hawaiʻi Press, 2010), 64–84.

46. Two panels of brick were used in representing each figure; the overall size of each figure (approximately seventy to seventy-five centimeters high) is much larger than later brick reliefs such as the Yanshi reliefs. See Xianyang shi wenwu kaogu yanjiusuo, *Wudai Fenghui mu,* 57–61. Composing one figure with two pieces of brick seems to have been a practical concern: given the fragility of clay brick compared to stone, it would have been much easier to work with smaller panels. A set of a similar type of reliefs that represent musicians and dancers was also found in the tomb of another military official, Li Maozhen, and his wife (ca. 924) in Baoji, Shanxi Province. See Baoji shi kaogu yanjiusuo, ed., *Wudai Li Maozhen fufu mu* (Beijing: Kexue chubanshe, 2008).

47. On either side of the entrance to both side chambers are the images of female attendants, standing in a three-quarter view toward the entrance. Although seriously damaged, there are fragmented images of several coiled bunches of coins, as well as of food and tea utensils on a table painted on the south wall. Except for these walls adjacent to the doorways, the rest of the walls in the chamber are painted with flower patterns. Xianyang shi wenwu kaogu yanjiusuo, *Wudai Fenghui mu,* 57–61.

48. Wu Hung, *The Double Screen: Medium and Representation in Chinese Painting* (Chicago: University of Chicago Press, 1996), 102.

49. For a discussion of the painterly effect of the stone reliefs, see Gustave Ecke and Paul Demiéville, *The Twin Pagodas of Zayton: A Study of Later Sculpture in China* (Cambridge, MA: Harvard University Press, 1935).

50. Maeda, "Some Sung, Chin, and Yuan Representations of Actors," 136.

51. See Guo Ruoxu, "Lun Cao Wu tifa," *Tuhua jianwen zhi,* juan 1, in Lu, ed., *Zhongguo shuhua quanshu* (Shanghai: Shanghai shuhua chubanshe, 1993), 1:469.

52. See Dong You, "Ba Li Xiang shou Wusheng renwu," *Guangchuan huaba,* juan 6, in Lu, ed., *Zhongguo shuhua quanshu,* 1:843. See also Zhang Yuanyan's account of Wu's sculptures in Xiangguo si and two students of Wu's, Zhang Xianqiao and Wang Nai'er, who were also famous for their excellent molding skills; Zhang Yanyuan, *Lidai minghua ji,* juan 8, in Lu, ed., *Zhongguo shuhua quanshu,* 1:153.

53. In this sense, Maeda's characterization of this particular visual effect as associated with the "realism" sought by contemporary court painters in the painting academy of emperor Huizong is misleading; Maeda, "Some Sung,

Chin, and Yuan Representations of Actors," 136. What was encouraged in Huizong's academy was the "resemblance" of a representation to its prototype in minute detail. The results of such a style, as seen in works by Huizong and other court painters, were paintings that faithfully sought the natural logic behind the prototypes—mostly birds and flowers—as species rather than as actual life in nature, and this hardly attempted to "deceive" the eyes of a beholder.

54. See Deng Chun, *Hua ji,* juan 9, in Lu, ed., *Zhongguo shuhua quanshu,* 2:723. I do not follow the common, literal translation of the term as "shadow," for reasons explained below. For brief discussions of this term in the pictorial context, see Susan Bush and Hsiao-yen Shih, eds., *Early Chinese Texts on Painting* (Cambridge, MA: Harvard-Yenching Institute and Harvard University Press, 1985), 122; and Valarie Ortiz, *Dreaming the Southern Song Landscape: The Power of Illusion in Chinese Painting* (Boston: Brill, 1999), 127.

55. See Liu Daochun, "Suzuomen di liu," in *Wudai minghua buyi,* in Lu, ed., *Zhongguo shuhua quanshu,* 1:463. For Zhang Sengyou's biography, see Zhang, *Lidai minghua ji,* juan 7, 1:147; and Wu Shichu, *Zhang Sengyao* (Shanghai: Shanghai renmin chubanshe, 1963).

56. For the most recent and thorough study of Guo's career and paintings, see Ping Foong, *The Efficacious Landscape: On the Authorities of Painting at the Northern Song Court* (Cambridge, MA: Harvard Asia Center, 2015).

57. See Xu Song, *Jiankang shilu,* juan 17, *SKQS* 370:24b. Use of shadowing effect along with contrasting colors such as brown, green, and black is abundantly found in Mogao cave murals in Dunhuang executed during the medieval period.

58. The term *Yingbi* here should not be confused with a term with identical characters, *yingbi* (also called *zhaobi*), a screen placed inside or outside a traditional *siheyuan* house or palace, or behind a host or occupant of a room. While it is one possibility that the later terms for screen walls might have derived from this special term in the Song dynasty, the folk beliefs on the function of screen walls have little to do with the Song term. The Qing dynasty author Shen Zinan, while recognizing the similarity of the two terms, makes no remarks about how they are related; see Shen Zinan, *Yilin huikao,* juan 8, "Dongyu pian," *SKQS* 859:86.

59. Mary Fong, "The Technique of 'Chiaroscuro' in Chinese Painting from Han to T'ang," *Artibus Asiae* 38, nos. 2–3 (1976): 96–127.

60. "Hua Yuntai shan ji," collected in Zhang, *Lidai minghua ji,* juan 5, 1:141.

61. See Zhang Yanyuan, *Lidai minghua ji,* juan 9, 152.

62. Zeng Zao, *Leishu,* juan 34, *SKQS* 873:596. This idea also applies to the well-known illusionistic painting *Double Screen (Zhong ping tu)* by tenth-century painter Zhou Wenju, which centers on the role of *ying* as a permeable sphere that both separates and connects various layers of space that exist between a viewer and the image. On the concept of illusionism and metapicture in this particular context, see Wu, *The Double Screen,* 102–121;

see also W. J. T. Mitchell, "Metapicture," in *Picture Theory: Essays on Verbal and Visual Representation* (Chicago: University of Chicago Press, 1994), 35–82.

63. This oft-cited discourse involves an actual mountain cave in Nagarahara in present-day Afghanistan and a "replica" of the cave temple in Mount Lu constructed by the Chinese monk Huiyuan (334–427). For the original tale, see Buddhabhadra, trans., *Fo shuo guanfo sanmei hai jing,* in *Taishō shīnshu Daizōkyō,* ed. Takakusu Junjirō and Watanabe Kaigyoku, vol. 15, no. 643 (Tokyo: Taishō Issaikyo Kankokai, 1914–1932), 681b; and Alexander Soper and Seigai Omura, *Literary Evidence for Early Buddhist Art in China* (Ascona, Switzerland: Artibus Asiae, 1959), 265–266. For the original passage on Huiyuan's cave temple in Mount Lu, see Huiyuan, "Foying ming," in Daoxuan, *Guang Hongming ji,* in Takakusu and Watanabe, eds., *Taishō shīnshu Daizōkyō,* vol. 52, no. 2103, 197c–198b. For a brief introduction to this sutra and translations of relevant passages, see Erik Zürcher, *Buddhist Conquest of China* (Leiden, Netherlands: Brill, 1959), 224–225.

64. Susan Bush introduces both translations; see Bush, "Tsung Ping's Essay on Painting Landscape and the 'Landscape Buddhism' of Mount Lu," in *Theories of the Arts in China,* ed. Susan Bush and Christian Murck (Princeton, NJ: Princeton University Press, 1983), 137, and n24. Raoul Birnbaum renders it "reflection," underlying the sense of emitting light from the Buddha's body; Birnbaum, "Buddhist Meditation Teachings and the Birth of 'Pure' Landscape Painting in China," *Journal of Chinese Religions* 9 (1981): 51. Eugene Wang characterizes this as a "luminous reflection on the wall . . . an image registered on a flat surface"; see Wang, *Shaping the Lotus Sutra: Buddhist Visual Culture in Medieval China* (Seattle: University of Washington Press, 2005), 246.

65. On Zong Bing's life, and a brief introduction to his two texts "Hua Shanshui xu" (Preface to *Painting Landscape*) and "Ming Fo lun" (Discussion on the illumination of the Buddha), see Nakamura Shigeo, *Chūgoku garon no tenkai: Shin To So Gen* (Kyoto, Japan: Nakayama Bunkadō, 1965), 59–81. For an insightful interpretation of "Hua Shanshui xu," see Jerome Silbergeld, "Re-reading Zong Bing's Fifth-Century Essay on Landscape Painting: A Few Critical Notes," in *A Life in Chinese Art: Essays in Honour of Michael Sullivan,* ed. Shelagh Vainker and Xin Chen (Oxford: Ashmolean Museum, 2012), 30–39.

66. Shen Kuo, *Mengxi bitan,* juan 17, in *Mengxi bitan jiaozheng* (Shanghai: Shanghai guji chubanshe, 1987), 1:549–550. The identical account appears in an essay collection by Jiang Shaoyu (fl. twelfth century); see Jiang Shaoyu, *Shishi leiyuan,* juan 54, *SKQS* 874:450.

67. One of the best-known examples of this discourse is Su Shi's appraisal of Wen Tong's principle of painting bamboos. See Su Shi, "Wen Yuke hua Xundang gu yan zhu ji," *Dongpo quanji,* juan 36, *SKQS* 1107:513–514, as translated in Bush and Shih, eds., *Early Chinese Texts on Painting,* 37.

68. Liu Daochun, *Shengchao minghua ping,* juan 3, in Lu, ed., *Zhongguo shuhua quanshu,* 1:456. Here I follow the translation in Charles H. Lachman, trans., *Evaluations of Sung Dynasty Painters of Renown: Liu Tao-ch'un's Sung-ch'ao ming-hua p'ing* (Leiden, Netherlands: Brill, 1989), 79.

69. On the importance of this topic, and for an in-depth discussion of the meanings of two forms of the "portrait" of the deceased, see Wu, *The Art of the Yellow Springs,* 68–84. By focusing on the performative potential of the imagery in a tomb, Jonathan Hay's study of murals in Tang-dynasty imperial tombs proposes an interesting framework for understanding the issue of viewership and gaze in tomb chambers; Jonathan Hay, "Seeing through Dead Eyes: How Early Tang Tombs Staged Afterlife," *Res: Anthropology and Aesthetics* 57–58 (2010): 17–54.

70. Dong, "Yanshi xian Jiuliu gou shuiku Song mu," 84. According to the report, the coffin bed, measuring 234 centimeters long, 100 centimeters wide, and 16 centimeters high, occupies the innermost section of the tomb, which covers almost half of the entire space.

71. When there is a representation of the deceased in the tomb, the dynamics of the gaze are altered; see the discussion in chapter 3.

72. Guo Tuan, *Kui che zhi,* juan 5, in Xu Lingyun and Xu Shanshu eds., *Tang Song biji xiaoshuo san zhong* (Hefei: Huangshan shushe, 1991), 139.

73. For a historical account on such a setting, see Xu Mengxin, *San chao bei meng huibian* (Shanghai: Shanghai guji chubanshe, 1987), 2:139.

74. For compilations of actors' words, see Wang Guowei, *Youyu lu,* in Xue Ruizhao, *Song Jin xiju shi gao* (Beijing: Sanlian shudian, 2005), appendix.

75. Yang Wanli, "Shi hua," *Chengzhai ji,* juan 115, *SKQS* 1161:453.

76. Ibid.

77. The original line is, "To govern them by means of not governing is that by which they are truly governed"; Su Shi, "Wangzhe buzhi yidi lun," *Dongpo quanji,* juan 40, *SKQS* 1107:554–555.

CHAPTER 3: THEATER OF THE DEAD

Portions of chapter 3 appeared as "Virtual Theater of the Dead: Actor Figurines and Their Stage in Houma Tomb No.1, Shanxi Province," in *Artibus Asiae* 71, no. 1 (2011): 75–114. Reprinted by permission.

1. Xu Mengxin, "Jingkang zhong zhi 52," in *San chao bei meng huibian,* juan 77 (Shanghai: Shanghai guji chubanshe, 1987), 1:583.

2. For the dating of this play, see Liao Ben, "Nanxi *Huanmen zidi cuo li shen* shidai kaobian," in *Zhongguo xiqu de chantui* (Beijing: Wenhua yishu chubanshe, 1989), 399–400. For English translations, see *Grandee's Son Takes the Wrong Career,* in *Eight Chinese Plays from the Thirteenth Century to the Present,* trans. William Dolby (New York: Columbia University Press, 1978), 30–52; and *A Playboy from a Noble House Opts for the Wrong Career,* trans. Wilt Idema and Stephen H. West in Idema and West, *Chinese Theater,*

1100–1450: A Source Book (Wiesbaden, Germany: Steiner Verlag, 1982), 205–235.

3. Shanxisheng wenwu guanli weiyuanhui Houma gongzuozhan, "Houma Jindai Dong shi mu jieshao," *Wenwu* 1959, no. 6 (1959): 50.

4. Wang Zhu, *Tujie jiaozheng dili xinshu,* 1192 ed. (Taipei: Jiwen shuju, 1985). A preface, "Jingjia jiaozheng buwan dili xinshu," which is included in the same volume, specifically mentions the popularity of this text in the area.

5. Both burials included a land deed with similar contents, identifying the occupants as brothers of a Dong family; Shanxisheng wenwu guanli weiyuanhui Houma gongzuozhan, "Houma Jindai Dong shi mu jieshao." Because the contents of the tombs, including the reliefs covering all the interior walls, have been reported to be identical, I refer here only to the main burial space—that is, to the older brother Dong Qijian's tomb. For an in-depth discussion of the significance in the furnishing of tombs with identical images, including portraits, see Jeehee Hong, "Changing Roles of the Tomb Portrait: Burial Practices and Ancestral Worship of Non-literati Elite in North China (1000–1400)," *Journal of Song-Yuan Studies* 44 (forthcoming).

6. There were two kinds of cremation practiced between the Song and Yuan periods: one was cremating a body and scattering the remains, and the other was a Buddhist practice in which the cremated bodies were enshrined in a sanctioned place; see Xu Pingfang, "Song Yuan shidai de huozang," *Wenwu cankao ziliao* 1956, no. 9 (1956): 21–26. See also Patricia Buckley Ebrey, "Cremation in Song China," *American Historical Review* 95, no. 2 (1990): 406–428.

7. For a discussion of three major burial types found in the Jin territory from the early twelfth through the early thirteenth centuries, see Qin Dashu, *Song Yuan Ming kaogu* (Beijing: Wenwu chubanshe, 2004), 212–214. On Jin dynasty tombs found in Shanxi, see Shi Xueqian, "Shilun Shanxi diqu de Jin mu," *Kaogu yu wenwu* 1988, no. 3 (1988): 88–92. For brief accounts on Jurchen-style burials, see *Da Jin guo zhi,* juan 39, in Yuwen Maozhao, ed., *Da Jin guo zhi jiaozheng,* annotated by Cui Wenyin (Beijing: Zhonghua shuju, 1986), 551–552.

8. See Tuo tuo, "Xizong benji (Huangtong si nian)," in *Jin shi* (Beijing: Zhonghua shuju, 1975), 80.

9. The administrative divisions were not affected by the dynastic shift either. Specifically, Houma city had belonged to Jiangzhou since the Song period, and this division did not change during the Jin. See Tuo tuo, *Song shi,* juan 86, "Dili zhi" 2 (Beijing: Zhonghua shuju, 1977); and Tuo tuo et al., *Jin shi,* juan 26, "Dili xia" (Beijing: Zhonghua shuju, 1975), 634–635.

10. Shanxisheng kaogu yanjiusuo Houma gongzuozhan, "Houma liangzuo Jindai jinianmu fajue baogao," *Wenwu jikan* 1996, no. 3 (1996): 65–78; Yang Fudou, "Shanxi Houma 104 hao Jin mu," *Kaogu yu wenwu* 1983, no. 6 (1983): 32–39; and Shanxisheng kaogu yanjiusuo Houma gongzuozhan, "Houma 65H4M102 Jin mu," *Wenwu jikan* 1997, no. 4 (1997): 17–27.

11. This cemetery belonged to the extended family of a local man named Duan Ji; see Shanxisheng kaogu yanjiusuo, "Shanxi Jishan Jin mu fajue jianbao,"

Wenwu 1983, no. 1 (1983): 45–63. Some of the burial chambers in this cemetery will be discussed in detail later in this chapter.

12. On the dramatists from middle and southern Shanxi in the Yuan period, see Wang Guowei, "Yuan xiqu jia xiao zhuan," in *Wang Guowei xiqu lunwenji* (Beijing: Zhongguo xiju chubanshe, 1957), 140–146. See also the lists of the Yuan dramatists in Zhong Sicheng, *Lugui bu,* juan *shang,* in *Lugui bu wai si zhong* (Shanghai: Shanghai guji chubanshe, 1978). For primary sources on regional printing, see Song Lian, *Yuan shi,* juan 2, "Taizong" (Beijing: Zhonghua shuju, 1977), 30; Kong Tianjian, "Cangshu ji," in *Jinwen zui,* ed. Zhang Jinwu, juan 28 (Guangzhou: Yue'ya tang, 1882), 5a–6b. For a brief introduction to this topic, see Zhang Xiumin, *Zhongguo yinshua shi* (Shanghai: Shanghai renmin chubanshe, 1989), 247. These two aspects—the flourishing of drama and print—seem to be closely interrelated, but this matter falls outside the scope of the current study.

13. When there is a discrepancy in patterns or colors on the figurines between what is observable now and what is drawn in the article as a visual documentation published just after the excavation, I follow the drawing. See Liu Nianzi, "Zhongguo xiqu wutai yishu zai shi san shiji chuye yijing xingcheng—Jin dai Houma Dong mu wutai diaocha baogao," *Xiju yanjiu* 2 (1959): 61–62.

14. Zhou Yibai, "Houma Dong shi mu zhong wuge zhuanyong de yanjiu," *Wenwu* 1959, no. 10 (1959): 50–52. The term *yuanben wuren* derives from Tao Zongyi's *Chuogeng lu,* in the section where five role types of Jin opera are described; see Tao Zongyi, *Nancun Chuogeng lu,* juan 25 (Beijing: Zhonghua shuju, 2004), 306.

15. Commonly called *dian qing* (blue [ink] dotting), tattoos or ink paintings on arms were popular during the Tang and Song periods; see Duan Chengshi, "Qing," in *Youyang zazu,* juan 8, *SKQS* 1047:686–689.

16. For the identification of the figurines, hereafter I largely rely on the study of the role types of the five figurines in Zhou Yibai, "Houma Dong shi mu zhong wuge zhuanyong de yanjiu," *Wenwu* 1959, no. 10 (1959): 50–52. According to the *Taihe zhengyin pu,* the term *gu* means a character on stage who dresses like an official; see Zhu Quan, "Cilin xuzhi," in *Taihe zhengyin pu,* in Zhong Sicheng, *Lugui bu wai si zhong,* 164. The fourteenth-century text *Chuogeng lu* states that a *guzhuang* was also called *wuhua cuannong*; the phrase derives from a Song period anecdote by Huizong (r. 1101–1126) about receiving tribute from the court of Cuanguo; see Tao Zongyi, *Nancun Chuogeng lu,* juan 25, 306. The origins of the terms *guzhuang* and *cuan* and the historical connection between them remain unclear; only by the late Yuan period did *wuhua cuannong* become a common term referring to five operatic role types. See Xia Tingzhi, *Qinglou ji,* in *Qinglou ji jianzhu,* annotated by Sun Chongtao and Xu Hongtu (Beijing: Zhongguo xiju chubanshe, 1990), 43.

17. Zhou, "Houma Dong shi mu," 52. According to the *Ducheng jisheng,* a *moni* plays the central role in drama; Nai Deweng, *Ducheng jisheng,* in *Dongjing menghua lu wai si zhong* (Beijing: Zhonghua shuhu, 1962), 96.

18. Zhou Yibai identifies this figurine as a *yinxi,* citing brief accounts of a character in texts such as the *Ducheng jisheng* and the thirteenth-century song suite (*sanqu*) "Zhuangjia bushi goulan"; see Zhou, "Houma Dong shi mu," 51. Note, however, that these texts tell us only the role that a *yinxi* plays—"opening the performance"—rather than providing any visual information that might be helpful in identifying the figurine.

19. Du Renjie, "Zhuangjia bushi goulan." The translation here is from "Introduction," in *Monks, Bandits, Lovers, and Immortals: Eleven Early Chinese Plays,* ed. Stephen H. West and Wilt Idema (Indianapolis, IN: Hackett, 2010), 14. For the original text and a brief note about the author, see "Du Renjie," in *Lidai quhua huibian,* ed. Yu Weimin and Sun Rongrong (Hefei: Huangshan shushe, 2006), 211–213. For discussions and other translations of this *sanqu,* see Ogawa Yōichi, "Du Shanfu saku Zhuangjia bushi goulan yakuchū," *Shūkan Tōyōgaku* 18 (1967): 78–86; Stephen H. West, *Vaudeville and Narrative: Aspects of Chin Theater* (Wiesbaden, Germany: Steiner Verlag, 1977), 11–17; and Idema and West, *Chinese Theater,* 64–83.

20. The sequence is clearly discussed and illustrated in Du Renjie [Du Shanfu], "Zhuangjia bushi goulan," in *Lidai quhua huibian,* ed. Yu Weimin and Sun Rongrong (Hefei: Huangshan shushe, 2006), 212–213.

21. See, for example, Sanmenxia shi wenwu gongzuodui and Yima shi wenwuguanli weiyuanhui, "Yima shi Jin dai zhuandiao mu fajue jianbao," *Huaxia kaogu* 41 (1993): 91. Valerie Hansen, in her discussion of the common positioning of a pair of identical tomb contracts (*maidiquan*) during a funerary ritual, suggests in passing that this stage was designed to be viewed by the gods. She reasons that the stage was positioned at the same height as the contract so that the gods could see both easily. The underlying assumption here is that stages in Chinese temples are often built in front of the main hall in order for the gods to see the performances. But this speculation is difficult to follow for two reasons: the miniature stage here was not necessarily modeled after a temple stage; and because tomb contracts buried in tombs belonged essentially to the dead, not to the gods, there is no reason to think that the contract (hence the theater as well) was to be seen by the gods, since they had their own copy of the contract. See Valerie Hansen, *Negotiating Daily Life in Traditional China: How Ordinary People Used Contracts, 600–1400* (New Haven, CT: Yale University Press, 1995), 178–179.

22. For studies on the ritual implications of tomb portraits in the middle period, see Li Qingquan, "'Yitang jiaqing' de xin yixiang: Song Jin shiqi de muzhu fufu xiang yu Tang Song muzang fengqi zhi bian," in *Gudai muzang meishu yanjiu,* ed. Wu Hung, Zhu Qingsheng, and Zheng Yan, vol. 2 (Changsha: Hunan meishu chubahshe, 2013), 317–335; Jeehee Hong, "Changing Roles of the Tomb Portrait: Burial Practices and Ancestral Worship of Non-Literati Elite in North China (1000–1400)," *Journal of Song-Yuan Studies* 44 (forthcoming).

23. Judging from the epitaph found in Tomb No. 7 of the same cemetery and dated coins also found there, the dates of the tombs in the Duan family

cemetery range between 1110 and 1181. See Shanxisheng kaogu yanjiusuo, "Shanxi Jishan Jin mu fajue jianbao," 45–63.

24. For the location of the figurines, see Liao Ben, *Song Yuan xiqu wenwu yu minsu* (Beijing: Wenhua yishu chubanshe, 1989), 99.

25. For two distinctive modes of portraying the deceased in a tomb space (i.e., figurative representation, and pictorial implication of its existence by rendering only an unoccupied seat), see Wu Hung, *The Art of the Yellow Springs: Understanding Chinese Tombs* (Honolulu: University of Hawai'i Press, 2010), 63–84.

26. The prominence of the actors in this burial space is even more accentuated than the Dong couple's in that there is no other image of humans except the two attendants. See Shanxisheng kaogu yanjiusuo Houma gongzuo zhan, "Jishan xian huafei chang Jin mu fajue baogao," *Wenwu shijie* 2011, no. 4 (2011): 6–9; and *Sheng si tong le*, ed. Shi Jinming and Hai Weilan (Beijing: Kexue chubanshe, 2012).

27. *Li Ji,* "Tangong xia," translated and annotated by Yang Tianyu, in *Li ji yizhu, shang* (Shanghai: Shanghai guji chubanshe, 1997), 151–152. On the historical significance of the discourse, see Wu Hung, "On Tomb Figurines: The Beginning of a Visual Tradition," in *Body and Face in Chinese Visual Culture,* ed. Wu Hung and Katherine R. Tsiang (Cambridge, MA: Harvard University Press, 2005), 13–14.

28. For new developments in *mingqi* making during the middle period, see Jeehee Hong, "Mechanism of Life for the Netherworld: Tranformations of *Mingqi* in Middle-Period China," *Journal of Chinese Religions* 43, no. 2 (2015): 161–193.

29. Although it chiefly introduces pre-Song stories, the *Taiping* is invaluable in understanding popular beliefs about supernatural phenomena including unnatural deaths and ghosts during the late Tang period; see Li Fang, *Taiping guangji* (Shanghai: Shanghai guji chubanshe, 1990). For a discussion of its circulation, see Zhang Guofeng, *Taiping guangji banben kaoshu* (Beijing: Zhonghua shuju, 2004).

30. Jessica Rawson, "Changes in the Representation of Life and the Afterlife as Illustrated by the Contents of Tombs of the T'ang and Sung Period," in *Arts of the Sung and Yuan,* ed. Maxwell Hearn and Judith Smith (New York: Metropolitan Museum of Art, 1996), 32–33. For an English translation of the text, see Glen Dudbridge, *Religious Experience and Lay Society in T'ang China: A Reading of Tai Fu's* Kuang-i chi (Cambridge: Cambridge University Press, 1995), appendix no. 159 and no. 162. For a revised edition of the original Chinese text, see Dai Fu, *Guang yi ji,* punctuated and annotated by Liu Dengge (Beijing: Beijing chubanshe, 2000).

31. Li Fang, "Cao Hui," *Taiping guangji,* juan 371 (Xiongqi shang), *SKQS* 1044: 632–633. Li Fang notes that the episode was originally recorded in the lost text *Xuanguai lu.*

32. Li, "Cao Hui," 633.

33. *Mengzi zhengyi,* annotated by Jiao Xun (Beijing: Zhonghua shuju, 1987), 63; *Li ji yizhu,* annotated by Yang Tianyu, 1:151–152. For an insightful discussion of this issue, see Wu Hung, "On Tomb Figurines," 13–14.

34. See Huan Kuan, *Yantie lun,* juan 7, *SKQS* 695:579.

35. See Liu Xi, *Shi ming,* juan 8, *SKQS* 221:423.

36. Ren Guang, *Shuxu zhinan,* juan 20, *SKQS* 920:594.

37. Gao Cheng, "Mingqi," *Shiwu jiyuan,* juan 9 (Beijing: Zhonghua shuju, 1989), 480.

38. Meng Yuanlao, "Zhongyuan jie," *Dongjing menghua lu,* juan 8, in *Dongjing menghua lu jianzhu,* annotated by Yi Yongwen (Beijing: Zhonghua shuju, 2006), 2:794–795.

39. Wu Zimu, "Tuanhang," *Mengliang lu,* juan 13, in *Dongjing menghua lu wai si zhong* (Beijing: Zhonghua shuhu, 1962), 239. Wu says at the beginning of the entry that these merchants were called *tuanhang,* as they were itinerant merchants working for the government.

40. *Da Han yuanling mizang jing,* in *Yongle dadian,* vol. 8199 (Beijing: Zhonghua shuju, 1959), 25a–27b. For an introduction to this text, see Xu Pingfang, "Tang Song muzang zhong de 'mingqi shensha' yu 'muyi' zhidu," *Kaogu* 1963, no. 2 (1963): 87–106.

41. Chen Chun, "Da Chen Baizao ba," *Beixi da quanji,* juan 27, *SKQS* 1168: 717–718. Even though Chen's text is mainly about his contemporaries in the Southern Song, when it is taken together with Zhao Yanwei's account, it seems most likely that the practice of making paper figurines had already begun in the northern Song and became widespread in the south as well as the north.

42. See Gu Yanwu, "*Han shu* zhu," *Rizhi lu,* juan 27, *SKQS* 858:1005.

43. Su Bai's suggestion is based on relevant accounts in the *Dongjing menghua lu, Zhenghe wuli xinyi, Liao shi,* and *Zizhi tongjian;* see Su Bai, *Baisha Song mu,* 2nd ed. (Beijing: Wenwu chubanshe, 2002), 94–95n39. See also Tuo tuo et al., *Song shi,* juan 124 (Xiong li 3), 2898.

44. Among the *mingqi* discovered in middle period tombs were a new type of object both visually plausible and physically operable for the living. See Hong, "Mechanism of Life for the Netherworld," 161–193.

45. Due to their perishable nature, wooden figurines buried in tombs rarely survived, but we know from the writings of eleventh-century author Gao Cheng that various kinds of wooden figurines were put in tombs at that time; see Gao Cheng, "Tong ren," *Shiwu jiyuan,* juan 9, 480.

46. There are, for example, two figurines of male and female attendants found in a Jin dynasty tomb excavated in Xinlifeng, Jiaozuo, Henan Province; see Henan bowuyuan ed., *Henan gudai taosu yishu* (Zhengzhou: Daxiang chubanshe, 2005), 357.

47. See Meng Yuanlao, "Qixi," *Dongjing menghua lu,* juan 8, 2:780–781.

48. Lu You, "Ba Song shan jingyu ji," *Weinan wenji,* juan 29, in *Lu You ji, SKQS* 1163:533.

49. Lu You, *Laoxue an biji*, juan 5, *SKQS* 865:39.

50. Wang Ye, "Henan zhongbu yibei faxian de zaoqi youshang duose caihui taoci," *Wenwu* 2006, no. 2 (2006): 54–95. The distribution of these ceramic figurines is extensive, including southern Shanxi, southern Hebei, central and northern Henan, central Shandong, Jiangsu, and Anhui provinces; a few were also found in Shanxi, Hubei, and Zhejiang provinces. Most, however, were found in central and northern Henan.

51. Su Ming, "Chengwu chutu Jin dai wu cai ciren," *Wenwu* 1993, no. 11 (1993): 88–89.

52. Shanxisheng wenwu guanli weiyuanhui Houma gongzuozhan, "Houma Jindai Dong shi mu jieshao," 55.

53. For a discussion of the concept and practice of *shengqi,* see Wu Hung, "Shengqi de gainian yu shijian," *Wenwu* 2010, no. 1 (2010): 87–96; and Wu, *The Art of the Yellow Springs*, 163–173.

54. The image of the Song actress Ding Dusai discussed in this volume's prelude is the only example excavated from tombs so far that had an actual real-life model. Yet this image can be identified as such only by the cartouche on the image that indicates her name, not by her physiognomic features or gesture.

55. For the concept of "type" in Chinese funerary context, see Ladislav Kesner, "Portrait Aspects and Social Functions of Chinese Ceramic Tomb Sculpture," *Orientations* 22, no. 8 (1991): 33–42.

56. Kesner, "Portrait Aspects and Social Functions of Chinese Ceramic Tomb Sculpture," 33–42.

57. For a useful discussion of the cross-cultural phenomenon of a multi-identity play, especially in literature and films, see Wendy Doniger, *The Woman Who Pretended to Be Who She Was: Myths of Self-Imitation* (New York: Oxford University Press, 2005).

58. Hong Mai, "Shi zhi chushi," in *Rongzhai suibi,* shang, juan 14 (Beijing: Zhonghua shuju, 2005), 180. Given the context, the *canjun* here most likely refers to an adjutant role (*canjun se*) that derived from the old adjutant play (*canjun xi*) in the Tang period, which was later developed into the *guzhuang* role; see Zhao Yanwei, *Yunlu manchao,* juan 5 (Beijing: Zhonghua shuju, 1998), 86. For a similar analogy, see Wang Anshi, *Linchuan wenji,* juan 10, "Gu shi," *SKQS* 1105:71; Li Bi, *Wang Jinggong shi zhu,* juan 14, *SKQS* 1106:98.

59. Wang Guowei, "Shanggu zhi Wudai zhi xiju," in *Song Yuan xiqu kao,* in *Wang Guowei xiqu lunwenji,* 9–12.

60. Wu Hung, "On Tomb Figurines," 22–25.

61. Given that the standardized sizes of architectural components were highly important in the Song period and afterward, the meaning of such downsizing would have also had equal weight; see Li Jie, *Yingzao fashi* (Beijing: Zhongguo shudian, 2006).

62. Ellen Johnston Laing, "Patterns and Problems in Later Chinese Tomb Decoration," *Journal of Oriental Studies* 16, nos. 1–2 (1978):16–17. The initial

observation of the structure as a *siheyuan* courtyard was made in the excavation report.

63. Ibid., 17–18.
64. For discussions of the development of the stage during the Song, Jin, and Yuan periods, see Ding Mingyi, "Shanxi zhongnan bu de Song Yuan wutai," *Wenwu* 1972, no. 4 (1972): 47–56; and Liao Ben, "Song Yuan xitai yiji—Zhongguo gudai juchang wenwu yanjiu zhi yi," *Wenwu* 1989, no. 7 (1989): 82–95.
65. The case of the Houma Tomb No. 104 makes a good comparison in that there are certain architectural elements that belong to imperial buildings rather than to commoners' houses, such as a high Mount Sumeru throne (*xumizuo*); see Yang, "Shanxi Houma 104 hao Jin mu," 38. Nancy Steinhardt suggests an architectural connection between most Jin tombs and the contemporaneous Buddhist humble hall (*tingtang*), which both consist of a single, rectangular room. Regardless of the question of how to define the interior space of the tombs, this suggests the interesting hypothesis that the builders of Jin tombs were familiar with the structure of Buddhist halls; see Nancy Steinhardt, "Death, Architecture, and Drama: Jin-Yuan Tombs in Southern Shanxi," in Shi et al. eds., *Sheng si tong le*, 27–36.
66. Li et al., *Yingzao fashi*, xia, juan 30, 740.
67. Liao, "Song Yuan xitai yiji," 90; and Liao Ben, *Zhongguo xiju tushi* (Zhengzhou: Henan jiaoyu chubanshe, 1996), 90–91. Nancy Steinhardt has concurred, further pointing out the similarity in the building frame and components between Dongyue Temple and the miniature theater. See Steinhardt, "Death, Architecture, and Drama," 31–32.
68. Liao, *Song Yuan xiqu wenwu yu minsu*, 187.
69. Xue Linping and Wang Jiqing, *Shanxi chuantong xichang jianzhu* (Beijing: Zhongguo jianzhu gongye chubanshe, 2005), 85–88.
70. For example, the top of the Jin-dated stage building in Erlang Temple (ca. 1183), located in Wangbao Village in Gaoping, Shanxi Province, is exposed, probably due to natural erosion over the centuries, which demonstrates the especially vulnerable nature of the roof compared to other architectural components. See Xue et al., *Shanxi chuantong xichang jianzhu*, color plate on p.1; also see pp. 59–60.
71. See, for example, Wei-cheng Lin, "Underground Wooden Architecture in Brick: A Changed Perspective from Life to Death in 10th- through 13th-Century Northern China," *Archives of Asian Art* 61 (2011): 27.
72. Luo Zhewen, ed., *Zhongguo gudai jianzhu* (Shanghai: Shanghai guji chubanshe, 2001), 156.
73. These include Houma Tomb No. 1, Houma Tomb No. 2, Macun Tomb No. 1, and Macun Tomb No. 3; they are the actor images framed in what appears to be an architectural (theater-evoking) structure. The rest of the actor representations listed in the appendix do not have any architectural frame.

74. Yang, "Shanxi Houma 104 hao Jin mu." Unfortunately, no photograph of the south wall in which actor figurines were located above the tomb gate was archived. For a photograph of the north wall, see fig. 3.17 in this volume.
75. Shanxisheng kaogu yanjiu suo, "Shanxi Jishan Jin mu fajue jianbao," 56.
76. Yang, "Shanxi Houma 104 hao Jin mu," 38–39.
77. For the development of the two-story *shanmen* combining a stage, see Gudai jianzhu xiuzheng suo, "Jin dongnan Lu'an, Pingxun, Gaoping he Jincheng si xian de gu jianzhu," *Wenwu cankao ziliao* 1959, no. 3 (1959): 26–42, 48.
78. In many middle period tombs, the back wall is distinguished from the other walls either by bearing an image of the deceased or by having an actual body enshrined in front of it. On the significance in the orientation of the portrait of the deceased in middle period tombs, see Hong, "Changing Roles of the Tomb Portrait."
79. Along with my discussion of this motif on coffin surface in chapter 1 of this volume, see Li Qingquan, "Kongjian luoji yu shijue yiwei," in *Gudai muzang meishu yanjiu*, vol. 1, ed. Wu Hung and Zheng Yan (Beijing: Wenwu chuban-she, 2011), 329–362; and Zheng Yan, "Lun 'Ban ji men,'" *Gugong bowuyuan yuankan* 3, no. 161 (2012): 16–36.
80. Many middle period burials in the north include similar types of furniture constructed of rectangular bricks and protrude from the walls; see Su, *Baisha Song mu*, fig. 31-II; Laing, "Patterns and Problems in Later Chinese Tomb Decoration," 6–7; Hebei sheng wenhuaju wenwu gongzuodui, "Hebei Jingjing xian Shizhuang Song mu fajue baogao," *Kaogu xuebao* 2 (1962): 31–73; and Zhengzhou shi wenwu kaogu yanjiusuo and Dengfeng shi wenwuju, "Henan Dengfeng Chengnanzhuang Song dai bihua mu," *Wenwu* 2005, no. 8 (2005): 62–70.
81. Shanxisheng wenwu guanli weiyuanhui Houma gongzuozhan, "Shanxi Houma Jin mu fajue jianbao," *Kaogu* 1961, no. 12 (1961): 681. See also *Da Han yuanling mizang jing*, 10a.
82. This idea is more fully explored in chapter 4.
83. Zhu Xizu, *Liu chao lingmu diaocha baogao* (Nanjing: Zhongyang guwu baoguan weiyuanhui, 1935).
84. Wu Hung, *Monumentality in Early Chinese Art and Architecture* (Stanford, CA: Stanford University Press, 1995), 254–255.
85. Wei-cheng Lin, "Underground Wooden Architecture in Brick," 20–26.
86. For a dominant medieval mode of visualizing these binary worlds that operated on the cognitive model, see Eugene Wang, *Shaping the Lotus Sutra: Buddhist Visual Culture in Medieval China* (Seattle: University of Washington Press, 2005), 277–316. See also chapter 4 and the postlude of the present volume, where I discuss this important issue in greater depth.
87. A helpful source for understanding this concept is Susan Stewart, *Nonsense: Aspects of Intertextuality in Folklore and Literature* (Baltimore: Johns Hopkins University Press, 1978), esp. 123–129, where she explores the sense of "nesting" as part of intertextual practice in literature.

88. Shanxisheng kaogu yanjiusuo, "Shanxi Jishan Jin mu fajue jianbao," 51–52. The genealogical content of his inscription, as well as the fact that it is the only one in the entire family tomb, implies that this text served as the introduction to the entire cemetery.

89. For a chart of this genealogy, see Tian Jianwen and Li Yongming, "Macun zhuandiao mu yu Duan shi kemingzhuan," *Wenwu shijie* 1 (2005), 15.

90. For recent scholarship on the ritual implications in the images of the deceased in middle period tombs, see chapter 1.

91. That the tomb inscription ends with a list of ancestral names indicates that the ancestral worship envisioned by Duan Ji was in harmony with the concept of the family cemetery. For general discussions of a relevant form of ancestral worship at graves (aboveground) during the Song and Yuan periods, see Patricia Buckley Ebrey, "Early Stages in the Development of Descent Group Organization," in *Kinship Organization in Late Imperial China, 1000–1940*, ed. Patricia Buckley Ebrey and James L. Watson (Berkeley: University of California Press, 1986): 16–61; Chang Jianhua, "Yuan dai muci ji zu wenti chutan," in *Shehui wenti de lishi kaocha*, ed. Zhao Qingzhu (Chengdu: Chengdu chubanshe, 1992): 67–75; and Wang Shanjun, "Songdai de zongzu jisi he zuxian chongbai," *Shijie zongjiao yanjiu* 3 (1999): 114–124.

92. On the historical significance of the genealogical interest manifested in such inscriptions as Duan Ji's in the formation of the nonliterati elite in northern China, see Hong, "Changing Roles of the Tomb Portrait." Because the descendants of the Jishan Duan as a clan still live in Jishan, with its ancestry traceable back to the Song period (see Tian, "Macun zhuandiao mu yu Duan shi Kemingzhuan"), it is reasonable to consider Duan Ji's patriline presented here as one of many localized descent groups. For a genealogy of another branch of the Jishan Duan from the Jin to the Yuan periods that consisted largely of literati, see Iiyama Tomoyasu, *Kin Gen jidai no Kahoku shakai to kakyo seido: mō hitotsu no "shijinsō"* (Tokyo: Waseda Daigaku Shuppanbu, 2011), 345–369.

93. Yang, "Shanxi Houma 104 hao Jin mu."

94. For an in-depth discussion of the issues of duplicability of the tomb portrait and its role in the ancestral worship of the nonliterati elite, see Hong, "Changing Roles of the Tomb Portrait."

95. See Hansen, *Negotiating Daily Life in Traditional China*, 150–188. On earlier forms of tomb contracts as tomb ordinance, see Fang Shiming, "Cong Xu Sheng diquan lun Han dai diquan zhi jianbie," *Wenwu* 1973, no. 5 (1973): 52–55; Li Shougang, "Ye tan 'diquan' de jianbie," *Wenwu* 1978, no. 7 (1978): 79–80; Anna Seidel, "Buying One's Way to Heaven: The Celestial Treasury in Chinese Religions," *History of Religions* 17 (1987): 419–432; and Terry Kleeman, "Land Contracts and Related Documents," in *Chūgoku no shūkyō, shisō to kagaku: Makio Ryōkai hakushi shōju kinen ronshū* (Tokyo: Kokusho kankōkai, 1984), 1–34.

CHAPTER 4: THEATER, BODY, AND PASSAGE

1. For a list of Yuan playwrights and their origins, see Zhong Sicheng, *Lugui bu*, juan 1, in *Lugui bu wai si zhong* (Shanghai: Shanghai guji chubanshe, 1978). The impact of such writers' works on the lives of the local elite was quite literal, as can be seen on tomb walls where lyrics of arias or poems attributed to Ma Zhiyuan were inscribed. For examples, see Shanxi daxue kexue jishu zhexue zhongxin, Shanxisheng kaogu yanjiusuo, Shanxi bowuyuan, "Shanxi Xing xian Hongyu cun Yuan Zhida er nian bihua mu," *Wenwu* 2011, no. 2 (2011): 40–46; Yang Jiyun and Gao Qingshang, "Houma Ershui M4 faxian mobi tishu de muzhi he sanpian zhugongdiao ciqu," *Zhonghua xiqu* 29 (2003): 1–5. For a discussion of these tombs, see the postlude of the present volume.

2. For accounts of a variety of entertainments, including theatrical performances in festivals in Dadu, see Song Lian, *Yuan shi*, juan 32 (Beijing: Zhonghua shuju, 1977), 711. For a general introduction to the Yuan *zaju*, see Wang Guowei, *Song Yuan xiqu shi* (Shanghai: Shanghai guji chubanshe, 1998); Yoshikawa Kojiro, *Gen zatsugeki kenkyū* (Tokyo: Iwanami shoten, 1948); Aoki Masaru, "Shina kinsei gikyokushi," in *Aoki Masaru zenshu* (Tokyo: Shunjusha, 1969–1975), vol. 3; and J. I. Crump, *Chinese Theater in the Days of Kublai Khan* (Tucson: University of Arizona Press, 1980).

3. On the intense battles in the area, see Zhou Jinggui, ed., *Puzhou fuzhi*, juan 23 (Taipei: Taiwan Xuesheng shuju, 1968), 33a, 34b. For discussions of prominent scholar-officials native to Yongle during the Yuan and Ming dynasties, see Wang Shangyi and Xu Hongping, "Song Yuan Ming Qing shiqi Shanxi wenren de dili fenbu ji wenhua fazhan tedian," *Shanxi daxue xuebao* 3 (1988): 38–46; and Zhang Zhenming, *Jinshang xingshuai shi* (Taiyuan: Shanxi renmin chubanshe, 1995): 206–213. For an informative discussion of the Yongle area as an important cultural center, see Paul Katz, *Images of the Immortal: The Cult of Lu Dongbin at the Palace of Eternal Joy* (Honolulu: University of Hawai'i Press, 1999), 24–33.

4. The Yongle gong was originally located sixteen miles to the southwest, at Yongle zhen. Half of the entire complex, including renowned wall paintings in the three halls, was moved to the current site due to the construction of a dam in Sanmen xia in 1958. For a history of this temple, see Katz, *Images of the Immortal*, 24–51; and Anning Jing, "Yongle Palace: The Transformation of the Daoist Pantheon during the Yuan Dynasty (1260–1368)," PhD diss., Princeton University, 1994.

5. Founded by Wang Zhe (1112–1170) during the Jin dynasty, the Complete Perfection sect became widespread in northern China by the early Yuan dynasty, attracting both literate and illiterate followers over the centuries. For historical studies on its philosophy and practice, see Kubo Noritada, "Zenshinkyo no seiritsu," *Tōyō Bunka Kenkyūjo kiyo* 42 (1966): 1–60; Hachiya Kunio, *Kindai dokyo no kenkyū: O Choyo to Ba Tanyo* (Tokyo: Shoin, 1992); Stephen Eskildsen, *The Teachings and Practices of the Early Quanzhen*

Taoist Masters (Albany: State University of New York Press, 2004); and Vincent Goossaert and Paul Katz, "New Perspectives on Quanzhen Taoism: The Formation of Religious Identity," *Journal of Chinese Religions* 29 (2001): 91–95. For a brief discussion of early Quanzhen activities in the Shanxi area, see Yang Xiaoguo, "Jin Yuan shiqi Quanzhenjiao zai Shanxi huodong tansuo," *Jinyang xuekan* 4 (2004): 25.

6. See Tudan Gonglü, "Chonghe zhenren pangong shendao zhi bei," *Ganshui xianyuan lu,* juan 5, in *Daojia jinshu lue,* ed. Chen Yuan (Beijing: Wenwu chubanshe, 1988), 554–556.

7. Pan's body was buried northwest of the Palace of Eternal Joy, and a shrine was built at the site. See Tudan, "Chonghe zhenren pangong shendao zhi bei," 556. This record corresponds to the location of the excavated tomb. For the archaeological report, see Shanxisheng wenwu guanli weiyuanhui kaogu yanjiusuo, "Shanxi Ruicheng Yonglegong jiuzhi Song Defang, Pan Dechong he 'Lüzu' mu fajue jianbao," *Kaogu* 1960, no. 8 (1960): 22–25.

8. Because some of the themes of many Yuan dynasty dramas are concerned with major figures of the Quanzhen sect, several scholars have suggested that the Quanzhen would have utilized theater for conversion and propagation of their ideas; see Zhan Shichuang, *Daojiao yu xiju* (Taipei: Wenjin chubanshe, 1997); and Wu Guofu, *Quanzhenjiao yu Yuanqu* (Nanchang shi: Jiangxi renmin chubanshe, 2005). It is difficult, however, to determine whether this link was the result of Quanzhen masters' strategy or the natural outcome of the burgeoning theater culture that infiltrated every level of society. See Wilt Idema and Stephen H. West, *Chinese Theater, 1100–1450: A Source Book* (Wiesbaden, Germany: Steiner, 1982), 300–301.

9. Katz, *Images of the Immortal,* 24–33.

10. For a history of the palace reconstructed through steles discovered in the area, see Su Bai, Yonge gong changjian shiliao biannian—Yongle gong zhaji zhi yi," *Wenwu* 1962, nos. 4–5 (1962): 80–87.

11. See Shanxisheng wenwu guanli weiyuanhui, "Shanxi Ruicheng Yonglegong jiuzhi Song Defang," 24.

12. An almost identical work is in the collection of the Metropolitan Museum of Art, New York (accession no. 1994.346a–g). In comparison with the quality of carvings on Pan's sarcophagus, the line carving of this piece is shallow and timid, which leads me to think that it may be a later imitation of Pan's sarcophagus or a product from the same workshop but created by less skillful hands.

13. According to a Qing text, the terminology itself derives from the Yuan period. See *Wushi weifu zhai suibi,* juan shang, Gongshuntang congshu ed., in *Yanpu zaji, Wushi weifu zhai suibi* (Taipei: Wenhai chubanshe, 1973), 25–26. For discussions of this motif in middle period funerary art, including the images on the two panels from Pan's tomb, see Shanxisheng wenwu guanli weiyuanhui, "Shanxi Ruicheng Yonglegong jiuzhi Song Defang," 24; Xu Pingfang, "Guanyu Song Defang he Pan Dechong mu de ji ge wenti," *Kaogu* 1960, no. 8 (1960): 42–45, 54; Wang Fucai, "Shanxi Ruicheng

Yonglegong Pan Dechong shiguo er shi si xiao xianketu benshi ji qi jumu kao," *Zhonghua xiqu* 22 (1999): 192–213; and Dong Xinlin, "Bei Song Jin Yuan muzang bishi suo jian er shi si xiao gushi yu Gaoli xiaoxing lu," *Huaxia kaogu* 2 (2009): 141–152.

14. Historian of Chinese architecture, Chai Zejun, describes this structure as "a two-story pavilion with a wide facade consisting of three sections"; see Chai Zejun, *Chai Zejun gujianzhu wenji* (Beijing: Wenwu chubanshe, 1999), 257.

15. My identification of the figures here generally relies on the fourteenth-century text *Chuogeng lu* by Tao Zongyi, who considered the basic structure of the Song *zaju* described in *Dongjing menghua lu* as still historically valid for understanding the origins of *zaju* in his time. See Tao Zongyi, *Nancun Chuogeng lu,* juan 25 (Beijing: Zhonghua shuju, 2004), 306–316.

16. Painted more than sixty years after the burial of the Pan sarcophagus, this mural shows diverse makeup, props, and costumes for the actors that suggest the fully mature form of Yuan drama. For a detailed discussion of the mural, see Anning Jing, *The Water God's Temple of Guangsheng Monastery: Cosmic Function of Art, Ritual, and Theater* (Leiden, Netherlands: Brill, 2002), 144–199.

17. Crump, *Chinese Theater in the Days of Kublai Khan,* 173. See also the discussion in chapter 3 of the present volume.

18. *Mo* roles are subdivided into the principal male role (*zhengmo*), the secondary male role (*fumo*), the auxiliary male role (*chongmo*), and the young male role (*xiaomo*). *Dan* roles are subdivided into four similar roles, except that instead of an auxiliary role corresponding to *chongmo* there is a female villain (*chadan*). Under the category of *jing* are the antagonist himself (*jing*) and the *jing*'s counterpart, the clown (*chou*). Thus, it is clear that the Pan sarcophagus only presents four prototypical roles, with the emphasis being on clown acting. For the standard form of Yuan drama, see Crump, *Chinese Theater in the Days of Kublai Khan,* 173. For a pictorial representation of an early *mo* type, see figure 4.6.

19. The burial history of Song Defang is recorded on stelae, including "Xuandu zhidao Piyun zhenren Song tianshi citing beiming bingyin," in *Daojia jinshi lue,* ed. Chen Yuan (Beijing: Wenwu chubanshe, 1988), 546–549; and on the epitaph found in his tomb; see Su Bai, "Yongle gong changjian shiliao biannian," 82–83. Because the dates of their burials are close to each other, and because both Pan's and Song's lives were deeply associated with the site of the Palace of Eternal Joy, it is reasonable to think that their sarcophagi would have been designed and carved by workshops in the same community, if not by a single workshop.

20. For a general discussion of *jiehua* painting, see Robert J. Maeda, "Chieh-hua: Ruled-line Painting in China," *Ars Orientalis* 10 (1975): 123–141. For its development in the eleventh century, see Heping Liu, "'The Water Mill' and Northern Song Imperial Patronage of Art, Commerce, and Science," *Art Bulletin* 84, no. 4 (2002): 566–567. For social and political implications of

jiehua during the Qing, see Anita Chung, *Drawing Boundaries: Architectural Images in Qing China* (Honolulu: University of Hawai'i Press, 2004). For new critical approaches on *jiehua* studies, see Chen Yunru, "'Jiehua' zai Song Yuan shiqi de zhuanzhe: yi Wang Zhenpeng de jiehua wei lie," *Meishushixue yanjiu jikan* 26 (2009): 135–192; Jerome Silbergeld, "Yi qu bai xie: fuzhi, bianhua, ji zhongguo jiehua yanjiu zhong de ruogan wenti," in *Qiannian danqing: Xi du Zhong Ri cang Tang Song Yuan huihua zhenpin,* ed. Shanghai bowuguan (Beijing: Beijing daxue chubanshe, 2010), 131–150.

21. See Shanxisheng kaogu yanjiusuo, "Shanxi Xinjiang Nanfanzhuang, Wuling-zhuang Jin Yuan mu fajue jianbao," *Wenwu* 1983, no. 1 (1983); and Liao Ben, *Song Yuan xiqu wenwu yu minsu* (Beijing: Wenhua yishu chubanshe, 1989), 210–212.

22. For detailed descriptions of the object, see Yang Houli and Wan Liangtian, "Jiangxi Fengcheng xian faxian Yuandai jinian qinghua youlilong ciqi," *Wenwu* 1981, no. 11 (1981): 72–74.

23. For a useful discussion on the ritual functions of medieval granary jars, see Albert Dien, "Developments in Funerary Practices in the Six Dynasties Period: The *Duisuguan* or 'Figured jar' as a Case in Point," in *Han Tang zhijian wenhua yishu de hudong yu jiaorong,* ed. Wu Hung (Beijing: Wenwu chubanshe, 2001), 509–546.

24. By the same token, whether this structure represents a *shanmen* of a contemporary temple can be better contextualized from this perspective. Xu Ping-fang has suggested that the stage building depicted on the Pan sarcophagus represents a *shanmen*. See Xu, "Guanyu Song Defang he Pan Dechong mu de ji ge wenti," 44.

25. Liao, *Song Yuan xiqu wenwu yu minsu,* 209.

26. For another good example of a four-leaf louvered door in tombs, see Shanxisheng wenwu guanli weiyuanhui, "Shanxi Xiaoyi Xiatujing he Liangjiazhuang Jin, Yuan mu fajue jianbao," *Kaogu* 1960, no. 7 (1960): 57–61.

27. Eugene Wang, *Shaping the Lotus Sutra* (Seattle: University of Washington Press, 2005), 285.

28. See Zhang Qingjin, "Shanxi Yongji faxian Jin dai Zhenyuan yuannian qingshiguan," *Wenwu* 1985, no. 8 (1985): 94; and Gao Wen and Gao Cheng-gang, *Zhongguo huaxiang shiguan yishu* (Taiyuan: Shanxi renmin chuban-she, 1996), 154. For the role of "virtual functionality" of such dummy doors and other burial objects in the larger context of *mingqi* making during the middle period, see Jeehee Hong, "Mechanism of Life for the Netherworld: Transformations of *Mingqi* in Middle-Period China," *Journal of Chinese Religions* 43, no. 2 (2015), 161–193.

29. For the entire inscription on the Yonghe sarcophagus, see Jie Xigong and Yan Jinzhu, "Shanxi Yonghe xian chutu Jin Da'an san nian shiguan," *Wenwu* 1989, no. 5 (1989): 71–74; and Gao, *Zhongguo huaxiang shiguan yishu,* 150–151. Carving genealogical information on the coffin's surface was an uncommon practice by that time period, which may be seen as a primordial

version of genealogical stele (*xianying bei*). For an in-depth study of the genealogical stelae from the Jin and Yuan periods, see Iiyama Tomoyasu, *Kin Gen jidai no Kahoku shakai to kakyo seido: mō hitotsu no "shijinsō"* (Tokyo: Waseda Daigaku Shuppanbu, 2011), chap. 3. For the practice of genealogical inscription by the nonliterati elite and its connection to literati practice, see Jeehee Hong, "Changing Roles of the Tomb Portrait: Burial Practices and Ancestral Worship of Non-literati Elite in North China (1000–1400)," *Journal of Song-Yuan Studies* 44 (forthcoming).

30. The other three sides of the sarcophagus are decorated with patterns of small auspicious figures, such as deer or peonies, framed in a floral outline in relief, and each of the long side panels bears five such figure-within-flower patterns; see Gao, *Zhongguo huaxiang shiguan yishu*, 152–153.

31. The "thingness" of things, notes Bill Brown, "How to Do Things with Things (A Toy Story)," *Critical Inquiry* 24, no. 4 (1998): 936, designates less the unalterably given material object world than "something that becomes visible or palpable only in (or as) its alteration."

32. The episode appears in Fan Ye, *Hou Han shu*, juan 112, xia, "Fei Changfang zhuan," Sibu beiyao duanxing ben ed. (Taipei: Taiwan Zhonghua shuju, 1965), 10a–11b.

33. These expressions are frequently found in poems and essays—especially Daoist ones—from the Tang and Song periods. See, for example, Zhang Junfang, *Yunji qijian*, juan 28, "Ershi ba zhi," Sibu chongkan chubian ed. (Shanghai: Shangwu yin shu guan, 1929), 11b–12a.

34. Rolf A. Stein, *World in Miniature: Container Gardens and Dwelling in Far Eastern Religious Thought*, trans. Phyllis Brooks (Stanford, CA: Stanford University Press, 1990), 58.

35. Ge Hong, "Hugong," *Shenxian zhuan*, juan 9, in *Liexian zhuan. Shenxian zhuan zhushe,* annotated and translated by Teng Xiuzhan and Deng Ansheng (Tianjin: Baihua wenyi chubanshe, 1996), 379–382; Fan, "Fei Changfang zhuan," 10a–11b.

36. According to the epitaph, the sponsors were indeed Feng's sons. For a transcription of the entire epitaph, see Gao, *Zhongguo huaxiang shiguan yishu*, 150.

37. This text is conventionally attributed to the renowned Tang dynasty astronomer Li Chunfeng (602–670), but Poul Andersen doubts this attribution. He suggests that if the book existed earlier, it did not come to the attention of the hagiographers before the twelfth century. For details, see Poul Andersen's introduction to "Jinsuo liuzhu yin," in *The Taoist Canon: A Historical Companion to the* Daozang, ed. Kristofer Schipper and Franciscus Verellen (Chicago: University of Chicago Press, 2004), 1076–1079. For the passage on Fei Changfang, see Li Chunfeng, "Jinsuo liuzhu yin," in *Zhengtong Daozang*, facs. 636, juan 27 (Shanghai: Shanghai Hanfen lou yingyin, 1924), 7b.

38. See Li, "Jinsuo liuzhu yin," 7b. In the commentary, the legend of Fei Changfang is first quoted, and then a detailed process of inner cultivation is given,

which is explained as a way for one to transform a pint container so that it contains heaven and earth.

39. See the commentaries by Dong Dening in "Wuzhenpian zhengyi," juan *zhong*, in *Daozang jinghua lu baizhong*, ed. Ding Fubao (Shanghai: Yixue shuju, 1921), 8:16b–17a.

40. Liu Guoliang and Lian Yao, trans., *Xin yi Wuzhen bian* (Taipei: Sanmin shuju, 2005), 159n2.

41. See "Xuan Hu zhenren taixi jue," in *Zhuzhen shengtaishen yongjue*, in *Zhengtong Daozang*, facs. 570, 3a–3b.

42. Kristofer Schipper, *The Taoist Body*, trans. Karen D. Duval (Berkeley: University of California Press, 1993), 100–112.

43. Here I use the term "icon" in a semiotic sense. See C. S. Peirce, "The Icon, Index, and Symbol," in *Collected Papers of Charles Sanders Peirce*, ed. Charles Hartshorne and Paul Weiss, vol. 2 (Cambridge: Harvard University Press, 1932), 156–173.

44. Anna Seidel, "*Post-Mortem* Immortality or the Daoist Resurrection of the Body," in *Gilgul: Essays on Transformation, Revolution, and Permanence in the History of Religions*, ed. Shaul Shaked and Gedaliahu A. G. Stroumsa (Leiden, Netherlands: Brill, 1987), 223–237.

45. There were at least one hundred Quanzhen Daoist temples in Shanxi by 1170, and the number tripled by the mid-fourteenth century. See Yang Xiaoguo, "Jin Yuan shiqi Quanzhenjiao zai shanxi huodong tansuo," *Jinyang xuekan* 4 (2004): 22.

46. Liao Ben, *Zhongguo gudai juchang shi* (Zhengzhou: Zhongzhou guji chubanshe, 1997), 49–50; Che Wenming, *Ershi shiji xiqu wenwu de fazhan yu quxue yanjiu* (Beijing: Wenwu yishu chubanshe, 2001), 35.

47. Zhou Yibai, "Zhongguo xiqu de shangxiachang," in *Zhou Yibai xiju lunwen xuan*, ed. Zhou Huawu (Changsha: Hunan renmin chubanshe, 1982), 182–193, notes that "the stage in Chinese drama is the entrances and exits of different characters."

48. Judith T. Zeitlin, *The Phantom Heroine: Ghosts and Gender in Seventeenth-Century Chinese Literature* (Honolulu: University of Hawai'i Press, 2007), 143.

49. Zeitlin has written extensively about an elaborate vocabulary of specialized entrances and exits that was developed in Chinese drama during the Ming and Qing periods, with abundant examples; see Zeitlin, *The Phantom Heroine*, 140–142.

50. Crump, *Chinese Theater in the Days of Kublai Khan*, 78–79.

51. Later the term coexisted with newer terms such as *houfang* or *neichang*. For the usages of these terms, see Liao, *Zhongguo gudai xiju shi*, 64; Zhou Yibai, "Zhongguo juchang shi," in *Zhou Yibai xiaoshuo xiqu lunji*, ed. Shen Xieyuan (Ji'nan: Qilu shushe, 1986), 185–186; and Zeitlin, *The Phantom Heroine*, 144.

52. Tao Zongyi, "Lianzhi xiu," *Nancun Chuogeng lu*, juan 12, 148.

53. Qian Nanyang has discussed the mutual influence between northern and southern dramas in the pre-Yuan and Yuan periods; see Qian Nanyang, *Xiwen gailun* (Shanghai: Shanghai guji chubanshe, 1981), 42–54.

54. The script is not dated, as is the case with the other two earliest extant examples of southern plays recorded in *Yongle dadian* (Documents from Yongle era). Judging from the form and structure of the script, however, most scholars of Chinese drama have agreed that *The Top Graduate Zhang Xie* would have been written in a rather early stage in the development of plays south of the Yangtze River over the twelfth and thirteenth centuries; see Qian, *Xiwen gailun*, 42–54.

55. *Zhang Xie zhuangyuan*, in *Yongle dadian xiwen sanzhong jiaozhu* (Beijing: Zhonghua shuju, 1979), 1–217. *The Top Graduate Zhang Xie* is attributed to a "talented man" (*cairen*) from the Jiushan Writing Club (Jiushan shuhui), one of two well-known literary groups that produced play texts in Wenzhou, Zhejiang Province. Note that in the juan 6 of *Wulin jiushi*, the term *shuhui* (writing club) appears under the category "zhu se jiyiren" (all sorts of entertainers). For discussions of writing clubs, see Idema and West, *Chinese Theater*, 130–131.

56. My research on the concepts of "inside" (*nei*) and "outside" (*wai*) was inspired by the insightful observations on these two concepts (and the terms for them) by Yan Dunyi and J. I. Crump. Although I do not entirely agree with Yan regarding the relationship between the two concepts, his observation drew my attention to the significance of that relationship. See Yan Dunyi, *Yuanju zhenyi* (Beijing: Zhonghua shuju, 1962), 162; and Crump, *Chinese Theater in the Days of Kublai Khan*, 150–151.

57. Fei Tangchen, *Su Zizhan fengxue pin Huangzhou zaju*, Maiwang guan chaoben ed., in *Yuanqu xuan waibian*, ed. Sui Shusen (Beijing: Zhonghua shuju, 1959), 356.

58. Marvin Carlson's characterization is based on the offstage *skene* of the ancient Greek theater, but its basic mechanism is shared by theaters of many other cultures. See Marvin Carlson, *Places of Performance: The Semiotics of Theater Architecture* (Ithaca, NY: Cornell University Press, 1989), 131.

59. Stephen H. West, "Text and Ideology: Ming Editors and Northern Drama," in *Ming Qing xiqu guoji yantaohui lunwenji*, ed. Hua Wei and Wang Ailing (Taipei: Zhongyang yanjiuyuan Zhongguo wenzhe yanjiusuo choubeichu, 1998), 235–284.

60. See Zheng Dehui, *Zhongli Chun zhiyong dingqi*, in *Guben xiqu congkan*, Maiwang guan chaoben ed. no. 34 (Shanghai: Shangwu yin shu guan, 1958), 12:24a, 24b; and Sui Shusen, ed., *Yuanqu xuan waibian* (Beijing: Zhonghua shuju, 1959), 507. For a brief introduction to the author, see Zhong, *Lugui bu*, xia, in *Lugui bu wai si zhong*, 31.

61. Yan, *Yuanju zhenyi*, 164–165.

62. For the Maiwang guan version, see *Duan yuanjia qianzhu*, in *Guben xiqu congkan* (Collectanea of dramas in old editions), 4 (fourth series), Maiwang guan chaoben ed., vol. 19, no. 51 (Shanghai: Shangwu yin shu guan, 1958),

19:2b. For the *Yuanqu xuan* version, see *Cui fujun duan yuanjia qianzhu,* in *Yuanqu xuan jiao zhu*, vol. 3, xia, ed. and annotated by Wang Xueqi (Shijiazhuang: Hebei jiaoyu chubanshe, 1994), 2853. For an overall narrative of this play, see Crump, *Chinese Theater in the Days of Kublai Khan,* 144–145.

63. Scholars of Chinese drama have widely accepted that most Ming period printings of the Yuan play texts were modified to a great degree by the literati of the time, usually adding more arias and reducing plain speech. For various aspects of such changes, see Wilt Idema, "The Many Shapes of Medieval Chinese Plays: How Texts Are Transformed in the Needs of Actors, Spectators, Censors, and Readers," *Oral Tradition* 20, no. 2 (2005): 320–334.

64. According to Yan Dunyi, the term *cheng da* in *wai cheng da* indicates some sort of assigned role, which derives from Jin and Yuan theater practice; see Yan, *Yuanju zhenyi*, 163.

65. Yan, *Yuanju zhenyi*, 162–166.

66. The scene from Fei Tangchen's *Su Zizhan fengxue pin Huangzhou zaju* quoted earlier in this chapter is a good example.

67. Yan limits this possible troupe member to a musician who would have been in charge of special sound effects or musical performance. But, as Crump implied, it is difficult to pin down who was supposed to do the invisible performance; see Crump, *Chinese Theater in the Days of Kublai Khan,* 151.

68. Yan, *Yuanju zhenyi*, 165.

69. Having the potential to alter the normal order and rhythm of everyday life, the spectacle would also have helped them to freely reverse the notions of inside and outside. On the power of spectacle and especially on its function in the reversal of perspectives, see Guy Debord, *The Society of the Spectacle,* trans. Donald Nicholson-Smith (New York: Zone Books, 1994).

70. For example, see Li Jie, *Yingzao fashi*, juan 28 (Beijing: Zhongguo shudian, 2006), vol. 2, 599.

71. See, for example, scene 2 (die er zhe) in *Dou'e yuan*, in *Yuanqu xuan jiao zhu*, vol. 4, shang, ed. and annotated by Wang Xueqi (Shijiazhuang: Hebei jiaoyu chubanshe, 1994), 3781. Also see Scene 2 in *Xiao Xiang*, in *Yuanqu xuan jiao zhu*, vol. 1, xia, ed. and annotated by Wang Xueqi (Shijiazhuang: Hebei jiaoyu chubanshe, 1994), 789.

72. See Yue Bochuan, *Lü Dongbin du Tieguai Li Yue zaju*, in *Yuanqu xuan jiao zhu*, vol. 2, shang, ed. and annotated by Wang Xueqi (Shijiazhuang: Hebei jiaoyu chubanshe, 1994), 1392. Yue Bochuan's name and works appear in different editions of *Lugui bu* by Zhong Sicheng. See Zhong, "Fulu Cao Lianting kan ben Xinbian Lugui bu," in *Lugui bu wai si zhong*, 66, 77.

73. See *Xixiang ji (er ben)*, "Cui Yingying ye tingqin," Xiezi, in *Yuanqu xuan waibian*, ed. Sui Shusen (Beijing: Zhonghua shuju, 1959), 274. See also the third segment (San zhe) in *Xixiang ji (san ben)*, in *Yuanqu xuan waibian*, 295.

74. It is unclear whether the doorway in each case refers to one of a pair (for exit and entrance), as depicted on the Pan sarcophagus, or a single doorway. On these two types of doorways, see Zhou Yibai, "Zhongguo juchang shi," in

Zhou Yibai xiaoshuo xiqu lunji, ed. Shen Xieyuan (Ji'nan: Qilu shushe, 1986), 482–485.

75. Carlson, *Places of Performance*, 131.

76. Zhu Quan, "Gui mendao," in *Taihe zhengyin pu shang*, in *Lugui bu wai si zhong*, 164. I follow the translation given in Zeitlin, *The Phantom Heroine*, 144. Compare this also with a later version of the same passage in *Yuanqu xuan jiao zhu*, vol. 1, shang, 89.

77. Scholars of Chinese architecture Xue Linping and Wang Jiqing, pointing out the nonexistence of Su's poem in the surviving works, still leave open the possibility that such a structure may have existed during the Song period; see Xue Lingping and Wang Jiqing, *Shanxi chuantong xichang jianzhu* (Beijing: Zhongguo jianzhu gongye chubanshe, 2005), 74. Indeed, the poem may well have been circulated in nonbook format, such as in a letter or the colophon of a painting.

78. Zeitlin, *The Phantom Heroine*, 145.

79. Crump, *Chinese Theater in the Days of Kublai Khan*, 151.

80. Shen Jiji, "Chen zhong ji," in Li Fang, *Wenyuan yinghua*, vol. 5, juan 833 (Beijing: Zhonghua shuju, 1982), 4396.

81. In terms of viewership, the same premise applies here as in the cases of the Yanshi reliefs and the Houma figurines. Even though the sarcophagus was not necessarily meant to be appreciated by living beings, its nature as an image-bearing object designed by an artisan who must have shared some visual references with his contemporaries makes it more likely that a certain kind of contemporary viewing practice or habit was exercised during the process of making it.

82. A stele inscription ("Zhong xiu Mingying wang dian zhi bei") cited in Xue Linping and Wang Jiqing, "Shanxi Yuan dai chuantong jianzhu yanjiu," *Tongji daxue xuebao* 14, no. 4 (2003): 31.

83. Jing Lihu, "Yongle gong Longhu dian kaolun," *Zhonghua xiqu* 8 (1989): 187–195; Xue and Wang, *Shanxi chuantong xichang jianzhu*, 251–252; and Luo Lirong, *Zhongguo shenmiao juchang shi* (Taipei: Liren shuju, 2006), 83–84.

84. Xue and Wang, *Shanxi chuantong xichang jianzhu*, 248–255.

85. One of the earliest architectural examples that combines a temple gate with a second-floor stage is recorded in a local gazetteer of Xugou County, in which an entertainment pavilion/stage (*yuelou*) was built on top of a temple gate during the Chenghua era (1465–1487); see Wang Xunxiang, *Xugou xian zhi*, juan 3, "Simiao," in *Zhongguo difang zhi jicheng: Shanxi fu xian zhi ji* (Nanjing: Fenghuang chubanshe, 2005).

86. For a historical discussion of *saishe* during the Song dynasty, see Noriyuki Kanai, "Sōdai no sonsha to shashin," *Tōyōshi kenkyū* 38, no. 2 (1979): 61–87. For anthropological research on *saishe*, see Wang Fucai, "Qinshui xian xia Gebei cun Shengwangxing gong Yuan bei ji saishe kao," *Minsu quyi* 107–108 (1997): 91–116; and Feng Junjie, ed., *Taixing shenmiao ji saishe yanju* (Taipei: Shi Hezheng minsu wenhua jijinhui chuban, 2000). For a study of contempo-

rary village rituals in north China, see David Johnson, *Spectacle and Sacrifice: The Ritual Foundations of Village Life in North China* (Cambridge, MA: Harvard University Asia Center, 2009).

POSTLUDE

1. Shanxi daxue kexue jishu zhexue zhongxin, Shanxisheng kaogu yanjiusuo, Shanxi bowuyuan, "Shanxi Xing xian Hongyu cun Yuan Zhida er nian bihua mu," *Wenwu* 2011, no. 2 (2011): 40–46.

2. For the lyrics of "Autumn Thoughts," see Sui Shusen ed., *Quan Yuan sanqu* (Beijing: Zhonghua suju, 1964), 242; for an English translation, see Wayne Schlepp, *San-ch'u: Its Technique and Imagery* (Madison: University of Wisconsin Press, 1970), 124; and Stephen Owen, trans. and ed., *An Anthology of Chinese Literature: Beginnings to 1911* (New York: Norton, 1996), 740.

3. Wayne Schlepp has pointed out that the song attributed to Ma Zhiyuan appears in both *Yuanren xiaoling ji* and *Quan Yuan sanqu,* but he regards it as an anonymous work. Schlepp, *San-ch'u,* 740. Fan Chunyi has also argued that the song existed as part of an anonymous yet popular song suite during the Yuan, but that later, in the Ming period, literati attributed it to Ma Zhiyuan. Given that versions of this song (with slight discrepancies in wording, yet with basically the same motif and form) were recorded in Yuan texts such as *Zhongyuan yinyun* (ca. 1324) and *Shuzhai laoxue congtan* (thirteenth century) as part of a popular song suite, Fan's suggestion is convincing. See Fan Chunyi, "Tianjingsha, Qiusi shi Ma Zhiyuan zuo de ma," *Gudian wenxue zhishi* 3 (2008): 46–51.

4. Among several examples, see the poem written on a ceramic pillow found in a Song tomb, published in Zhongguo guisuanyan xuehui, ed., *Zhongguo taoci shi* (Beijing: Wenwu chubanshe, 1982), 247; see also a poem written on the wall of a Jin tomb, published in Shanxisheng wenwu guanli weiyuanhui, "Shanxi Xiaoyi Xiatujing he Liangjiazhuang Jin, Yuan mu fajue jianbao," *Kaogu* 1960, no. 7 (1960): 57–61.

5. For an introduction to *sanqu,* see Schlepp, *San-ch'u,* 3–19; Li Changji, *Zhongguo gudai sanqu shi* (Shanghai: Huadong shifan daxue chubanshe, 1991), 5–238; and Owen, *An Anthology of Chinese Literature,* 728–743.

6. As with the other cases discussed in this book, both the elaborateness of the tomb and the absence in the tomb inscription of any record of Wu Qing's achievement as an official or literatus suggest that the couple belonged to nonliterati local elite.

7. For the archaeological report, see Yang Jiyun and Gao Qingshang, "Houma Ershui M4 faxian mobi tishu de muzhi he sanpian zhugongdiao ciqu," *Zhonghua xiqu* 29 (2003): 1–5. For a discussion of the *zhugongdiao* written in this tomb, see Ning Xiyuan, "Zaoqi zhugongdiao keci de zhongda faxian," *Zhonghua xiqu* 31 (2004): 14–17. For an introduction to this tomb in English, see Fan Jeremy Zhang, "'Drama Sustains the Spirit': Art, Ritual, and Theater in

Jin and Yuan Period Pingyang, 1150–1350," PhD diss., Brown University, 2011, 80–110.

8. My understanding of the term benefits from Bruno Latour's discussion of the social; see Bruno Latour, *Reassembling the Social: An Introduction to Actor-Network-Theory* (Oxford: Oxford University Press, 2007). For Latour, "'social' is not some glue that could fix everything including what the other glues cannot fix; it is *what* is glued together by many *other* types of connectors" (5; emphasis in the original). This definition also resonates with the etymology of the term: the root of "social" is *seq-/ sequi,* and the primary meaning is "to follow," while the Latin *socius* denotes a companion, an associate. The immense scope of Latour's overall argument falls outside the basic conception of the social that I adopt here, but it essentially conforms to the way I envision the social grouping of the local elites under discussion.

9. Here I am not concerned with the Chinese term *shehui,* which refers to society in the contemporary world. While the term as a compound was derived from a group of people or a place organized for worshiping the earth god (*sheshen*) during the middle period, the adoption of that term as referring to the modern notion of society was (re)imported from the Japanese translation of the English word "society" in the nineteenth century, *shakai.* For examples of *shehui* in the Song, see Meng Yuanlao, "Qiushe," in *Dongjing menghua lu jianzhu,* annotated by Yi Yongwen (Beijing: Zhonghua shuju, 2005), vol. 2, juan 8, 810–813. For a detailed discussion of the translation projects in modern Japan as well as the notion of *shakai,* see Yanabu Akira, *Hon'yakugo seiritsu jijō* (Tokyo: Iwanami shoten, 1982), esp. 4–19.

10. See chapter 1 of the present volume; also see Jeehee Hong, "'Hengzai' zhong de zangyi," in *Gudai muzang meishu yanjiu,* ed. Wu Hung, Zhu Qingsheng, and Zheng Yan, vol. 3 (Changsha: Hunan meishu chubanshe, 2015), 196–226.

11. Michael Loewe, *Ways to Paradise: The Chinese Quest for Immortality* (London: Allen and Unwin, 1979); Anna Seidel, "*Post-Mortem* Immortality or the Taoist Resurrection of the Body," in *Gilgul: Essays on Transformation, Revolution, and Permanence in the History of Religions,* ed. Shaul Shaked and Gedaliahu A. G. Stroumsa (Leiden, Netherlands: Brill, 1987), 223–237; Ying-Shih Yü, "'O Soul, Come Back!' A Study in the Changing Conceptions of the Soul and Afterlife in Pre-Buddhist China," *Harvard Journal of Asiatic Studies* 47, no. 2 (1987): 363–395; Kenneth Brashier, "Han Thanatology and the Division of 'Souls,'" *Early China* 21 (1996): 125–158.

12. For a series of excellent historical studies on this issue, with varying degrees of agreement and disagreement within the scope of the large historical narrative described herein, see Edward A. Kracke Jr., "Region, Family and Individual in the Chinese Examination System," in *Chinese Thought and Institutions,* ed. John K. Fairbank (Chicago: University of Chicago Press, 1967), 251–268; Robert M. Hartwell, "Demographic, Political, and Social Transformations of China, 750–1550," *Harvard Journal of Asiatic Studies*

42, no. 2 (1982): 365–442; Robert P. Hymes, *Statesmen and Gentlemen: The Elite of Fu-chou, Chiang-hsi, in Northern and Southern Sung* (Cambridge: Cambridge University Press, 1986); Patricia Buckley Ebrey, "The Dynamics of Elite Domination in Sung China," *Harvard Journal of Asiatic Studies* 48, no. 2 (1988): 493–519; Peter Bol, *"This Culture of Ours": Intellectual Transitions in T'ang and Sung China* (Stanford, CA: Stanford University Press, 1992); Beverly J. Bossler, *Powerful Relations: Kinship, Status, and the State in Sung China (960–1279)* (Cambridge, MA: Council on East Asian Studies, 1998); and Chang Woei Ong, *Men of Letters within the Passes: Guanzhong Literati in Chinese History, 907–1911* (Cambridge, MA: Harvard University Asia Center, 2008).

13. The socialization of the funerary realm was manifested in various visual forms during the middle period. For a pictorial example that encapsulates this phenomenon, see Jeehee Hong, "Theatricalizing Death and Society in *The Skeletons' Illusory Performance* by Li Song," *Art Bulletin* 93, no. 1 (2011): 60–78.

14. On early Buddhist images, see Wu Hung, "Buddhist Elements in Early Chinese Art (2nd and 3rd Centuries AD)," *Artibus Asiae* 47, nos. 3–4 (1986): 263–352. For a short introduction to the Buddhist images in tomb spaces of the middle period, see Ran Wanli, "Songdai sangzang xisu zhong fojiao yinsu de kaoguxue guancha," *Kaogu yu wenwu* 2009, no. 4 (2009): 77–85. For an in-depth discussion of the striking representation of *parinirvāṇa* painted in the Hancheng Song tomb in Shanxi Province, see Jeehee Hong and T. J. Hinrichs, "Unwritten Life (and Death) of a 'Pharmacist' in Song China: Decoding Hancheng Tomb Murals," *Cahiers d'Extrême-Asie* 24 (forthcoming).

15. See Hebei sheng wenwu yanjiusuo ed., *Xuanhua Liao mu—1974~1993 nian kaogu fajue baogao*, 2 vols. (Beijing: Wenwu chubanshe, 2001). For a comprehensive discussion of the tombs, see Li Qingquan, *Xuanhua Liao mu* (Beijing: Wenwu chubanshe, 2008). On the origins and role of the exorcist image in Xuanhua Tomb No. 7 and how it reveals the socialization of the tomb space, see Jeehee Hong, "Exorcism from the Streets to the Tomb: Image of the Judge and Minions in the Xuanhua Liao Tomb No. 7," *Archives of Asian Art* 63, no. 1 (2013): 1–25. Like the images of different religious connotations (as in the figures shown here), the treatment of the body was also hybridized. As in other tombs in the Xuanhua cemetery, Zhang Wenzao and his wife were placed in the coffin in the form of mannequins—two figures made of straw, containing cremated ashes of the deceased. A highly complex form of the corpse treatment, this practice has been addressed in depth by only a few scholars; see Hsueh-man Shen, "Body Matters: Manikin Burials in Liao Tombs of Xuanhua, Hebei Province," *Artibus Asiae* 65, no. 1 (2005): 133–134; Li, *Xuanhua Liao mu*, 262–273; and Wu Hung, *The Art of the Yellow Springs: Understanding Chinese Tombs* (Honolulu: University of Hawai'i Press, 2010), 142–146.

16. Among numerous excellent studies, see Eric Zürcher, *The Buddhist Conquest of China* (Leiden, Netherlands: Brill, 1959); C. K. Yang, *Religion in Chinese Society* (Berkeley: University of California Press, 1961); Steven Sangren, *History and Magical Power in a Chinese Community* (Stanford, CA: Stanford University Press, 1987); James L. Watson and Evelyn S. Rawski, eds., *Death Ritual in Late Imperial and Modern China* (Berkeley: University of California Press, 1988); Valerie Hansen, *Changing Gods in Medieval China, 1127–1276* (Princeton, NJ: Princeton University Press, 1990); Patricia Buckley Ebrey and Peter Gregory, eds., *Religion and Society in T'ang and Sung China* (Honolulu: University of Hawai'i Press, 1993); Edward L. Davis, *Society and the Supernatural in Song China* (Honolulu: University of Hawai'i Press, 2001); and Richard von Glahn, *The Sinister Way: The Divine and Demonic in Chinese Religious Culture* (Berkeley: University of California Press, 2004).

GLOSSARY

Anyang 安陽
ao 凹
Baoji 寶雞
Baojin lou 寶津樓
Beiping 北平
Bianjing 汴京
bozang 薄葬
bu zai tianya 不在天涯
cairen 才人
cang 藏
canghu 蒼鶻
Cangshan 蒼山
canjun 參軍
Cao Hui 曹惠
chadan 搽旦

chang 場
Changning 長寧
Changzhi 長治
chaoyuan 朝元
Chen 陳
Chen Chun 陳淳
Chen Yongzhi 陳用之
Chen Yuanjing 陳元靚
Cheng Yi 程頤
Chengwu 成武
Chenliu 陳留
chongmo 沖末
chou 丑
chu shi 處世
chuling 芻陵

Chuogeng lu 輟耕錄
ci 詞
Cuanguo 爨國
Da Han yuanling mizangjing
    大漢原陵秘葬經
Dadu 大都
dahun 打諢
Dai Fu 戴孚
Dali 大曆
dan 旦
dao shu 到書
Daogongbu chang 大攻布裳
Deng Chun 鄧椿
Dengfeng 登封
Dengzhou 鄧州

197

Diaozuo zhidu 彫作制度

Dili xinshu 地理新書

Ding Dusai 丁都賽

Dong Hai 董海

Dong Ming 董明

Dong Qijian 董屺堅

Dong You 董逌

Dongpo mao 東坡帽

Dongyue 東岳

du 度 (to cross)

Du Renjie 杜仁杰

Duan 段

Duan Ji 段楫

duanchang ren 斷腸人

duansong 斷送

Ducheng jisheng 都城紀勝

Er shi si xiao 二十四孝

Erlang 二郎

Ershui 二水

Fan Ye 范曄

Fan Zuyu 范祖禹

fang 房

fangmu 仿木

Fei Tangchen 費唐臣

Feihu 飛虎

Feng Hui 馮暉

Feng Rong 馮榮

Feng Yan 封演

Fengcheng 豐城

fuban 負板

fujing 副淨

fumo 副末

Fusheng si 福勝寺

Gao Cheng 高承

Gaoping 高平

ge 閣

Ge Hong 葛洪

gong 工

gongjiang 工匠

Gu Kaizhi 顧愷之

gu mendao 古門道 (ancient doorways)

gu mendao 鼓門道 (drum doorways)

Gu Yanwu 顧炎武

Guan Hanqing 關漢卿

Guang yi ji 廣異記

Guangsheng 光勝

guanjiang 官匠

Guanyin 觀音

gui mendao 鬼門道

Guo Ruoxu 郭若虛

Guo Xi 郭熙

guzhuang 孤裝

Han Qi 韓琦

Han Xizai yeyan tu 韓熙載夜宴圖

Hanlin shuhua yuan 翰林書畫院

Hedong 河東

Heishangou 黑山溝

Hong Mai 洪邁

Hongdong 洪洞

Hongmen 鴻門

Hongyu 紅峪

houbi 後壁

houdai zisun 後代子孫

houmian 後面

houyi 侯乙

houzang 厚葬

hu 壺

hu zhong riyue 壺中日月

Hua ji 畫繼

"Hua Yuntai shan ji" 画雲臺山記

huajiang 畫匠

huan 幻

Huang Tingjian 黃庭堅

Huanmen zidi cuo lishen 宦門子弟錯立身

Huiyuan 慧远

huji 戶籍

"Hunzuo diao" 混作彫

hushao 胡哨

hutian 壺天

ji 己 (I; myself)

ji 畿 (satellite town)

Jia Gongyan 賈公彥

jiandi 減地

jiang 匠

jiangji 匠籍

jiangshi 講史

jianzang 儉葬

Jiaozuo 焦作

jiehua 界畫

jili 吉禮

Jincheng 晉城

jing 景 (scenery)

Jing 景 (name)

jing 淨 (role type)

"Jinsuo liuzhu yin" 金鎖流珠引

Jiuliugou 酒流溝

Jiushan shuhui 九山書會

Li Chunfeng 李淳風

Li Daochun 劉道醇

Li Maozhen 李茂貞

Li Yishan 李義山

Liang 梁

liang duan 兩段

Li ji 禮記

lingwei 靈位

lingzuo 靈座

Linzi 臨淄

Liu Bang 劉邦

Liu Nianzi 劉念玆

Longhu dian 龍虎殿

lou 樓

louzeyuan 漏澤園

Lu 盧

Lü Pin 呂品

Lu You 陸游

Lugui bu 錄鬼簿

Luolong 洛龍

Luoning 洛寧

Luoyang 洛陽

Lushan 蘆山

Lutai dizi 露臺弟子

Ma Zhiyuan 馬致遠

Macun 馬村

Mahao 麻浩

maidi quan 買地券

Maiwang guan 脈望舘

mendao 門道

Meng Yuanlao 孟元老

Mengliang lu 夢梁錄

ming'an 冥暗

mingjing 銘旌

mingqi 明器

mingqi fenzuo 冥器分作

Mingying wang 明應王

minjiang 民匠

mo 末

moni 末泥

mu ouren 木偶人

mubiao 墓表

muzhi 墓誌

muzhiming 墓誌銘

Nanchui 南垂

naobo 鐃鈸

nei 內

nei ying 內應

neidan 內丹

Nie Chongyi 聶崇義

paiban 拍板

Pan Dechong 潘德衝

Pingmo 平陌

Pingyang 平陽

po 婆

Puzhou 蒲州

puzuo 鋪作

Qiao Zhou 譙周

Qidong 齊東

qiejiang 砌匠

qin 寢

Qinghong 輕紅

Qingming 清明

Qingsu 輕素

Qiushe 秋社

"Qiusi" 秋思

Quanzhen 全真

Quanzhou 泉州

que 闕

Qufu 曲阜

Ren Guang 任廣

Ruicheng 芮城

saishe 賽社

sanduan 散段

sangjiu 喪柩

Sanli tu 三禮圖

Sanmen xia 三門峽

Sanqing dian 三清殿

sanqu 散曲

Sengqie 僧伽

shakai 社会 (shehui in
    Japanese)

shanhua 山花

shanmen 山門

shanqiang 山牆

shanshui bi 山水壁

shaozhuanjiang 燒磚匠

shehui 社會

Shen Jiji 沈既濟

Shen Yue 沈約

shendao 神道

shengqi 生器

sheshen 社神

shi 尸 (corpse)

shi 詩 (poetry)

shi 士 (literati)

shi'e 十惡

Shi ming 釋名

shijiang 石匠

Shilin guangji 事林廣記

shizao wanzao 事造剜鑿

shizi xieshan 十字歇山

Shu Han 蜀漢

Shuang ta 雙塔

Sicui chang 緦衰裳

siheyuan 四合院

Sima Guang 司馬光

Sizhou dasheng 四洲大聖

Song Defang 宋德方

Song Di 宋迪

Song Yingxing 宋應星

Su Shi 蘇軾

suo 塑

Taiping guangji 太平廣記

tian qu 天趣

Tiangong kaiwu 天工開物

tingtang 廳堂

tu 凸

tuanhang 團行

Tujue 突厥

wai 外

wai chengda 外呈答

wai ying 外應

wai zhai 外宅

Wang Chuzhi 王處直

Wang Hui 王暉

Wang Yong 王枺

Wang Zhe 王嚞

Wangbao 王報

washe 瓦舍

Weichi Jingde 尉遲敬德

Wen 文 (emperor)

Wen Tong 文同

weng 翁

Wenxian 溫縣

Wenzhou 溫州

Wohu 卧虎

Wu Daozi 吳道子

wu fu 五服

Wu Qing 武慶

wu zhuang 吳裝

Wugu cangsuo 五穀倉所

wuhua cuannong 五花爨弄

Wuji men 無極門

Wulin jiushi 武林舊事

Wulingzhuang 吳嶺莊

Wuzhen pian 悟真篇

Xiang Yu 項羽

xianying bei 先塋碑

xiaomo 小末

Xie Tiao 謝朓

xieshan 歇山

xiezi 楔子

xifang 戲房

xiju 戲具

xin gong 信工

Xing 興

Xinmi 新密

xiong li 凶禮

Xiwangmu 西王母

xiwen 戲文

Xixiang ji 西廂記

Xu Xi 徐熙

Xuanhua 宣化

Xuanzang 玄奘

Yan Dunyi 嚴敦易

yanduan 艷段

Yang Huizhi 楊惠之
Yangjiayuan 楊家院
Yanshi 偃師
Yantie lun 鹽鐵論
Yao 姚 (family name)
Yicheng si 一乘寺
yidou sansheng 一斗三升
Yijing 義淨
Yili 儀禮
ying 影
yingbi (also *Yingbi*) 影壁
yingtang 影堂
Yingzao fashi 營造法式
yinxi 引戲
yinyang 陰陽
Yongji 永濟
Yongle dadian 永樂大典
Yongle gong 永樂宮
Yuanben wu ren 院本五人
Yuanqu xuan 元曲選
Yue Bochuan 岳伯川
Yue Shou 岳壽
yuesang 樂喪

yuji 虞際
yushi 愉尸
za 雜
zaju 雜劇
zang 葬
Zeng 曾 (state)
zhaiyan 齋筵
zhancui 斬衰
zhancui chang 斬衰裳
Zhang 張 (family name, for both Madam Zhang and Xuanhua cemetery)
Zhang Boduan 張伯端
Zhang Sengyou 張僧繇
zhang su bai bi 張素敗壁
Zhang Xie zhuangyuan 張協狀元
zhao hun 招魂
zhaobi 照壁
zhen 真
Zhen zhong ji 枕中記
Zheng Tingyu 鄭庭玉
Zheng Xuan 鄭玄

zheng zaju 正雜劇
zhengmo 正末
zhi yidi 治夷狄
Zhong ping tu 重屏圖
Zhong Sicheng 鍾嗣成
Zhongyuan jie 中元節
Zhou Wenju 周文矩
Zhu Quan 朱權
Zhu Sanweng 朱三翁
zhu se jiyiren 諸色技藝人
Zhu Yunjian 朱允建
zhuanggu 裝孤
"Zhuangjia bushi goulan" 莊家不識構欄
zhugan zi 竹竿子
zhugongdiao 諸宮調
Zhulin qixian 竹林七賢
zhuokuai 斫膾
zhuoshi 斫事
zi mingfu 資冥福
Zizhan yang 子瞻樣
Zoucheng 邹城
Zouying ge 走鸎歌

BIBLIOGRAPHY

PRIMARY SOURCES

Ban Gu. *Han shu* (History of the Han dynasty). Beijing: Zhonghua shuju, 1962.

Buddhabhadra, trans. *Fo shuo guanfo sanmei hai jing* (Sutra on the ocean samādhi of visualizing the Buddha). In *Taishō shinshū Daizōkyō*, edited by Takakusu Junjirō and Watanabe Kaigyoku, vol. 15, no. 643. Tokyo: Taishō Issaikyo Kankokai, 1914–1932.

Chao Ruyu. *Song mingchen zouyi* (Memorials by famous statesmen of the Song dynasty). Taipei: Taiwan shangwu yin shuguan, 1983.

Chen Chun. *Beixi da quanji* (Complete works of Chen Chun). *SKQS* vol. 1168.

Chen Pengnian and Li Suchang. *Zhongxiu Guang yun* (Revised Broad Rhymes). *SKQS* vol. 236.

Chen Shan. *Menshi xinhua* (New notes taken while squeezing lice). In *Xuxiu Siku quanshu* (Revised continuation of *SKQS*), 1122. Shanghai: Shanghai guji chubanshe, 1995–2002.

Chen Yuanjing. *Shilin guangji* (Comprehensive record of the forest of matters). Beijing: Zhonghua shuju, 1999.

Cheng Dachang. *Yanfanlu* (Extending the Fanlu). In *Congshu jicheng chubian* (First edition of the collected collectanea), vol. 293. Beijing: Zhonghua shuju, 1991.

"Chonghe zhenren pangong shendao zhi bei" (Memorial stele for Pan Dechong). In *Ganshui xianyuan lu* (Accounts of the immortals who appeared at Ganshui), edited by Li Daoqian. In *Daojia jinshi lue* (Collection of Daoist epigraphy), edited by Chen Yuan. Beijing: Wenwu chubanshe, 1988.

Cui fujun duan yuanjia qianzhu (Officer Cui judges villains and rewards the hero). In Zang Maoxun, *Yuanqu xuan jiao zhu* (Selected Yuan dramas, collated and annotated), vol. 3, xia, edited and annotated by Wang Xueqi. Shijiazhuang: Hebei jiaoyu chubanshe, 1994.

Da Han yuanling mizang jing (Secret burial classic of the original sepulchers of the Great Han). In *Yongle dadian* (Great canon of the Yongle era), vol. 8199. Beijing: Zhonghua shuju, 1959.

Dai Fu. *Guang yi ji* (Extensive records of marvels). In *Guang yi ji*. Punctuated and annotated by Liu Dengge. Beijing: Beijing chubanshe, 2000.

Daocheng. *Shishi yaolan* (Essential readings for Buddhists). In *Taishō shinshū Daizōkyō*, edited by Takakusu Junjirō and Watanabe Kaigyoku, vol. 54, no. 2127. Tokyo: Taishō Issaikyo Kankokai, 1914–1932.

Deng Chun. *Hua ji* (Painting continued). In *Zhongguo shuhua quanshu* (Complete collection of writings on calligraphy and painting in China), vol. 2, edited by Lu Fusheng. Shanghai: Shanghai shuhua chubanshe, 1993.

Ding Fubao, ed. *Daozang jinghua lu baizhong* (Selection of one hundred essential texts from the Daoist Canon), vol. 8. Shanghai: Yixue shuju, 1921.

Dong You. *Guangchuan huaba* (Dong You's colophons on paintings). In *Zhongguo shuhua quanshu* (Complete collection of writings on calligraphy and painting in China), vol. 1, edited by Lu Fusheng. Shanghai: Shanghai shuhua chubanshe, 1993.

Dou Yi. *Song xingtong* (The Song panel code). Beijing: Zhonghua shuju, 1984.

Du Renjie. "Zhuangjia bushi goulan" (Country bumpkin knows nothing of theater). In Yu Weimin and Sun Rongrong. *Lidai quhua huibian* (Collection of dramas through history). Hefei: Huangshan shushe, 2006.

Duan Chengshi. *Youyang zazu* (Miscellaneous morsels from Youyang). *SKQS* vol. 1047.

Duan yuanjia qianzhu ([Officer Cui] judges villains and rewards the hero). In *Guben xiqu congkan* (Collectanea of dramas in old editions), 4, Maiwang guan chaoben ed., vol. 19, no. 51. Shanghai: Shangwu yin shu guan, 1958.

Fan Ye. *Hou Han shu* (History of the Later Han dynasty). Sibu beiyao duanxing ben ed. Taipei: Taiwan Zhonghua shuju, 1965.

Fei Tangchen. *Su Zizhan fengxue pin Huangzhou zaju* (Su Shi in a snowstorm banished to Huangzhou). In *Yuanqu xuan waibian* (Supplementary collection of Selected Yuan Dramas), edited by Sui Shusen. Beijing: Zhonghua shuju, 1959.

Feng Yan. *Feng shi wenjian ji* (Record of things seen and heard by Feng Yan). In *Feng shi wenjian ji jiaozhu* (Annotated Record of Things Seen and Heard by Feng Yan), annotated by Zhao Zhenxin. Beijing: Zhonghua shuju, 2005.

Gao Cheng. *Shiwu jiyuan* (Record of the origins of things and affairs). Beijing: Zhonghua shuju, 1989.

Ge Hong. *Shenxian zhuan* (Biographies of immortals). In *Liexian zhuan. Shenxian zhuan zhushe* (Annotations and translations of Collected Biographies of Immortals and Biographies of immortals), annotated and translated by Teng Xiuzhan and Deng Ansheng. Tianjin: Baihua wenyi chubanshe, 1996.

Gu Kaizhi. "Hua Yuntai shan ji" (Note on painting Cloud Terrace Mountain). In Zhang Yanyuan, *Lidai minghua ji* (Famous paintings through history), in *Zhongguo shuhua quanshu* (Complete collection of writings on calligraphy and painting in China), vol. 1, edited by Lu Fusheng. Shanghai: Shanghai shuhua chubanshe, 1993.

Gu Yanwu. *Rizhi lu* (Daily accumulation of knowledge). *SKQS* vol. 858.

Guan Hanqing. *Dou'e yuan* (The injustice to Dou E). In *Yuanqu xuan jiao zhu*, vol. 4, shang, edited and annotated by Wang Xueqi. Shijiazhuang: Hebei jiaoyu chubanshe, 1994.

Guo Ruoxu. *Tuhua jianwen zhi* (Paintings seen and heard). In *Zhongguo shuhua quanshu* (Complete collection of writings on calligraphy and painting in China), vol. 1, edited by Lu Fusheng. Shanghai: Shanghai shuhua chubanshe, 1993.

Guo Tuan. *Kui che zhi* (Collection of ghost stories). In Xu Lingyun and Xu Shanshu, *Tang Song biji xiaoshuo san zhong* (Miscellaneous notes and trivial anecdotes of the Tang and Song periods: Three selections). Hefei: Huangshan shushe, 1991.

Han Taihua. *Wushi weifu zhai suibi* (Random notes from the wushi weifu study). Gongshuntang congshu ed. In *Yanpu zaji, Wushi weifu zhai suibi* (Miscellaneous Notes of Yanpu and Random Notes from the Wushi weifu Study). Taipei: Wenhai chubanshe, 1973.

Hong Mai. *Rongzhai suibi* (Miscellaneous notes from the Rong Study). Beijing: Zhonghua shuju, 2005.

Huan Kuan. *Yantie lun* (Discourses on salt and iron). *SKQS* vol. 695.

Huang Minzhi. "Jining Li shi zuyingbei" (Genealogical stele of Mr. Li from Jining). In *Quan Liao Jin wen* (Complete writings from the Liao and Jin periods), vol. 2. Taiyuan: Shanxi guji chubanshe, 2002.

Huiyuan. "Foying ming" (Inscription on the reflection of the Buddha). In Daoxuan, *Guang Hongming ji* (Expanded collection on the propagation and clarification [of Buddhism]), in *Taishō shinshū Daizōkyō*, edited by Takakusu Junjirō and Watanabe Kaigyoku, vol. 52, no. 2103. Tokyo: Taishō Issaikyo Kankokai, 1914–1932.

Jiang Shaoyu. *Shishi leiyuan* (A categorized account of events [of the Song]). *SKQS* vol. 874.

Kangxi, ed. *Yu ding Quan Tang shi* (Complete Tang poems). *SKQS* vol. 1431.

Kong Tianjian. "Cangshu ji" (Record of book collecting). In *Jinwen zui* (The best of Jin dynasty writings), edited by Zhang Jinwu. Guangzhou: Yue'ya tang, 1882.

Li Bi. *Wang Jinggong shi zhu* (Annotations to the poems of Wang Anshi). *SKQS* vol. 1106.

Li Chunfeng. "Jinsuo liuzhu yin" (Guide to the golden lock and the moving pearls). In *Zhengtong Daozang* (Daoist canon), facs. 636. Shanghai: Shanghai Hanfen lou yingyin, 1924.

Li Ding. "Xuandu zhidao Piyun zhenren Song tianshi citing beiming bingyin." In *Daojia jinshi lue* (Collection of Daoist epigraphy), edited by Chen Yuan. Beijing: Wenwu chubanshe, 1988.

Li Fang. *Taiping guangji* (Extensive records of the Taiping era). *SKQS* vol. 1044.

Li Jie. *Yingzao fashi* (Treatise on architectural methods). 2 vols. Beijing: Zhongguo shudian, 2006.

Li Jifu. *Yuanhe junxian zhi* (Gazetteer of the Yuanhe region). *SKQS* vol. 468.

Li Zhi. *Shiyou tanji* (Record of conversations between the master and his friends). Beijing: Zhonghua shuju, 2002.

Liu Daochun. *Shengchao minghua ping* (Evaluations of renowned painters of the Song dynasty). In *Zhongguo shuhua quanshu* (Complete collection of writings on calligraphy and painting in China), vol. 1, edited by Lu Fusheng. Shanghai: Shanghai shuhua chubanshe, 1993.

———. *Wudai minghua buyi* (A complementary to renowned painters of five dynasties). In *Zhongguo shuhua quanshu* (Complete collection of writings on calligraphy and painting in China), vol. 1, edited by Lu Fusheng. Shanghai: Shanghai shuhua chubanshe, 1993.

Liu Xi. *Shi ming* (Explanation of words). In *Congshujicheng chubian*, vol. 1151, edited by Wang Yunwu. Changsha: Shangwu yin shu guan, 1939.

Liu Yiqing. *Shishuo xinyu jiaojian* (A new account of tales of the world). Annotated by Xu Zhen'e. 2 vols. Beijing: Zhonghua shuju, 1984.

Lu You. *Fangweng jiaxun* (Family instruction of Lu You). In *Zhibuzuzhai congshu* (Collectanea of Zhibuzhai). Baibu congshu jicheng (One hundred collectanea), no. 29 (box 22). Taipei: Yiwen, 1966.

———. *Laoxue an biji* (Miscellaneous notes from Laoxue an). *SKQS* vol. 865.

———. *Lu Fangweng quanji* (Complete writings of Lu You). Beijing: Zhongguo shudian, 1986.

———. *Weinan wenji* (Collected writings of Lu You). In *Lu You ji* (Collected works of Lu You). *SKQS* vol. 1163.

Maozhao Yuwen. *Da Jin guo zhi* (History of the Great Jin). In Cui Wenyin et al., *Da Jin guo zhi jiaozheng* (History of the Great Jin, collated and corrected). Beijing: Zhonghua shuju, 1986.

Meng Yuanlao. *Dongjing menghua lu* (Record of dreamy splendors of the eastern capital). In *Dongjing menghua lu jianzhu* (Record of Dreamy Splendors of the Eastern Capital, collated and annotated). Annotated by Yi Yongwen. 2 vols. Beijing: Zhonghua shuju, 2006.

Mengzi zhengyi (Explanations on Mencius). Annotated by Jiao Xun. Beijing: Zhonghua shuju, 1987.

Nai Deweng. *Ducheng jisheng* (Record of the splendors of the capital). In *Dongjing menghua lu wai si zhong* (Record of Dreamy Splendors of the Eastern Capital and four other books). Beijing: Zhonghua shuhu, 1962.

Nie Chongyi. *Xin ding Sanli tu* (Newly edited pictures for the three compendia for ritual). 2 vols. Beijing: Zhonghua shuju, 1963.

Ouyang Min. *Yudi guangji* (Broad description of the world). Chengdu: Sichuan daxue chubanshe, 2003.

Ouyang Xiu. *Xin Tang shu* (New history of the Tang dynasty). Beijing: Zhonghua shuju, 1975.

Ren Guang. *Shuxu zhinan* (Guide to the correspondence). *SKQS* vol. 920.

Shao Bowen. *Shaoshi jianwen lu* (Record of things seen and heard by Shao Bowen). Beijing: Zhonghua shuju, 1983.

Shen Jiji. "Zhen zhong ji" (Record of the world in a pillow). In Li Fang et al., *Wenyuan yinghua* (The finest blossoms in the garden of literature), vol. 5. Beijing: Zhonghua shuju, 1982.

Shen Kuo. *Mengxi bitan* (Brush Talks from Dream Brook). In *Mengxi bitan jiaozheng* (Brush Talks from Dream Brook, collated), annotated by Hu Daozheng. 2 vols. Shanghai: Shanghai guji chubanshe, 1987.

Shen Zinan. *Yilin huikao* (Compendium of studies on the arts). *SKQS* vol. 859.

Sima Guang. *Chuanjia ji* (The works of Ouyang Xiu). *SKQS* vol. 1094.

——. *Sima shi shuyi* (Etiquette for writing and other occasions), vol. 1040. Congshu jicheng chubian ed. Beijing: Zhonghua shuju, 1985.

Sima Qian. *Shi ji* (Historical records). Beijing: Zhonghua shuju, 1959.

Song Lian. *Yuan shi* (History of the Yuan dynasty). Beijing: Zhonghua shuju, 1977.

Song Yingxing. *Tiangong kaiwu* (The works of heaven and inception of things). Guangzhou: Guangdong renmin chubanshe, 1976.

Su Shi. *Dongpo quanji* (Complete works of Su Shi). *SKQS* vol. 1107.

Sui Shusen, ed. *Yuanqu xuan waibian* (A supplementary collection of selected Yuan dramas). Beijing: Zhonghua shuju, 1959.

——, ed. *Quan Yuan sanqu* (Complete collection of Yuan dramas and song suites). Beijing: Zhonghua shuju, 1964.

Tao Zongyi. *Nancun Chuogeng lu* (Notes taken by Tao Zongyi while at rest from plowing). Beijing: Zhonghua shuju, 2004.

Tuo tuo. *Jin shi* (History of the Jin dynasty). Beijing: Zhonghua shuju, 1975.

——. *Song shi* (History of the Song dynasty). Beijing: Zhonghua shuju, 1977.

Wang Anshi. *Linchuan wenji* (Literary works of Wang Anshi). *SKQS* vol. 1105.

Wang Dang. *Tang yulin jiaozheng* (Forest of anecdotes on the Tang, collated). Annotated by Zhou Xunchu. 2 vols. Beijing: Zhonghua shuju, 1987.

Wang Qinruo. *Cefu yuan gui* (Models from the archives). Beijing: Zhonghua shuju, 1989.

Wang Shifu. *Xixiang ji er ben* (Story of the western chamber, second edition). In *Yuanqu xuan waibian* (Addenda to the Selections of the Dramas of the Yuan Dynasty). 3 vols, edited by Sui Shusen. Beijing: Zhonghua shuju, 1959.

Wang Xunxiang. *Xugou xian zhi* (Gazetteer of Xugou County). In *Zhongguo difang zhi jicheng: Shanxi fu xian zhi ji* (Collected gazetteers of China: Prefectures and counties in Shanxi Province). Nanjing: Fenghuang chubanshe, 2005.

Wang Zhu. *Tujie jiaozheng dili xinshu* (Illustrated and collated new book of earth patterns). 1192 ed. Taipei: Jiwen shuju, 1985.

Wu Zimu. *Mengliang lu* (Record of reminiscing on the past). In *Dongjing menghua lu wai si zhong* (*Dongjing menghua lu* and four other texts). Shanghai: Shanghai gudian wenxue chubanshe, 1956.

Xia Tingzhi. *Qinglou ji* (Green bower collection). In *Qinglou ji jianzhu* (Annotations to Green Bower Collection). Annotated by Sun Chongtao and Xu Hongtu. Beijing: Zhongguo xiju chubanshe, 1990.

Xu Mengxin. *San chao bei meng huibian* (Compilation of documents on the treaties with the north during the three reigns). 2 vols. Shanghai: Shanghai guji chubanshe, 1987.

Xu Song. *Jiankang shilu* (Veritable records of Jiankang). Siku quanshu ed., vol. 370. Shanghai: Shanghai guji chubanshe, 1987.

"Xuan Hu zhenren taixi jue" (Embryonic breathing of the perfected person of the mysterious gourd). In *Zhuzhen shengtai shenyongjue* (Spiritual method of the embryonic breathing of all sages), in *Zhengtong Daozang* (Daoist canon), facs. 570. Shanghai: Shanghai Hanfen lou yingyin, 1924.

Xuanhe huapu (Catalogue of paintings in the Xuanhe era). In *Zhongguo shuhua quanshu* (Complete collection of writings on calligraphy and painting in China), edited by Lu Fusheng, vol. 2. Shanghai: Shanghai shuhua chubanshe, 1993.

Xuanzang. *Da Tang Xiyue ji* (Great Tang records on the western regions). Annotated by Zhou Guolin. Changsha: Yuelu shushe, 1999.

Yang Tianyu. *Li ji yizhu* (Book of rites, translated and annotated), 3 vols. Shanghai: Shanghai guji chubanshe, 1997.

Yang Wanli. *Chengzhai ji* (Collected works of Yang Wanli). *SKQS* vol. 1161.

Yang Yinliu. *Zhongguo gudai yinyueshi kao.* 4 vols. Beijing: Renmin yinyue chubanshe, 1986.

Yijing. *Foshuo tiandi bayang shenzhou jing* (Scripture on the spell of the eight yang spirits of heaven and earth). In *Taishō shinshū Daizōkyō,* edited by Takakusu Junjirō and Watanabe Kaigyoku, vol. 85, no. 2897. Tokyo: Taishō Issaikyo Kankokai, 1914–1932.

Yili zhushu (Annotations and commentaries on Ceremonies and Rites). With commentary by Zheng Xuan and compiled by Jia Gongyan. 3 vols. Shanghai: Shanghai guji chubanshe, 2008.

Yue Bochuan. *Lü Dongbin du Tieguai Li Yue zaju* (Lü Dongbin leads Iron Crutch Li Yue to enlightenment). In *Yuanqu xuan jiao zhu* (Selected Yuan dramas, collated and annotated), vol. 2, shang, edited by Wang Xueqi. Shijiazhuang: Hebei jiaoyu chubanshe, 1994.

Yue Shi. *Taiping huanyu ji* (Universal geography of the Taiping era). 2 vols. Taipei: Wenhai chubanshe, 1963.

Yuwen Maozhao, ed. *Da Jin guo zhi* (History of the great Jin kingdom). In *Da Jin guo zhi jiaozheng* (Annotations to history of the great Jin kingdom). Annotated by Cui Wenyin. Beijing: Zhonghua shuju, 1986.

Zang Maoxun. *Yuanqu xuan jiao zhu* (Selected Yuan dramas, collated and annotated), edited and annotated by Wang Xueqi. 4 vols. Shijiazhuang: Hebei jiaoyu chubanshe, 1994.

Zanning. *Song Gaoseng zhuan* (Biographies of eminent monks compiled during the Song). Beijing: Zhonghua shuju, 1987.

Zeng Zao. *Leishu* (Encyclopedia). *SKQS* vol. 873.

Zhang Junfang. *Yunji qijian* (Seven tablets in a cloudy satchel). Sibu chongkan chubian ed. Shanghai: Shangwu yin shu guan, 1929.

Zhang Xian. *Anlu ji* (Collected works of Zhang Xian). In Zhang You, *Fugu bian* (Compilation of restored graphs). Yangzhou: Huainan shuju, 1903.

Zhang Xie zhuangyuan (The top graduate Zhang Xie). In *Yongle dadian xiwen sanzhong* (Three southern dramas selected from documents of the Yongle era). Taipei: Chang'an chubanshe, 1978.

Zhang Yanyuan. *Lidai minghua ji* (Record of renowned paintings through history). In *Zhongguo shuhua quanshu* (Complete collection of writings on calligraphy and painting in China), vol. 1, edited by Lu Fusheng. Shanghai: Shanghai shuhua chubanshe, 1993.

Zhao Yanwei. *Yunlu manchao* (Random jottings recorded at Yunlu). Beijing: Zhonghua shuju, 1998.

Zheng Dehui. *Zhongli Chun zhiyong dingqi* (Zhongli Chun brings peace to Qi through her wisdom and courage). In *Guben xiqu congkan* (Collectanea of dramas in old editions). Maiwang guan chaoben ed., vol. 12, no. 34. Shanghai: Shangwu yin shu guan, 1958.

Zheng Juzhong et al. *Zhenghe wuli xinyi* (New ceremonies for the five rites of the Zhenghe period). Taipei: Taiwan shangwu yin shuguan, 1983.

Zhipan. *Fozu tongji* (A chronicle of the patriarch of Buddhism). In *Taishō shinshū Daizōkyō*, vol. 49, no. 2035, edited by Takakusu Junjirō and Watanabe Kaigyoku. Tokyo: Taishō Issaikyo Kankokai, 1914–1932.

Zhong Sicheng. *Lugui bu* (Register of ghosts). In *Lugui bu wai si zhong* (Register of Ghosts and four other texts). Shanghai: Shanghai guji chubanshe, 1978.

Zhou Jinggui, ed. *Puzhou fuzhi* (Prefectural gazetteer of Puzhou). Taipei: Taiwan Xuesheng shuju, 1968.

Zhou Nan. *Shanfang ji* (Collected works of Zhou Nan). Siku quanshu zhenben san ji (Third collection of rare works from *SKQS*), vol. 242, edited by Wang Yunwu. Taipei: Taiwan Shangwu yin shu guan, 1972.

Zhu Jingxuan. *Tang chao minghua lu* (Record of renowned paintings of the Tang). In *Zhongguo shuhua quanshu* (Complete collection of writings on calligraphy and painting in China), vol. 1, edited by Lu Fusheng. Shanghai: Shanghai shuhua chubanshe, 1993.

Zhu Mu. *Gujin shiwen leiju* (Complete collection of the affairs and writings of ancient and modern times). *SKQS* vol. 925.

Zhu Quan. *Taihe zhengyin pu* (Record of correct tones of the Taihe era). In *Lugui bu wai sizhong* (Register of Ghosts and four other texts). Shanghai: Shanghai guji chubanshe, 1978.

Zhu Xi. *Chu Hsi's Family Rituals: A Twelfth-Century Chinese Manual for the Performance of Cappings, Weddings, Funerals, and Ancestral Rites,* translated and annotated by Patricia Buckley Ebrey. Princeton, NJ: Princeton University Press, 1991.

———. *Jiali* (Family rituals). *SKQS* vol. 142.

Zong Bing. "Hua Shanshui xu" (Preface to painting landscape). In *Zhongguo hualun leibian* (Classified anthology of Chinese writings on painting), vol. 1, edited by Yu Jianhua. Taipei: Huazheng shuju, 1984.

———. "Ming Fo lun" (Essay explaining Buddhism). In Sengyou, *Hongming ji* (Extended collection [of documents] for propagating enlightenment), in *Taishō shinshū Daizōkyō,* edited by Takakusu Junjirō and Watanabe Kaigyoku, vol. 52, no. 2102 (Tokyo: Taishō Issaikyo Kankokai, 1914–1932).

SECONDARY SOURCES

Aoki Masaru. "Shina kinsei gikyokushi" (History of drama in early modern China). In *Aoki Masaru zenshu* (Complete writings of Aoki Masaru), vol. 3. Tokyo: Shunjusha, 1969–1975.

Asim, Ina. "Status Symbol and Insurance Policy: Song Land Deeds for the Afterlife." In *Burial in Song China,* edited by Dieter Kuhn. Heidelberg: Edition Forum, 1994.

Bao Weimin. "Song dai minjiang chagu zhidu shulue." In *Chuantong guojia yu shehui.* Beijing: Shangwu yin shu guan, 2009.

Barbieri-Low, Anthony J. *Artisans in Early Imperial China.* Seattle: University of Washington Press, 2007.

Barthes, Roland. *Image, Music, Text.* Trans. Stephen Heath. New York: Hill and Wang, 1977.

Beckman, Joy E. "Layers of Being: Bodies, Objects, and Spaces in Warring States Burials." PhD diss., University of Chicago, 2006.

Berling, Judith. "Orthopraxy." In *Encyclopedia of Religion,* vol. 11, edited by Mircea Eliade. New York: Macmillan, 1987.

Birnbaum, Raoul. "Buddhist Meditation Teachings and the Birth of 'Pure' Landscape Painting in China." *Journal of Chinese Religions* 9 (1981): 42–58.

———. "Light in the Wutai Mountains." In *The Presence of Light: Divine Radiance and Religious Experience,* edited by Mathew T. Kapstein. Chicago: University of Chicago Press, 2004.

Bol, Peter K. *Neo-Confucianism in History.* Cambridge, MA: Harvard University Asia Center, 2008.

———. *"This Culture of Ours": Intellectual Transitions in T'ang and Sung China.* Stanford, CA: Stanford University Press, 1992.

Bossler, Beverly J. *Powerful Relations: Kinship, Status, and the State in Sung China (960–1279).* Cambridge, MA: Council on East Asian Studies, 1998.

Bourdieu, Pierre. *Outline of a Theory of Practice.* Trans. Richard Nice. Cambridge: Cambridge University Press, 2009.

Brashier, Kenneth. "Han Thanatology and the Division of 'Souls.'" *Early China* 21 (1996): 125–158.

Brown, Bill. "How to Do Things with Things (A Toy Story)." *Critical Inquiry* 24, no. 4 (1998): 935–964.

Bush, Susan. "Tsung Ping's Essay on Painting Landscape and the 'Landscape Buddhism' of Mount Lu." In *Theories of the Arts in China,* edited by Susan Bush and Christian Murck. Princeton, NJ: Princeton University Press, 1983.

Bush, Susan, and Hsiao-yen Shih, eds. *Early Chinese Texts on Painting.* Cambridge, MA: Harvard-Yenching Institute, 1985.

Cahill, James, ed. *An Index of Early Chinese Painters and Paintings.* Warren, CT: Floating World Editions, 2003.

Čapek, Abe. *Chinese Stone Pictures: A Distinctive Form of Chinese Art.* London: Spring Books, 1962.

Carlson, Marvin. *Places of Performance: The Semiotics of Theater Architecture.* Ithaca, NY: Cornell University Press, 1989.

Chai Zejun. *Chai Zejun gujianzhu wenji* (Collected works of Chai Zejun). Beijing: Wenwu chubanshe, 1999.

Chang Jianhua. "Yuan dai muci jizu wenti chutan" (Initial inquiry into the issue of the grave rite and ancestral worship during the Yuan). In *Shehui wenti de lishi kaocha* (Historical investigation of social issues), edited by Zhao Qingzhu. Chengdu: Chengdu chubanshe, 1992.

Chang Wen-chang. *Zhili yi jiao tianxia—Tang Song lishu yu guojia shehui* (Cultivating the world through ordering rites: Books on rites and Tang–Song society). Taipei: Guoli Taiwan daxue chubanshe, 2012.

Che Wenming. *Ershi shiji xiqu wenwu de fazhan yu quxue yanjiu* (Development of the material study of theater and studies on drama in the twentieth century). Beijing: Wenhua yishu chubanshe, 2001.

Chen Chang'an. "Luoyang chutu Sizhou dasheng shidiaoxiang" (On the stone sculpture of Sengqie excavated in Luoyang). *Zhongyuan wenwu* 1997, no. 2 (1997): 93–109.

Chen Yunru. "'Jiehua' zai Song Yuan shiqi de zhuanzhe: yi Wang Zhenpeng de jiehua wei lie" (A shift in "ruled-line painting" during the Song and Yuan periods: The case of Wang Zhenpeng's ruled-line painting). *Meishushixue yanjiu jikan* 26 (2009): 135–192.

Chung, Anita. *Drawing Boundaries: Architectural Images in Qing China.* Honolulu: University of Hawai'i Press, 2004.

Crump, J. I. *Chinese Theater in the Days of Kublai Khan.* Tucson: University of Arizona Press, 1980.

———. "Yuan-pen, Yuan's Rowdy Ancestor." *Literature East and West* 14, no. 4 (1970): 473–490.

Davis, Edward L. *Society and the Supernatural in Song China.* Honolulu: University of Hawai'i Press, 2001.

Debord, Guy. *The Society of the Spectacle.* Trans. Donald Nicholson-Smith. New York: Zone Books, 1994.

Deng Fei. "Guanyu Song Jin muzang zhong xiaoxingtu de sikao" (Reflections on the images of filial piety found in tombs of Song and Jin periods). *Zhongyuan wenwu* 2009, no. 4 (2009): 75–81.

Dien, Albert. "Developments in Funerary Practices in the Six Dynasties Period: The *Duisuguan* or "Figured Jar" as a Case in Point." In *Han Tang zhijian wenhua yishu de hudong yu jiaorong* (Between Han and Tang: Cultural and artistic interaction in a transformative period), edited by Wu Hung. Beijing: Wenwu chubanshe, 2001.

Ding Mingyi. "Shanxi zhongnan bu de Song Yuan wutai" (Stages of Song and Yuan periods in central and southern Shanxi). *Wenwu* 1972, no. 4 (1972): 47–56.

Dolby, William. *Grandee's Son Takes the Wrong Career.* In *Eight Chinese Plays from the Thirteenth Century to the Present.* Translated and with an introduction by William Dolby. New York: Columbia University Press, 1978.

Dong Xiang. "Yanshi xian Jiuliu gou shuiku Song mu" (On the Song dynasty tomb found in Jiuliu, Yanshi County). *Wenwu* 1959, no. 9 (1959): 84–85.

Dong Xinlin. "Bei Song Jin Yuan muzang bishi suo jian er shi si xiao gushi yu Gaoli xiaoxing lu" (The Twenty-Four Exemplars of Filial Piety as seen through wall adornment in the tombs of Northern Song, Jin, and Yuan dynasties and the record of filial deeds of the Goryeo dynasty). *Huaxia kaogu* 2 (2009): 141–152.

Doniger, Wendy. *The Woman Who Pretended to Be Who She Was: Myths of Self-Imitation.* New York: Oxford University Press, 2005.

Dudbridge, Glen. *Religious Experience and Lay Society in T'ang China: A Reading of Tai Fu's* Kuang-i chi. Cambridge: Cambridge University Press, 1995.

Ebrey, Patricia Buckley. *Confucianism and Family Rituals in Imperial China: Social History of Writing about Rites.* Princeton, NJ: Princeton University Press, 1991.

——. "Cremation in Song China." *American Historical Review* 95, no. 2 (1990): 406–428.

——. "Early Stages in the Development of Descent Group Organization." In *Kinship Organization in Late Imperial China, 1000–1940,* edited by Patricia Buckley Ebrey and James L. Watson. Berkeley: University of California Press, 1986.

——. "The Response of the Sung State to Popular Funeral Practices." In *Religion and Society in T'ang and Sung China,* edited by Patricia Buckley Ebrey and Peter N. Gregory. Honolulu: University of Hawai'i Press, 1993.

Ecke, Gustave, and Paul Demiéville. *The Twin Pagodas of Zayton: A Study of Later Sculpture in China*, edited by Cambridge, MA: Harvard University Press, 1935.

Eschenbach, Silvia Freiin Ebner von. "Public Graveyards of the Song Dynasty." In *Burial in Song China,* edited by Dieter Kuhn. Heidelberg: Edition Forum, 1994.

Eskildsen, Stephen. *The Teachings and Practices of the Early Quanzhen Taoist Masters.* Albany: State University of New York Press, 2004.

Fan Chunyi. "Tianjingsha, Qiusi shi Ma Zhiyuan zuo de ma" (Are "Tianjingsha" and "Qiusi" the works of Ma Zhiyuan?). *Gudian wenxue zhishi* 3 (2008): 46–51.

Fang Shiming. "Cong Xu Sheng diquan lun Han dai diquan zhi jianbie" (Discussion on discerning land deeds of the Han period through the Xu Sheng land deed). *Wenwu* 1973, no. 5 (1973): 52–55.

Feng, Jiren. *Chinese Architecture and Metaphor: Song Culture in the Yingzao Fashi Building Manual*. Honolulu: University of Hawai'i Press, 2012.

Feng Junjie. *Shanxi xiqu beike jikao* (A study of stelae in Shanxi Province related to dramas). Beijing: Zhonghua shuju, 2002.

———. *Xiju yu kaogu* (Theatrical performance and archaeology). Beijing: Wenhua yishu chubanshe, 2002.

———, ed. *Taixing shenmiao ji saishe yanju* (A study of theatrical performances at temples in the Taixing region). Taipei: Shi Hezheng minsu wenhua jijinhui chuban, 2000.

Fong, Mary C. "The Technique of 'Chiaroscuro' in Chinese Painting from Han to T'ang." *Artibus Asiae* 38, nos. 2–3 (1976): 96–127.

Foong, Ping. *The Efficacious Landscape: On the Authorities of Painting at the Northern Song Court*. Cambridge, MA: Harvard University Asia Center, 2015.

Foster, Hal. *Vision and Visuality*. Seattle: Bay Press, 1988.

Fraser, Sarah. *Performing the Visual: The Practice of Buddhist Wall Painting in China and Central Asia, 618–960*. Stanford, CA: Stanford University Press, 2004.

Gao Wen and Gao Chenggang. *Zhongguo huaxiang shiguan yishu* (A study of images on sarcophagi in China). Taiyuan: Shanxi renmin chubanshe, 1996.

Glahn, Else. "On the Transmission of the Ying-Tsao Fa-Shih." *T'oung Pao* 61, nos. 4–5 (1974): 232–265.

Goossaert, Vincent, and Paul Katz. "New Perspectives on Quanzhen Taoism: The Formation of Religious Identity." *Journal of Chinese Religions* 29 (2001): 91–95.

Gudai jianzhu xiuzheng suo. "Jin dongnan Lu'an, Pingxun, Gaoping he Jincheng si xian de gu jianzhu" (Old architecture in southern Shanxi area). *Wenwu cankao ziliao* 1959, no. 3 (1959): 26–42, 48.

Hachiya Kunio. *Kindai dokyo no kenkyū: O Choyo to Ba Tanyo* (A study of Taoism in the Jin dynasty: Wang Zhongyang and Ma Danyang). Tokyo: Shoin, 1992.

Hansen, Valerie. *Changing Gods in Medieval China, 1127–1276*. Princeton, NJ: Princeton University Press, 1990.

———. *Negotiating Daily Life in Traditional China: How Ordinary People Used Contracts, 600–1400*. New Haven, CT: Yale University Press, 1995.

Hartwell, Robert M. "Demographic, Political, and Social Transformations of China, 705–1550." *Harvard Journal of Asiatic Studies* 42, no. 2 (1982): 365–442.

Hay, Jonathan. "Seeing through Dead Eyes: How Early Tang Tombs Staged Afterlife." *Res: Anthropology and Aesthetics* 57–58 (2010): 17–54.

Hebei sheng wenhuaju wenwu gongzuodui. "Hebei Jingjing xian Shizhuang Song mu fajue baogao" (Excavation report of a Song tomb found in Shizhuang in Jingjing County, Hebei Province). *Kaogu xuebao* 2 (1962): 31–73.

Hebei sheng wenwu yanjiusuo, ed. *Xuanhua Liao mu—1974~1993 nian kaogu fajue baogao* (Liao-dynasty tombs in Xuanhua: A report of excavations from 1974 to 1993). 2 vols. Beijing: Wenwu chubanshe, 2001.

Hebei sheng wenwu yanjiusuo and Baoding shi wenwu guanlichu. *Wudai Wang Chuzhi mu* (The tomb of Wang Chuzhi of the Five Dynasties period). Beijing: Wenwu chubanshe, 1998.

Henan bowuyuan, ed. *Henan gudai taosu yishu* (The art of ancient clay sculpture in Henan Province). Zhengzhou: Daxiang chubanshe, 2005.

Hong, Jeehee. "Changing Roles of the Tomb Portrait: Burial Practices and Ancestral Worship of Non-literati Elite in North China (1000–1400)." *Journal of Song-Yuan Studies* 44 (forthcoming).

———. "Exorcism from the Streets to the Tomb: Image of the Judge and Minions in the Xuanhua Liao Tomb No. 7." *Archives of Asian Art* 63, no. 1 (2013): 1–25.

———. "'Hengzai' zhong de zangyi: Song Yuan shiqi zhongyuan muzang de yili shijian" (Funeral in the permanent present: Ritual time in middle period tombs of northern China). In *Gudai muzang meishu yanjiu* (Studies on tomb art in traditional China), vol. 3, edited by Wu Hung, Zhu Qingsheng, and Zheng Yan. Changsha: Hunan meishu chubanshe, 2015.

———. "Mechanism of Life for the Netherworld: Tranformations of *Mingqi* in Middle-Period China." *Journal of Chinese Religions* 43, no. 2 (2015): 161–193.

———. "Theatricalizing Death and Society in *The Skeletons' Illusory Performance* by Li Song." *Art Bulletin* 93, no. 1 (2011): 60–78.

Hong, Jeehee, and T. J. Hinrichs. "Unwritten Life (and Death) of a 'Pharmacist' in Song China: Decoding Hancheng Tomb Murals." *Cahiers d'Extrême-Asie* 24 (forthcoming).

Howard, Angela Falco, et al. *Chinese Sculpture*. New Haven, CT: Yale University Press, and Beijing: Foreign Language Press, 2006.

Huang Minglan and Gong Dazhong. "Luoyang Bei Song Zhang Jun mu huaxiang shiguan" (On the sarcophagus of Zhang Jun of the Northern Song excavated in Luoyang). *Wenwu* 1984, no. 7 (1984): 79–81.

Hurvitz, Leon. "Tsung Ping's Comments on Landscape Painting." *Artibus Asiae* 32, nos. 2–3 (1970): 146–156.

Hymes, Robert P. *Statesmen and Gentlemen: The Elite of Fu-chou, Chiang-hsi, in Northern and Southern Sung.* Cambridge, MA: Cambridge University Press, 1986.

Idema, Wilt. "The Many Shapes of Medieval Chinese Plays: How Texts Are Transformed in the Needs of Actors, Spectators, Censors, and Readers." *Oral Tradition* 20, no. 2 (2005): 320–334.

Idema, Wilt, and Stephen H. West. *Chinese Theater, 1100–1450: A Source Book.* Wiesbaden, Germany: Steiner Verlag, 1982.

Iiyama Tomoyasu. *Kin Gen jidai no Kahoku shakai to kakyo seido: mō hitotsu no "shijinsō"* (The society and examination system in northern China during the Jin and Yuan periods). Tokyo: Waseda Daigaku Shuppanbu, 2011.

Jiangyinshi bowuguan. "Jiangsu Jiangyinshi Qingyangzhenli Jingba Song mu" (A Song dynasty tomb discovered in Jingba in Jiangyin City, Jiangsu Province). *Kaogu* 2008, no. 3 (2008): 92–96.

Jie Xigong and Yan Jinzhu. "Shanxi Yonghe xian chutu Jin Da'an san nian shiguan" (On the sarcophagus [4th year of Da'an reign era of the Jin] excavated in Yonghe County, Shanxi Province). *Wenwu* 1989, no. 5 (1989): 71–74.

Jing, Anning. *The Water God's Temple of the Guangsheng Monastery: Cosmic Function of Art, Ritual and Theater.* Leiden, Netherlands: Brill, 2002.

———. "Yongle Palace: The Transformation of the Daoist Pantheon during the Yuan Dynasty (1260–1368)." PhD diss., Princeton University, 1994.

Jing Lihu. "Yongle gong Longhu dian kaolun" (An examination of Longhu Hall in Yongle Palace). *Zhonghua xiqu* 8 (1989): 187–195.

Johnson, David G. *Spectacle and Sacrifice: The Ritual Foundations of Village Life in North China.* Cambridge, MA: Harvard University Asia Center, 2009.

Katz, Paul. *Images of the Immortal: The Cult of Lu Dongbin at the Palace of Eternal Joy.* Honolulu: University of Hawai'i Press, 1999.

Kesner, Ladislav. "Portrait Aspects and Social Functions of Chinese Ceramic Tomb Sculpture." *Orientations* 22, no. 8 (1991): 33–42.

Kieschnick, John. *The Impact of Buddhism on Chinese Material Culture.* Princeton, NJ: Princeton University Press, 2003.

Kiyohiko Munakata. "Concepts of Lei and Kan-lei in Early Chinese Art Theory." In *Theories of the Arts in China,* edited by Susan Bush and Christian Murck. Princeton, NJ: Princeton University Press, 1983.

Kleeman, Terry. "Land Contracts and Related Documents." In *Chūgoku no shūkyō, shisō to kagaku: Makio Ryōkai hakushi shōju kinen ronshū* (Religion, thought, and science in China: A collection of studies in celebration of the longevity of Dr. Makio Ryōkai). Tokyo: Kokusho kankōkai, 1984.

Kracke, Edward A., Jr. "Region, Family and Individual in the Chinese Examination System." In *Chinese Thought and Institutions,* edited by John K. Fairbank. Chicago: University of Chicago Press, 1967.

Kubo Noritada. "Zenshinkyo no seiritsu" (The establishment of the Quanzhen sect). *Tōyō Bunka Kenkyūjo kiyo* 42 (1966): 1–60.

Kuhn, Dieter. "Decoding Tombs of the Song Elite." In *Burial in Song China,* edited by Dieter Kuhn. Heidelberg: Edition Forum, 1994.

———. "Religion in the Light of Archaeology and Burial Practices." In *Modern Chinese Religion,* vol. 1, edited by John Lagerway. Leiden, Netherlands: Brill, 2015.

Lachman, Charles H., trans. *Evaluations of Sung Dynasty Painters of Renown: Liu Tao-ch'un's Sung-ch'ao ming-hua p'ing.* Leiden, Netherlands: Brill, 1989.

Laing, Ellen Johnston. "Patterns and Problems in Later Chinese Tomb Decoration." *Journal of Oriental Studies* 16, nos. 1–2 (1978): 3–20.

Latour, Bruno. *Reassembling the Social: An Introduction to Actor-Network-Theory.* Oxford: Oxford University Press, 2007.

Lee, De-nin D. *The Night Banquet: A Chinese Scroll through Time*. Seattle: University of Washington Press, 2010.

Lee, Sonya S. *Surviving Nirvana: Death of the Buddha in Chinese Visual Culture*. Hong Kong: Hong Kong University Press, 2010.

Legge, James, trans. *The Chinese Classics*. 5 vols. Oxford: Oxford University Press, 1861–1872.

Leidy, Denise Patry. "A Portrait of the Monk Sengqie in the Metropolitan Museum of Art." *Oriental Art* 49, no. 1 (2003): 52–64.

Leidy, Denise Patry, and Donna Straham. *Wisdom Embodied: Chinese Buddhist and Daoist Sculpture in the Metropolitan Museum of Art*. New Haven, CT: Yale University Press, 2010.

Li Changji. *Zhongguo gudai sanqu shi* (A history of sanqu in China). Shanghai: Huadong shifan daxue chubanshe, 1991.

Li Qingquan. "Kongjian luoji yu shijue yiwei—Song Liao Jin mu 'furen jimen tu' xinlun" (Spatial logic and visual meaning: A new discussion of the motif of "woman opening doors" in tombs of the Song, Liao, and Jin periods). In *Gudai muzang meishu yanjiu* (Studies on tomb art in traditional China), vol. 1, edited by Wu Hung and Zheng Yan. Beijing: Wenwu chubanshe, 2011.

——. *Xuanhua Liao mu—Muzang yishu yu Liao dai shehui* (Liao dynasty tombs at Xuanhua: Tomb art and society of the Liao period). Beijing: Wenwu chubanshe, 2008.

——. "'Yitang jiaqing' de xin yixiang: Song Jin shiqi de muzhu fufu xiang yu Tang Song muzang fengqi zhi bian." In *Gudai muzang meishu yanjiu*, vol. 2, edited by Wu Hung, Zhu Qingsheng, and Zheng Yan. Changsha: Hunan meishu chubanshe, 2013.

Li Shougang. "Ye tan 'diquan' de jianbie" (Another discussion on discerning land deeds). *Wenwu* 1978, no. 7 (1978): 79–80.

Li Xianqi and Wang Liling. "Henan Luoning Bei Song Lezhongjin huaxiang shiguan" (On the sarcophagus found in Lezhong in Luoyang, Henan Province). *Wenwu* 1993, no. 5 (1993): 30–39.

Liao Ben. "Guangyuan Nan Song mu zaju, daqu shike kao" (Examination of the stone carving representing zaju and daqu excavated in a Southern Song tomb in Guangyuan). *Wenwu* 1986, no. 12 (1986): 25–35.

——. "Nanxi *Huanmen zidi cuo li shen* shidai kaobian" (Study on the date of the southern drama A Playboy from a Noble House Opts for the Wrong Career). In *Zhongguo xiqu de chantui* (Transformations of Chinese drama), edited by Liu Yanjun and Liao Ben. Beijing: Wenhua yishu chubanshe, 1989.

——. *Song Yuan xiqu wenwu yu minsu* (A material study of theater and folk custom of the Song and Yuan periods). Beijing: Wenhua yishu chubanshe, 1989.

——. "Song Yuan xitai yiji—Zhongguo gudai juchang wenwu yanjiu zhi yi" (Traces of stages of Song and Yuan periods: A material study of ancient Chinese theater). *Wenwu* 1989, no. 7 (1989): 82–95.

——. *Xiqu wenwu fafu* (Initiation of the material study of theater). Xiamen: Xiamen daxue chubanshe, 2003.

——. *Zhongguo gudai juchang shi* (A history of ancient Chinese theater). Zheng-zhou: Zhongzhou guji chubanshe, 1997.

——. *Zhongguo xiju tushi* (Illustrated history of Chinese theater). Zhengzhou: Henan jiaoyu chubanshe, 1996.

——. *Zhongguo xiqu shi* (A history of Chinese drama). Shanghai: Shanghai renmin chubanshe, 2004.

Lin, Wei-cheng. "Underground Wooden Architecture in Brick: A Changed Perspective from Life to Death in 10th- through 13th-Century Northern China." *Archives of Asian Art* 61 (2011): 3–36.

Liu Guoliang and Lian Yao, trans. *Xin yi Wuzhen bian* (A new translation of Wuzhen bian). Taipei: Sanmin shuju, 2005.

Liu Haiwen et al. "Hebei Xuanhua jinian Tang mu fajue jianbao" (A brief archaeological report of dated Tang dynasty tombs in Xuanhua, Hebei Province). *Wenwu* 2008, no. 7 (2008): 23–28.

Liu, Heping. "'The Water Mill' and Northern Song Imperial Patronage of Art, Commerce, and Science. *Art Bulletin* 84, no. 4 (2002): 566–567.

Liu Nianzi. "Song zaju Ding Dusai diaozhuan kao" (An examination of the brick relief representing the actress Ding Dusai of the Song). *Wenwu* 1980, no. 2 (1980): 58–62.

——. *Xiqu wenwu congkao* (Comprehensive research on material evidence of theater). Beijing: Zhongguo xiju chubanshe, 1986.

——. "Zhongguo xiqu wutai yishu zai shi san shiji chuye yijing xingcheng—Jin dai Houma Dong mu wutai diaocha baogao" (Chinese art of theater had already begun to develop in the thirteenth century: A research report on the theater found in the Jin dynasty tomb of a certain Dong in Houma). *Xiju yanjiu* 2 (1959): 61–62.

Liu Zhiyuan, Yu Dezhang, and Liu Wenjie. *Sichuan Han dai huaxiang zhuan yu Han dai shehui* (Image-bearing bricks from Sichuan and the society of the Han period). Beijing: Wenwu chubanshe, 1983.

Loewe, Michael. *Ways to Paradise: The Chinese Quest for Immortality*. London: Allen and Unwin, 1979.

Lu Jie. *Zhongguo chuantong jianzhu yishu daguan* (Survey of traditional Chinese architecture). Chengdu: Sichuan renmin chubanshe, 2000.

Lü Pin. "Henan Xingyang Bei Song shiguan xianhua kao" (Examination of the line drawing on the Northern Song sarcophagus found in Xingyang, Henan Province). *Zhongyuan wenwu* 1983, no. 4 (1983): 91–96.

Luo Lirong. *Zhongguo shenmiao juchang shi* (A history of temple stages in China). Taipei: Liren shuju, 2006.

Luo Zhewen, ed. *Zhongguo gudai jianzhu* (Ancient Chinese architecture). Shanghai: Shanghai guji chubanshe, 2001.

Luoyangshi wenwu gongzuodui. "Luoyang Luolongqu guanlinmiao Song dai zhuandiaomu fajue jianbao." *Wenwu* 2011, no. 8 (2011): 31–46.

Maeda, Robert J. "Chieh-hua: Ruled-line Painting in China." *Ars Orientalis* 10 (1975): 123–141.

——. "Some Sung, Chin, and Yüan Representations of Actors." *Artibus Asiae* 41, nos. 2–3 (1979): 132–156.

Mair, Victor. *Painting and Performance: Chinese Picture Recitation and Its Indian Genesis.* Honolulu: University of Hawaiʻi Press, 1988.

Manovich, Lev. *The Language of New Media.* Cambridge, MA: MIT Press, 2001.

Matsumura Takumi. "Tenmon jido ko" (An examination of tianmen and dihu). In *Chūgoku ko dokyo shi kenkyū* (A study of ancient Daoism in China), edited by Yoshikawa Tadao. Kyoto: Toho gakkai, 1993.

McKnight, Brian E., ed. *Law and the State in Traditional East Asia: Six Studies on the Sources of East Asian Law.* Honolulu: University of Hawaiʻi Press, 1987.

Mitchell, W. J. T. "Metapicture." In *Picture Theory: Essays on Verbal and Visual Representation.* Chicago: University of Chicago Press, 1994.

Miyazaki Ichisada. *Tōyō teki kinsei* (East Asia's early modern age). In *Miyazaki Ichisada zenshū* (Complete writings of Miyazaki Ichisada). Tokyo: Iwanami shoten, 1991.

Morohashi Tetsuji. *Dai kan wa jiten* (Classical Chinese-Japanese dictionary). 12 vols. Tokyo: Taishukan shoten, 1955–1960.

Mulvey, Laura. *Visual and Other Pleasures.* Bloomington: Indiana University Press, 1989.

Nakamura Shigeo. *Chūgoku garon no tenkai: Shin To So Gen* (Development of painting theories in China: Jin, Tang, Song, and Yuan dynasties). Kyoto: Nakayama Bunkadō, 1965.

Nelson, Robert, ed. *Visuality before and beyond the Renaissance.* Cambridge: Cambridge University Press, 2000.

Ning Xiyuan. "Zaoqi zhugongdiao keci de zhongda faxian" (A significant discovery of an early print of zhugongdiao). *Zhonghua xiqu* 31 (2004): 14–17.

Noriyuki Kanai. "Sōdai no sonsha to shashin" (Village rituals and deities during the Song period). *Tōyōshi kenkyū* 38, no. 2 (1979): 61–87.

Ogawa Yōichi. "Du Shanfu saku Zhuangjia bushi goulan yakuchū" (Du Shanfu's Country Bumpkin Knows Nothing of Theater, translated and annotated). *Shūkan Tōyōgaku* 18 (1967): 78–86.

Ong, Chang Woei. *Men of Letters within Passes: Guanzhong Literati in Chinese History, 907–1911.* Cambridge, MA: Harvard University Asia Center, 2008.

Ortiz, Valarie. *Dreaming the Southern Song Landscape: The Power of Illusion in Chinese Painting.* Boston: Brill, 1999.

Overmyer, Daniel L. "Buddhism in the Trenches: Attitudes toward Popular Religion in Chinese Scriptures Found at Tun-Huang." *Harvard Journal of Asiatic Studies* 50, no. 1 (1990): 197–222.

Owen, Stephen, trans. and ed. *An Anthology of Chinese Literature: Beginnings to 1911.* New York: Norton, 1996.

Peirce, C. S. "The Icon, Index, and Symbol." In *Collected Papers of Charles Sanders Peirce,* vol. 2, edited by Charles Hartshorne and Paul Weiss. Cambridge: Harvard University Press, 1932.

Postlewait, Thomas, and Tracy C. Davis, eds. *Theatricality.* New York: Cambridge University Press, 2003.

Qian Nanyang. *Xiwen gailun* (A general study of southern drama). Shanghai: Shanghai guji chubanshe, 1981.

Qin Dashu. *Song Yuan Ming kaogu* (Archaeology of the Song, Yuan, and Ming periods). Beijing: Wenwu chubanshe, 2004.

———. "Songdai sangzang xisu de biange ji qi tixian de shehui yiyi" (Funerary practice of the Song period and its social meaning). *Tang yanjiu* 11 (2005): 313–336.

Ran Wanli. "Songdai sangzang xisu zhong fojiao yinsu de kaoguxue guancha" (Archaeological research on Buddhist elements in the funerary practice of the Song period). *Kaogu yu wenwu* 2009, no. 4 (2009): 77–85.

Rawson, Jessica. "Changes in the Representation of Life and the Afterlife as Illustrated by the Contents of Tombs of the T'ang and Sung Period." In *Arts of the Sung and Yuan,* edited by Maxwell Hearn and Judith Smith. New York: Metropolitan Museum of Art, 1996.

Ricoeur, Paul. "Narrative Time." *Critical Inquiry* 7, no. 1 (1980): 169–190.

Sangren, Steven. *History and Magical Power in a Chinese Community.* Stanford, CA: Stanford University Press, 1987.

Sanmenxia shi wenwu gongzuodui and Yima shi wenwuguanli weiyuanhui. "Yima shi Jin dai zhuandiao mu fajue jianbao" (A brief archaeological report of the Jin dynasty tomb with brick reliefs excavated in Yima City). *Huaxia kaogu* 4 (1993): 87–91.

Sanmenxia wenwu gongzuodui. *Bei Song Shanzhou louzeyuan* (A mass grave of the Northern Song period in Shanzhou). Beijing: Wenwu chubanshe, 1999.

Santoro, Marco, ed. "On the Shoulders of Pierre Bourdieu: A Contemporary Master in Chiascuro." Special issue, *Cultural Sociology* 5, no. 1 (2011).

Satake Yasuhiko. "Kandai no hunbo saishi gazo ni okeru teimon, teiketsu to shaba gyoretsu" (Tingmen, tingque, and chariot processions in the images of funerary rites found in the tombs of the Han period). *Jinbun gakuho Tokyo Toritsu daigaku* 325 (2002): 1–150.

Schipper, Kristofer. *The Taoist Body.* Translated by Karen D. Duval. Berkeley: University of California Press, 1993.

Schipper, Kristofer, and Franciscus Verellen, eds. *The Taoist Canon: A Historical Companion to the* Daozang. Chicago: University of Chicago Press, 2004.

Schlepp, Wayne. *San-ch'u: Its Technique and Imagery.* Madison: University of Wisconsin Press, 1970.

Schottenhammer, Angela. "Characteristics of Song Epitaphs." In *Burial in Song China,* edited by Dieter Kuhn. Heidelberg: Edition Forum, 1994.

Seidel, Anna. "Buying One's Way to Heaven: The Celestial Treasury in Chinese Religions." *History of Religions* 17 (1987): 419–432.

———. "*Post-Mortem* Immortality or the Taoist Resurrection of the Body." In *Gilgul: Essays on Transformation, Revolution, and Permanence in the History of Religions,* edited by Shaul Shaked and Gedaliahu A. G. Stroumsa. Leiden, Netherlands: Brill, 1987.

Shandongsheng bowuguan and Cangshan xian wenhua guan. "Shandong Cangshan Yuanjia yuan nian huaxiangshi mu" (On the tomb [first year of the Yuanjia reign era] with pictorial stone slabs excavated in Cangshan, Shandong Province). *Kaogu* 1975, no. 2 (1975): 124–134.

Shanxi daxue kexue jishu zhexue zhongxin, Shanxisheng kaogu yanjiusuo, Shanxi bowuyuan. "Shanxi Xing xian Hongyu cun Yuan Zhida er nian bihua mu" (On the tomb with murals [second year of the Zhida reign era of the Yuan dynasty] found in Hongyu Village in Xing County, Shanxi Province). *Wenwu* 2011, no. 2 (2011): 40–46.

Shanxi shifan daxue xiqu wenwu yanjiusuo. *Song Jin Yuan xiqu wenwu tulun* (Illustrations and discussions of archaeological materials related to the theater of Song, Jin, and Yuan dynasties). Taiyuan: Shanxi renmin chubanshe, 1987.

Shanxisheng kaogu yanjiusuo. "Shanxi Jishan Jin mu fajue jianbao" (A brief archaeological report of a Jin dynasty tomb excavated in Jishan, Shanxi Province). *Wenwu* 1983, no. 1 (1983): 45–63.

———. "Shanxi Xinjiang Nanfanzhuang, Wulingzhuang Jin Yuan mu fajue jianbao." (A brief archaeological report of Jin and Yuan dynasty tombs excavated in Nanfanzhuang and Wulingzhuang in Xinjiang, Shanxi Province). *Wenwu* 1983, no. 1 (1983): 64–72.

———, ed. *Zoujin kaogu buru Song Jin—Yi ci gongzhong kaogu huodong de tansuo yu shiqian* (Entering Song–Jin periods through archaeology—Discussions and practices of the first archaeological event for the public). Beijing: Kexue chubanshe, 2009.

Shanxisheng kaogu yanjiusuo Houma gongzuozhan. "Houma liangzuo Jindai jinianmu fajue baogao" (Archaeological report of two dated tombs of the Jin period in Houma). *Wenwu jikan* 1996, no. 3 (1996): 65–78.

———. "Houma 65H4M102 Jin mu" (On the Jin dynasty tomb excavated at Houma, 65H4M102). *Wenwu jikan* 1997, no. 4 (1997): 17–27.

———. "Jishan xian huafei chang Jin mu fajue baogao" (Archaeological report of the Jin dynasty tomb found at a chemical fertilizer factory site in Jishan County). *Wenwu shijie* 2011, no. 4 (2011): 6–9.

Shanxisheng wenwu guanli gongzuo weiyuanhui. *Yongle gong* (Yongle Palace). Beijing: Renmin meishu chubanshe, 1964.

Shanxisheng wenwu guanli weiyuanhui et al. "Shanxi Xiaoyi Xiatujing he Liangjiazhuang Jin, Yuan mu fajue jianbao" (A brief archaeological report of Jin and Yuan dynasty tombs excavated in Xiatujing and Liangjiazhuang in Xiaoyi, Shanxi Province). *Kaogu* 1960, no. 7 (1960): 57–61.

Shanxisheng wenwu guanli weiyuanhui Houma gongzuozhan. "Houma Jindai Dong shi mu jieshao." (Introductory report of the Jin dynasty tomb of a certain Dong in Houma). *Wenwu* 1959, no. 6 (1959): 50–55.

———. "Shanxi Houma Jin mu fajue jianbao." (A brief archaeological report of the Jin dynasty tomb excavated in Houma, Shanxi Province). *Kaogu* 1961, no. 12 (1961): 681–683.

Shanxisheng wenwu guanli weiyuanhui kaogu yanjiusuo. "Shanxi Ruicheng Yonglegong jiuzhi Song Defang, Pan Dechong he 'Lüzu' mu fajue jianbao" (A brief archaeological report of the tombs of Song Defang, Pan Dechong, and "Lü Dongbin" excavated in Yongle Palace in Ruicheng, Shanxi Province). *Kaogu* 1960, no. 8 (1960): 22–25.

Shen, Hsueh-man. "Body Matters: Manikin Burials in Liao Tombs of Xuanhua,
    Hebei Province." *Artibus Asiae* 65, no. 1 (2005): 99–141.
Sheng Lei. "Sichuan 'bankaimen zhong tan shen renwu' ticai chubu yanjiu" (A
    preliminary study of the motif of "figure peeking from behind half-open doors"
    from Sichuan). *Zhongguo Han hua yanjiu* 1 (2004): 70–88.
Shi Jinming and Hai Weilan. *Sheng si tong le* (Theater, life, and the afterlife: Tomb
    decor of the Jin dynasty from Shanxi). Beijing: Kexue chubanshe, 2012.
Shi Xueqian. "Shilun Shanxi diqu de Jin mu" (A preliminary discussion on Jin
    dynasty tombs in the Shanxi region). *Kaogu yu wenwu* 1998, no. 3 (1988): 88–92.
Shi Zhilian. "Bei Song funü huaxiangzhuan" (Brick reliefs representing women
    found in tombs of the Northern Song period). *Wenwu* 1979, no. 3 (1979):
    87–103.
Shiba Yoshinobu. *Sōdai shōgyōshi kenkyū* (A study of commercial history of the
    Song period). Tokyo: Kazama shobo, 1968.
Shih Shou-chien. "Cheng Tang baihua zhi chengli yu bimiao nengli zhi kuazhan"
    (Establishment of the *baimiao* painting and the development of brushwork
    in the early eighth century). In *Feng'ge yu shibian: Zhongguo huihua shi lun*
    (Style in transformation: Ten studies on the history of Chinese painting).
    Taipei: Yunchen wenhua shiye gufen youxian gongsi, 1996.
Silbergeld, Jerome. "Re-reading Zong Bing's Fifth-Century Essay on Landscape
    Painting: A Few Critical Notes." In *A Life in Chinese Art: Essays in Honour of
    Michael Sullivan,* edited by Shelagh Vainker and Xin Chen. Oxford: Ash-
    molean Museum, 2012.
——. "Yi qu bai xie: fuzhi, bianhua, ji zhongguo jiehua yanjiu zhong de ruogan
    wenti" (A hundred lines converging on a single point: Replication, transforma-
    tion, and some issues regarding the study of Chinese ruled-line painting). In
    Qiannian danqing: Xi du Zhong Ri cang Tang Song Yuan huihua zhenpin
    (Paintings from the Tang to Yuan dynasties in Japanese and Chinese collec-
    tions), edited by Shanghai bowuguan. Beijing: Beijing daxue chubanshe, and
    Shanghai: Dong fang chuban zhong xi, 2010.
Sirén, Osvald. *Chinese Painting: Leading Masters and Principles.* London: Lund,
    Humphries, 1956.
Soper, Alexander, and Seigai Omura. *Literary Evidence for Early Buddhist Art in
    China.* Ascona, Switzerland: Artibus Asiae, 1959.
Stein, Rolf A. *World in Miniature: Container Gardens and Dwelling in Far
    Eastern Religious Thought.* Translated by Phyllis Brooks. Stanford, CA:
    Stanford University Press, 1990.
Steinhardt, Nancy. "Death, Architecture, and Drama: Jin-Yuan Tombs in Southern
    Shanxi." In *Sheng si tong le* (Theater, life, and the afterlife: Tomb decor of the
    Jin dynasty from Shanxi), edited by Shi Jinming and Hai Weilan. Beijing:
    Kexue chubanshe, 2012.
Stewart, Susan. *Nonsense: Aspects of Intertextuality in Folklore and Literature.*
    Baltimore: Johns Hopkins University Press, 1978.
Su Bai. *Baisha Song mu* (Song dynasty tombs at Baisha). 2nd ed. Beijing: Wenwu
    chubanshe, 2002. Originally published 1957.

———. "Baisha Song mu zhong de zaju zhuandiao" (Brick reliefs representing zaju found in a Song dynasty tomb at Baisha). *Kaogu* 1960, no. 9 (1960): 59–60.

———. "Yongle gong changjian shiliao biannian—Yongle gong zhaji zhi yi" (Chronology of historical sources on the establishment of Yongle Palace: The first research on Yongle Palace). *Wenwu* 1962, nos. 4–5 (1962): 80–87.

Su Ming. "Chengwu chutu Jin dai wu cai ciren" (Multicolor ceramic figurines of the Jin period excavated in Chengwu). *Wenwu* 1993, no. 11 (1993): 88–89.

Sullivan, Michael. *The Birth of Chinese Landscape Painting in China.* Berkeley: University of California Press, 1962.

Sutton, Donald S. "Ritual, Cultural Standardization, and Orthopraxy in China: Reconsidering James L. Watson's Ideas." Special issue, *Modern China* 33, no. 1 (2007).

Tackett, Nicholas. *The Destruction of the Medieval Chinese Aristocracy.* Cambridge, MA: Harvard University Asia Center, 2014.

Tananka Tan. *Chūgoku kenchikushi no kenkyū* (A study of ritual dramas in China). Tokyo: Kōbundō, 1989.

Tang Shan. "Jiangxi Poyang faxian Song dai xiju yong" (Actor figurines of the Song period found in Poyang, Jiangxi Province). *Wenwu* 1979, no. 4 (1979): 6–9, 99–100.

Thomson, Lydia duPont. "The Yi'nan Tomb: Narrative and Ritual in Pictorial Art of the Eastern Han (25–220 CE)." PhD diss., New York University, 1998.

Thôte, Alain. "The Double Coffin of Leigudun Tomb No.1: Iconographic Sources and Related Problems." In *New Perspectives on Chu Culture during the Eastern Zhou Period,* edited by Thomas Lawton. Princeton, NJ: Princeton University Press, 1991.

Tian Jianwen and Li Yongmin. "Macun zhuandiao mu yu Duan shi kemingzhuan" (On tombs furnished with reliefs in Macun and bricks with carved names of a Duan lineage). *Wenwu shijie* 2005, no. 1 (2005): 12–19.

Tseng, Lillian Lan-ying. "Funerary Spatiality: Wang Hui's Sarcophagus in Han China." *Res: Anthropology and Aesthetics* 61–62 (2012): 116–131.

———. *Picturing Heaven in Early China.* Cambridge, MA: Harvard Asia Center, 2011.

———. "Zuofang, getao yu diyuzhe chuantong: Cong Shandong Anqu Dongjiazhuang Han mu de zhizuo henji tanqi" (Workshop, repertories, and regional visual traditions: traces of the Han carved tomb at Anqiu in Shandong). *Taida meishushi yanjiujikan* 8 (2000): 33–86.

Von Glahn, Richard. *The Sinister Way: The Divine and Demonic in Chinese Religious Culture.* Berkeley: University of California Press, 2004.

Wang, Eugene. *Shaping the Lotus Sutra: Buddhist Visual Culture in Medieval China.* Seattle: University of Washington Press, 2005.

Wang Fucai. "Qinshui xian xia Gebei cun Shengwangxing gong Yuan bei ji saixi kao" (A study on theatrical performances in deity-welcoming rituals and the content of a Yuan dynasty stele in Shengwangxing Palace in Gebei Village, Qinshui County). *Minsu quyi* 107–108 (1997): 91–116.

———. "Shanxi Ruicheng Yonglegong Pan Dechong shiguo er shi si xiao xianketu benshi ji qi jumu kao" (A study of the original stories of the Twenty-Four

Exemplars of Filial Piety and drama titles relevant to the line drawing carved on the sarcophagus of Pan Dechong in Yongle Palace, Ruicheng, Shanxi Province). *Zhonghua xiqu* 22, no. 1 (1999): 192–213.

Wang Guowei. *Guantang jilin, bieji* (Collected writings of Wang Guowei, additional volumes). Beijing: Zhonghua shuju, 1959.

——. *Song Yuan xiqu shi* (A history of drama during the Song and Yuan periods). Shanghai: Shanghai guji chubanshe, 1998.

——. *Wang Guowei xiqu lunwenji* (Collected articles on drama by Wang Guowei). Beijing: Zhongguo xiju chubanshe, 1957.

Wang Jinxian and Zhu Xiaofang. "Shanxi Changzhi Anchang Jin mu" (On a Jin dynasty tomb excavated in Anchang village of Changzhi City, Shanxi Province). *Wenwu* 1990, no. 5 (1990): 76–85.

Wang Shangyi and Xu Hongping. "Song Yuan Ming Qing shiqi Shanxi wenren de dili fenbu ji wenhua fazhan tedian" (On the distribution of literati in Shanxi area and features of cultural development during the Song, Yuan, Ming, and Qing periods). *Shanxi daxue xuebao* 3 (1988): 38–46.

Wang Shanjun. "Songdai de zongzu jisi he zuxian chongbai" (On the memorial rite for lineage and ancestral worship during the Song period). *Shijie zongjiao yanjiu* 3 (1999): 114–124.

Wang Ye. "Henan zhongbu yibei faxian de zaoqi youshang duose caihui taoci" (On multicolor ceramic figurines found in the north of Middle Henan Province). *Wenwu* 2006, no. 2 (2006): 54–95.

Watson, James L. "Rites or Beliefs? The Construction of a Unified Culture in Late Imperial China." In *China's Quest for National Identity,* edited by Lowell Dittmer and Samuel S. Kim. Ithaca: Cornell University Press, 1993.

——. "The Structure of Chinese Funerary Rites: Elementary Forms, Ritual Sequence, and the Primacy of Performance." In *Death Ritual in Late Imperial and Modern China,* edited by James L. Watson and Evelyn S. Rawski. Berkeley: University of California Press, 1988.

West, Stephen H. "Some Remarks on the Development of Northern Music-Drama." *Chinoperl Papers* 6 (1976): 23–44.

——. "Text and Ideology: Ming Editors and Northern Drama." In *Ming Qing xiqu guoji yantaohui lunwenji* (Proceedings of the International Conference on Drama of the Ming and Qing Periods), edited by Hua Wei and Wang Ailing. Taipei: Zhongyang yanjiuyuan Zhongguo wenzhe yanjiusuo choubeichu, 1998.

——. *Vaudeville and Narrative: Aspects of Chin Theater.* Wiesbaden, Germany: Steiner Verlag, 1977.

West, Stephen H., and Wilt Idema, eds. and trans. *Monks, Bandits, Lovers, and Immortals: Eleven Early Chinese Plays.* Indianapolis, IN: Hackett, 2010.

Wu Guofu. *Quanzhenjiao yu Yuanqu* (Quanzhen Taoism and Yuan drama). Nanchang shi: Jiangxi renmin chubanshe, 2005.

Wu Hung. *The Art of the Yellow Springs: Understanding Chinese Tombs.* Honolulu: University of Hawai'i Press, 2010.

——. "Beyond the 'Great Boundary': Funerary Narrative in Early Chinese Art." In *Boundaries in China,* edited by John Hay. London: Reaktion, 1994.

——. "Buddhist Elements in Early Chinese Art (2nd and 3rd Centuries AD)." *Artibus Asiae* 47, nos. 3–4 (1986): 263–352.

——. "A Case of Cultural Interaction: House-Shaped Sarcophagi of the Northern Dynasties." *Orientations* 137, no. 5 (2002): 34–41.

——. *The Double Screen: Medium and Representation in Chinese Painting.* Chicago: University of Chicago Press, 1996.

——. *Monumentality in Early Chinese Art and Architecture.* Stanford, CA: Stanford University Press, 1995.

——. "Myths and Legends in Han Funerary Art." In *Stories from China's Past: Han Dynasty Pictorial Tomb Reliefs and Archaeological Objects from Sichuan Province, People's Republic of China,* edited by Lucy Lim. San Francisco: Chinese Culture Foundation of San Francisco, 1987.

——. "On Tomb Figurines: The Beginning of a Visual Tradition." In *Body and Face in Chinese Visual Culture,* edited by Wu Hung and Katherine R. Tsiang. Cambridge, MA: Harvard University Press, 2005.

——. "Shengqi de gainian yu shijian" (The concept and practice of shengqi). *Wenwu* 2010, no. 1 (2010): 87–96.

——. *The Wu Liang Shrine: The Ideology of Early Chinese Pictorial Art.* Stanford, CA: Stanford University Press, 1989.

Wu Lan and Xue Yong. "Shanxi Mizhi xian Guanzhuang Dong Han huaxiang shi mu" (On the Eastern Han tomb furnished with brick reliefs excavated in Guangzhuang in Mizhi County, Shanxi Province). *Kaogu* 1987, no. 2 (1987): 997–1001.

Xianyang shi wenwu kaogu yanjiusuo. *Wudai Fenghui mu* (Tomb of Feng Hui of the Five Dynasties period). Chongqing: Chongqing chubanshe, 2001.

Xie Baofu. *Beichao hunsang lisu yanjiu* (A study on the ritual custom of wedding and funeral in northern dynasties). Beijing: Shoudu shifan daxue chubanshe, 1998.

Xu Guangju, ed. *Zhongguo chutu bihua quanji* (Complete collection of tomb murals in China). 10 vols. Beijing: Kexue chubanshe, 2012.

Xu Huadang. *Zhongguo chuantong nisu* (Traditional Chinese clay sculpture). Beijing: Renmin meishu chubanshe, 2005.

Xu Pingfang. "Guanyu Song Defang he Pan Dechong mu de ji ge wenti" (On a few issues regarding the tombs of Song Defang and Pan Dechong). *Kaogu* 1960, no. 8 (1960): 42–45, 54.

——. "Sengqie zaoxiang de faxian he Sengqie chongbai" (On the discovery of the sculpture of Sengqie and the worshiping of Sengqie). *Wenwu* 1996, no. 5 (1996): 50–67.

——. "Song Yuan mu zhong de zaju diaoke" (Representations of zaju found in tombs from the Song to Yuan periods). In *Zhongguo lishi kaoguxue luncong* (Collected articles on Chinese archaeology). Taipei: Yunchen wenhua shiye gufen youxian gongsi, 1995.

——. "Song Yuan shidai de huozang" (Cremation during the Song and Yuan periods). *Wenwu cankao ziliao* 1956, no. 9 (1956): 21–26.

———. "Songdai de zaju diaozhuan" (On brick reliefs representing zaju from the Song period). *Wenwu* 1960, no. 5 (1960): 40–42.

———. "Tang Song muzang zhong de 'mingqi shensha' yu 'muyi' zhidu" (The system of the "mingqi" and "shensha" figurines and the "muyi" system in Tang and Song period tombs: Reading of the Secret Burial Classic of the Original Sepulchers of the Great Han). *Kaogu* 1963, no. 2 (1963): 87–106.

Xue Linping and Wang Jiqing. *Shanxi chuantong xichang jianzhu* (Traditional theater architecture in Shanxi Province). Beijing: Zhongguo jianzhu gongye chubanshe, 2005.

———. "Shanxi Yuan dai chuantong jianzhu yanjiu" (A study of Yuan dynasty architecture in Shanxi Province). *Tongji daxue xuebao* 14, no. 4 (2003).

Xue Ruizhao. *Song Jin xiju shi gao* (A study of theatrical performances in the Song and Yuan periods). Beijing: Sanlian shudian, 2005.

Yan Dunyi. *Yuanju zhenyi* (Consideration of doubts in Yuan dramas). Beijing: Zhonghua shuju, 1962.

Yan Xiaohui. "Shanxi Changzi xian Shizhe Jin dai bihua mu" (On a Jin dynasty tomb with murals found in Shizhe, Changzi County, Shanxi Province). *Wenwu* 1985, no. 6 (1985): 45–54.

Yanabu Akira. *Hon'yakugo seiritsu jijō* (The context of the standardization of translated words). Tokyo: Iwanami shoten, 1982.

Yang Baoshun. "Jiaozuo Jin mu fajue jianbao" (A brief archaeological report of a Jin dynasty tomb found in Jiaozuo). *Zhongyuan wenwu* 1979, no. 1 (1979): 14–24.

Yang, C. K. *Religion in Chinese Society*. Berkeley: University of California Press, 1961.

Yang Fudou. "Shanxi Houma 104 hao Jin mu" (Archaeological report of Houma Tomb No. 104 from the Jin period). *Kaogu yu wenwu* 1983, no. 6 (1983): 32–39.

Yang Houli and Wan Liangtian. "Jiangxi Fengcheng xian faxian Yuandai jinian qinghua youlilong ciqi" (On underglazed blue-and-red ware from the Yuan period discovered in Fengcheng County, Jiangxi Province). *Wenwu* 1981, no. 11 (1981): 72–74.

Yang Hsien-yi and Gladys Yang, trans. *Selected Plays of Kuan Han-ch'ing*. Shanghai: New Art and Literature Publishing House, 1958. Repr. as *Selected Plays of Guan Hanqing,* Beijing: Foreign Language Press, 1979.

Yang Jianmin. *Zhongzhou xiqu lishi wenwu kao* (A study of the history of theater in Zhongzhou). Beijing: Wenwu chubanshe, 1992.

Yang Jiyun and Gao Qingshang. "Houma Ershui M4 faxian mobi tishu de muzhi he sanpian zhugongdiao ciqu" (On the handwritten epitaph and three groups of zhugongdiao lyrics discovered in Ershui Tomb No. 4, Houma City). *Zhonghua xiqu* 29 (2003): 1–5.

Yang Xiaoguo. "Jin Yuan shiqi Quanzhenjiao zai Shanxi huodong tansuo" (Investigation into the activities of Quanzhen Daoists in Shanxi area during the Jin and Yuan periods). *Jinyang xuekan* 4 (2004): 22–26.

Yang, Xiaoshan. *Metamorphosis of the Private Sphere: Gardens and Objects in Tang-Song Poetry*. Cambridge, MA: Harvard University Asia Center, 2003.

Yi Qing. "Song Jin zhongyuan diqu bihua mu 'muzhuren dui (bing) zuo' tuxiang
    tanxi" (Discussion on the images of tomb occupants depicted in tombs of the
    Song and Jin periods in the Central Plain). *Zhongyuan wenwu* 2011, no. 2
    (2011): 73–80.
Yili (Ceremonies and rites). In *Yili zhushu* (Annotated Ceremonies and Rites). With
    commentary by Zheng Xuan and compiled by Jia Gongyan. 3 vols. Shanghai:
    Shanghai guji chubanshe, 2008.
Yoshikawa Kojiro. *Gen zatsugeki kenkyū* (A study on Yuan drama). Tokyo:
    Iwanami shoten, 1948.
Yü, Ying-Shih. "'O Soul, Come Back!' A Study in the Changing Conceptions of the
    Soul and Afterlife in Pre-Buddhist China. *Harvard Journal of Asiatic Studies*
    47, no. 2 (1987): 363–395.
Yuan Quan. "Song Jin muzang maoque ticai kao" (Research on the motif of cat and
    bird in tombs of the Song and Jin periods). *Kaogu yu wenwu* 2008, no. 4 (2008):
    105–112.
Zeitlin, Judith T. *The Phantom Heroine: Ghosts and Gender in Seventeenth-
    Century Chinese Literature.* Honolulu: University of Hawai'i Press, 2007.
Zeng Zhaoyu, Jiang Baogeng, and Li Zhongyi. *Yinan gu huaxiangshi mu fajue
    baogao* (Archaeological report of an ancient tomb with stone reliefs discovered
    in Yinan). Shandong: Wenwubu wenwu guanliju, 1956.
Zhan Shichuang. *Daojiao yu xiju* (Daoism and theatrical performance). Taipei:
    Wenjin chubanshe, 1997.
Zhang, Fan. "Drama Sustains the Spirit: Art, Ritual, and Theater in Jin and Yuan
    Period Pingyang, 1150–1350." PhD diss., Brown University, 2011.
Zhang Guofeng. *Taiping guangji banben kaoshu* (Discussion on editions of
    Taiping guangji). Beijing: Zhonghua shuju, 2004.
Zhang Qingjin. "Shanxi Yongji faxian Jin dai Zhenyuan yuannian qingshiguan"
    (On a Jin dynasty limestone sarcophagus [first year of the Zhenyuan reign era
    of the Jin dynasty] discovered in Yongji, Shanxi Province). *Wenwu* 1985, no. 8
    (1985): 94–96.
Zhang Siqing and Wu Yongzheng. "Wenxian Song mu fajue jianbao" (A brief
    archaeological report of a Song dynasty tomb excavated in Wen County).
    Zhongyuan wenwu 1983, no. 1 (1983): 19–20.
Zhang Xiumin. *Zhongguo yinshua shi* (A history of print in China). Shanghai:
    Shanghai renmin chubanshe, 1989.
Zhang Zhenming. *Jinshang xingshuai shi* (History of the prosperity and decline of
    Shanxi merchants). Taiyuan: Shanxi renmin chubanshe, 1995.
Zhao Chao. *Gudai muzhi tonglun* (A survey of ancient tomb inscriptions). Beijing:
    Zijincheng chubanshe, 2003.
Zhao Dianzeng and Yuan Shuguang. "'Tianmen' kao—jian lun Sichuan Han
    huaxiangzhuan (shi) de zuhe yu zhuti" (Research on "tianmen" and discussion
    on the combination of types and motifs of Han dynasty bricks and stones
    bearing images). *Sichuan wenwu* 1990, no. 6 (1990): 2–11.
——. "Tianmen xukao" (A sequel to the research on tianmen). *Zhongguo Han hua
    yanjiu* 1 (2004): 27–34.

Zhao Jingshen. *Xiqu bitan.* Beijing: Zhonghua shuju, 1962.

Zheng Yan. "Lun 'Ban ji men'" (Discussion on the motif of "figure peeking out from behind the door"). *Gugong bowuyuan yuankan* 3 (2012): 16–36.

Zhengzhou shi wenwu kaogu yanjiusuo, ed. *Zhengzhou Song Jin bihua mu* (Song and Jin dynasty tombs with murals excavated in Zhengzhou). Beijing: Kexue chubanshe, 2005.

Zhengzhou shi wenwu kaogu yanjiusuo and Dengfeng shi wenwuju. "Henan Dengfeng Chengnanzhuang Song dai bihua mu" (On a Song dynasty tomb with murals discovered in Chengnanzhuang, Dengfeng, Henan Province). *Wenwu* 2005, no. 8 (2005): 62–70.

Zhongguo guisuanyan xuehui, ed. *Zhongguo taoci shi* (A history of Chinese pottery). Beijing: Wenwu chubanshe, 1982.

Zhongguo xiqu zhi bianzhi weiyuanhui. *Zhongguo xiqu zhi: Shaanxi juan* (Chinese opera gazetteer: Shaanxi volume). Beijing: Wenhua yishu chubanshe, 1990.

Zhou Dao. "Wenxian Song zaju diaozhuan zhitan." *Xiqu yishu* 2 (1984): 56–59.

———. "Xingyang Songdai shiguan zaju tu kao" (A study of a Song dynasty sarcophagus excavated in Xingyang). *Xiqu wenwu* 4 (1983): 104–105.

Zhou Dao and Wang Xiao. *Han hua: Henan Handai huaxiang yanjiu* (Han dynasty pictures: A study of Han dynasty images from Henan Province). Zhengzhou: Zhongzhou guji chubanshe, 1996.

Zhou Yibai. "Bei Song muzang zhong renwu diaozhuan de yanjiu" (A study of brick reliefs representing human figures discovered in tombs of the Northern Song). *Wenwu* 1961, no. 10 (1961): 41–46.

———. "Houma Dong shi mu zhong wuge zhuanyong de yanjiu" (A study of the five clay figurines found in the tomb of a certain Dong in Houma). *Wenwu* 1959, no. 10 (1959): 50–52.

———. "Zhongguo juchang shi" (A history of Chinese theater). In *Zhou Yibai xiaoshuo xiqu lunji* (Collected articles by Zhou Yibai on novels and dramas), edited by Shen Xieyuan. Ji'nan: Qilu shushe, 1986.

———. *Zhongguo xiju shi* (A history of Chinese theater). Shanghai: Zhonghua shuju, 1953.

———. "Zhongguo xiqu de shangxiachang" (Entering and exiting in Chinese drama). In *Zhou Yibai xiju lunwen xuan* (Selected works of Zhou Yibai on drama), edited by Zhou Huawu. Changsha: Hunan renmin chubanshe, 1982.

Zhu Xizu. *Liu chao lingmu diaocha baogao* (Investigation report on the Six Dynasties Mausoleum). Nanjing: Zhongyang guwu baoguan weiyuanhui, 1935.

Zoucheng shi wenwu guanli ju. "Shandong Zoucheng shi Wohu shan Han huaxiangshi mu" (On a Han dynasty tomb with pictorial stone discovered at Mount Wohu in Zhoucheng City, Shandong Province). *Kaogu* 1999, no. 6 (1999): 43–51.

Zürcher, Eric. *The Buddhist Conquest of China.* Leiden, Netherlands: Brill, 1959.

INDEX

Page numbers in boldface type refer to illustrations.

227

ABOUT THE
AUTHOR

JEEHEE HONG is an assistant professor in the Department of Art and Music Histories at Syracuse University. Her research focuses on the ritual art and visual culture of middle period China (the ninth through fourteenth centuries). Hong has worked on themes as diverse as theatricality in painting, the shifting role of tomb portraits, cultural patterns of emerging local elites, temporality in tomb imageries, and new conceptions and practices of "spirit articles" in middle period funerary art. Her research has been funded by the Andrew W. Mellon Foundation, the Asian Cultural Council and, most recently, the American Council of Learned Society.